LIFE/DEATH RHYTHMS OF CAPITALIST REGIMES–DEBT BEFORE DISHONOUR

LIFE/DEATH RHYTHMS OF CAPITALIST REGIMES–DEBT BEFORE DISHONOUR

Timetable of World Dominance 1400 to 2100 AD

PART II   DEMOCRATIC CAPITALISM

WILL SLATYER

PARTRIDGE
A Penguin Random House Company

To order additional copies of this book, contact
Toll Free 800 101 2657 (Singapore)
Toll Free 1 800 81 7340 (Malaysia)
orders.singapore@partridgepublishing.com

www.partridgepublishing.com/singapore

CONTENTS

PART II
Democratic Capitalism

CHAPTER 4

The East India Company to Nationalised British Empire in Asia 1700-1900AD

Chronology of Company Dominance

The East India Company (EIC), chartered in 1600 as the Governor and Company of Merchants of London trading into the East Indies, and often called the Honourable East India Company, was an English and later (from 1707) British joint-stock company. In an act aimed at strengthening the power of the EIC, King Charles II in 1670 provisioned the EIC with the rights to autonomous territorial acquisitions, to mint money, to command fortresses and troops and form alliances, to make war and peace, and to exercise both civil and criminal jurisdiction over the acquired areas.

Initially, the Company struggled in the spice trade due to the competition from the already well established Dutch East India Company. The Company built its first factory in south India and, benefiting from the imperial patronage, soon expanded its commercial trading operations, eclipsing the Portuguese. The Company sought a permanent establishment, while the Parliament would not willingly allow it greater autonomy and so relinquish the opportunity to exploit the Company's profits. The Company developed a lobby in the English parliament.

The Seven Years War meant Britain and France clashed on Indian soil, between the EIC troops and the French company forces. Then national troops were provided by respective governments. After General Clive was successful during the war, the Company officials had discovered that there was more money to be made from military adventures than trade, and that India could be plundered.

I place the commencement of the EIC military dominance in India as 1757 when the Law Officers of the Crown delivered the Pratt-Yorke opinion distinguishing overseas territories acquired by right of conquest from those acquired by private treaty. The opinion asserted that, while the Crown of Great Britain enjoyed sovereignty over both, only the property of the former was vested in the Crown. The Company enjoyed British government support particularly after loss of the American colonies in 1783.

The EIC peak could have been reached in 1816 after the Anglo-Nepalese War 1814-1816. By 1815 the Company's debt was £40million and just over three-quarters of its annual budget was consumed by the expenses of its army which was then 150,000 strong. There had been brief signs of a financial resurgence in the mid-1760s as the land taxes of Bengal began to pour in, but these quickly vanished and the Company lurched from crisis to crisis. In order to stay afloat, it had fallen back on the dubious expedient of raising capital by regular share issues, and had created what in effect was the private version of the national debt.

The Company lost power with Government of India Act 1858 when its responsibilities were assumed by the Crown, and its army absorbed into the Indian army. The company ceased to exist when the company dissolved through the East India Stock Dividend Redemption Act 1873.

Company Leaders in War and Defence in Asia

India

Under pressure from English competitors, an Act was passed by parliament in 1694 which basically allowed any English firm to trade with India. The EIC developed a lobby in parliament that resulted in 1698 of an Act establishing the English Company trading to the East Indies which was floated under a state backed indemnity. The new company was dominated by stockholders of the old company. The two companies competed vigorously but then merged in 1708, together with a state indenture, to become the United Merchants of England Trading to the East Indies. The merged company, still known as the East India Company, lent £3.2million to the Treasury in return for three years exclusive trading privileges. By Acts in 1712 and 1730 the licence was prolonged to 1766. In 1742, in apprehension of a war with France, the British government extended exclusive trading until 1783 in return for a further loan of £1million. The British government did not own shares in the Company (though prominent courtiers and politicians certainly did).

In 1744 the youthful renegade Robert Clive arrived at Fort St. George, in Madras (Chennai) on the Coromandel Coast to work as a factor. Over the forty years since the death of the Mughal Emperor Aurangzeb in 1707, the power of the emperor had gradually fallen into the hands of his provincial viceroys or *soobedars*. The dominant rulers on the Coromandel Coast were the Nizam of Hyderabad, Asaf Jah I, and the Nawab of the Carnatic, Anwaruddin Mohammed Khan. The Nawab nominally owed fealty to the Nizam, but in many respects acted independently. The French *Compagnie des Indes* under governor Marquis Dupleix was based at Pondicherry. The First Carnatic War (1746-1748) reflected the Indian conflict between Britain and France in the wider War of Austrian Succession.

Madras was surrendered to French forces in 1746. Clive and some others escaped and decided to join the Company army. He helped repel a French attack on Fort St. David (100miles south of Madras) in 1747 and was given a commission as ensign. Clive distinguished himself in the 1748 Siege of Pondicherry, before the end of the War. Madras was returned to the British as part of the peace agreement in early 1749.

Lieutenant Clive had command of 30 British soldiers and 300 *sepoys* (Indian soldiers) under Major Lawrence when confronted by a large Indian (Tanjorean) army. Indian soldiers responded well to daring and courageous officers such as Clive. The actions of his unit were credited in the capture of the fort of Devikottai after which the Rajah of Tanjore negotiated peace. Clive was denied a promotion and demobbed when the Company slashed the military. Lawrence secured Clive a lucrative position as the commissary of Fort St George.

The struggle for succession of the Nizam of Hyderabad led to the Second Carnatic War in which the French backed Muzaffar Jung and Chanda Sahib who wished to be Nawab of Arcot. The British supported Nasir Jung/Muhammad Ali Khan. Initially the French succeeded in installing their protégés on the thrones in 1749. The Company military was still in a mess when in 1751 Clive volunteered to lead a mission to attack Arcot if he was given a commission as Captain. After a series of forced marches Clive's motley crew occupied a deserted Arcot. The subsequent siege defence by Clive's small force was successful with minimum casualties. To end a stalemate, the governors requested government troops from their governments. The governments agreed and changed a commercial battle into an international war for India. The War ended with the Treaty of Pondicherry 1754.

The French leader Dupleix was asked to return to France when the Directors of *Compagnie des Indes* were dissatisfied with his political ambitions. He was replaced by Charles Godeheu. The Directors of the EIC voted Clive a sword worth $700. Clive returned to England in 1753.

Lieutenant Colonel Clive of the British Army came back to India in 1755 to act as deputy governor of Fort St. David. In 1756, coincident with the Seven Years War in Europe, the new Nawab of Bengal, Siraj-ud-Daulah, took the fort at Calcutta, and imprisoned the British in the notorious "Black Hole" following abuse of commercial privileges. Admiral Charles Watson and Clive were diverted from the Third Carnatic War to remove the Nawab from Calcutta (Kolkata) by force. Calcutta was taken with relative ease but the huge army of the Nawab returned.

The British intrigued to bribe the Nawab's commander-in-chief, Mir Jafar, to betray his forces in exchange for the office of viceroy and paying a huge sum of money. In 1757 Clive's outnumbered army drew up against the Nawab's huge forces at Plassey. In the subsequent battle Mir Jafar led a large portion of the Nawab's army way from the battle, allowing for a British victory with minimum casualties. Mir Jafar was installed as Nawab and distributed funds as agreed. Clive personally received £160,000 and later an annuity of £27,000 for life to make him one of the richest British men. He extended his largesse to other officials in Calcutta. This battle, in which most of the Nawab's treasury millions vanished, ensured British control of the commercially important province of Bengal. British forces captured the French settlement of Chandernagore.

In 1760 the Governor of Bengal, Clive, returned to England with his personal fortune and left Bengal impoverished trying to recoup the outlay by Mir Jafar. He was made Baron Clive of Plassey, County Clare and began an effort to reform the home system of the East India Company. The Company had become mired in corruption, civil and military, and had been plundered of its share of the Bengal bribe. Employees were allowed not only to choose how to fulfill their orders, but also to trade on their own account.

The Third Carnatic War was then won in the south when the British commander Sir Eyre Coote decisively defeated the French under Comte de Lally at the Battle of Wandiwash in 1760. Pondicherry was taken in 1761. The Company captured Manila in the Philippines in 1762. The Treaty of Paris 1763 returned Chandernagore and Pondicherry to the French but confirmed Britain as the dominant foreign power in India. The French retained outposts for the next two hundred years but were no threat to the British.

The Company had created another powerful East India lobby in Parliament, a caucus of MPs who had either directly or indirectly profited from its business. The Company army was able to expand by paying Indian regular soldiers higher wages that the Nawabs could afford, by expropriating land revenue. The army was well equipped with muskets, artillery, bullock wagons and cavalry horses. The British secured Ganges-Jumna Doab, the Delhi-Agra region, parts of Bundelkhand, Broach, some districts of Gujarat, fort of Ahmmadnagar, province of Cuttack (which included Mughalbandi/the coastal part of Odisha, Garjat/the princely states of Odisha, Balasore Port, parts of Midnapore district of West Bengal), Bombay (Mumbai) and the surrounding areas. This led to a formal end of the Maratha Empire and firm establishment of the British East India Company in India.

The Court of Proprietors forced the Directors to send Lord Clive to Bengal with the powers of Governor and Commander in Chief. General Clive arrived back in India in 1765 to find that Mir Jafar had died, so that his son Kasim Ali was the Nawab of Bengal. Kasim Ali had induced the Nawab of Awadh and the Emperor of Delhi to invade Bihar, north of Bengal. The Bengal Company army scattered the Indian armies on the field of Buxar from which the Emperor withdrew. The Nawab of Awadh threw himself on the mercies of the British. Clive returned to the Nawab of Awadh all territory except the provinces of Allahabad and Kora which he presented to the weak emperor. The price to the Emperor for the provinces was the granting of Bengal to Clive. By the *firman* (royal mandate) the Company became the real sovereign rulers of thirty million people, yielding annual revenue of four million pounds sterling. Clive also received a charter for the Carnatic and the Deccan.

Unfortunately London had now realised the high cost of maintaining a Company army even as the recipients of the largesse freely spent their fortunes in Britain. From the 1760s when profits fell and Company stock became speculative, Indian allies were backed by state loans and guarantees. In 1769-70 there was a terrible famine in Bengal but land revenues remained high. In the 1770s the Company began to incur even greater costs from its wars, expansion of territory and administration.

The Company repaid the state not just in taxes and tariffs, but also in ideas. It was one of the 18th and 19th centuries' great innovators in the art of governing—more innovative by some way than the British government, not to mention its continental rivals, and surpassed only by the former colonies of America.

Clive sought to institute a strong administration which unfortunately had little effect on corruption that remained widespread. He reorganised the army into three brigades, making each a complete force equal to any single Indian army. Lord Clive left India for the last time in 1767. In 1772, Clive was invested in the Order of the Bath and was appointed Lord Lieutenant of Shropshire. He committed suicide in 1774, possibly from an overdose of opium.

Low Chinese demand for European goods, and high European demand for Chinese goods, including tea, silk, and porcelain, forced European merchants to purchase these goods with silver, the only commodity the Chinese would accept. With India and its poppy fields under Britain's command, the logical option to fix the imbalance of trade was to start trading opium in exchange for tea.

Recognising the growing number of addicts, the Chinese Yongzheng Emperor had prohibited the sale and smoking of opium in 1729. The East India Company established an elaborate trading scheme partially relying on legal markets, and partially leveraging illicit ones. British merchants carrying no opium would buy tea in Canton on credit, and would balance their debts by selling opium at auction in Calcutta. From there, the opium would reach the Chinese coast hidden aboard British ships then smuggled into China by native merchants. In 1773 the Company created a British monopoly on opium buying in Bengal and for fifty years the opium trade was key to its hold on the Far East.

Warren Hastings was appointed the first Governor-General of India, under Lord North's Regulating Act 1773, having already spent eighteen years in the Company's Indian service. In 1784, after a further ten years of service, during which he helped extend and regularise the nascent *Raj* (Sanskrit - reign) created by Clive of India, Hastings resigned. On his return to England he was charged in Parliament with high crimes and misdemeanours by Edmund Burke, who was encouraged by Sir Philip Francis, whom Hastings had wounded during a duel in India. He was impeached in 1787, but the trial, which ran from 1788 to 1795, ended in acquittal. Hastings spent most of his replenished fortune on his defence.

During the period of the Napoleonic Wars, the East India Company arranged for letters of marque for its vessels. This was not so that they could carry cannons to fend off warships, privateers and pirates on their voyages to India and China (that they could do without permission) but so that, should they have the opportunity to take a prize, they could do so without being guilty of piracy. The company also had its own navy, the Bombay Marine, equipped with warships. These vessels often accompanied vessels of the Royal Navy on expeditions, such as the invasion of Java (1811).

In 1786 Charles Cornwallis finally accepted Prime Minster Pitt's appointment to be Governor-General and Commander in Chief of India. Cornwallis engaged in reforms of all types, which had an impact on many areas of civil, military, and corporate administration. Cornwallis was responsible for *"laying the foundation for British rule throughout India and setting standards for the services, courts, and revenue collection that remained remarkably unaltered almost to the end of the British era."* He also enacted important reforms in the operations of the British East India Company, and, with the notable exception of the Kingdom of Mysore, managed to keep the company out of military conflicts during his tenure.

The company was unavoidably drawn into war with Mysore in 1790. Tipu Sultan, Mysore's ruler, had expressed contempt for the British not long after signing the 1784 Treaty of Mangalore, and also expressed a desire to renew conflict with them. In late 1789 he invaded the Kingdom of Travancore, a company ally according to treaty, because of territorial disputes and Travancore's harbouring of refugees from other Mysorean actions. Cornwallis ordered company and Crown troops to mobilise in response. An Indo-Muslim with French republican tendencies could not be allowed to dictate to the *Raj*. The 1790 campaign against Tipu was conducted by General William Medows, and it was a limited success. Medows successfully occupied the Coimbatore district, but Tipu counterattacked and was able to reduce the British position to a small number of strongly held outposts. Tipu then invaded the Carnatic, where he attempted unsuccessfully to draw the French into the conflict.

Because of Medows' weak campaigning, Cornwallis personally took command of the British forces in 1791. After an ineffectual campaign in 1791, the replenished army was successful in a siege of Seringapatam. Cornwallis negotiated peace which demanded the cessation of half of Mysorean territory, most of which went to the British allies. To guarantee the Tipu's performance two of his sons became hostage.

Cornwallis had the Company take over the few remaining judicial powers of the Nawab of Bengal, the titular local ruler of much of the Bengal Presidency, and gave some judicial powers to company employees. In 1790 he introduced circuit courts with company employees as judges, and set up a court of appeals in Calcutta. He had the legal frameworks of Muslim and Hindu law translated into English, and promulgated administrative regulations and a new civil and criminal code. This work, introduced in 1793, was known as the Cornwallis Code. One consequence of the code was that it instituted a type of racism, placing the British as an elite class on top of the complex status hierarchy of caste and religion that existed in India at the time.

Cornwallis's attitude toward the lower classes did, however, include a benevolent and somewhat paternalistic desire to improve their condition. He introduced legislation to protect native weavers who were sometimes forced into working at starvation wages by unscrupulous company employees, outlawed child slavery, and established in 1791 a Sanskrit college for Hindus. He also established a mint in Calcutta that, in addition to benefiting the poor by providing a reliable standard currency, was a forerunner of India's modern currency.

Cornwallis left India in 1793 the same year that revolutionary France declared war on Great Britain. Richard Wellesley, Earl of Mornington, had been a member of the Board of Control over Indian Affairs before in 1797 he accepted the office of Governor-General of India. Soon after landing in 1798 Mornington ordered preparations for war against the Sultan of Mysore. The invasion of Mysore followed in early 1799 which resulted in the killing of the Tipu Sultan and the capture of Seringapatam. In 1799 Mornington became Marquess Wellesley. After the end of the war, Wellesley's brother Arthur Wellesley was promoted to brigadier-general as the new governor of Seringapatam and Mysore. In 1803 Arthur, now promoted to major-general, was sent to command an army to success in the Second Anglo-Maratha War. Wellesley's other brother, Henry, was his private secretary and diplomatic advisor.

The result of these wars and of the treaties which followed them was that French influence in India was extinguished, and forty million people and ten millions of revenue were added to the British dominions. The powers of the Maratha and all other princes were so reduced that the Company/ Britain became the true dominant authority over all India with an army of 192,000 men. This was the empire of the East India Company *Raj*. The traditional principles of English aristocratic government were applied to the people of India, mingling firmness with benevolent paternalism. Wellesley rode a magnificently bedecked elephant to demonstrate his power. Of course the debts of the Company had trebled to the point that it was an institutionally funded organisation. A free-trader like Pitt, Wellesley endeavoured to remove some of the restrictions on the trade between Britain and India.

In 1804 Arthur applied for permission to return to England and returned with his brother the Marquess in 1805. Arthur was made Knight of the Bath and was elected Tory Member of Parliament in 1806, before returning to the army as lieutenant-general in 1808. Richard, as Lord Wellesley, declined to join the Portland government in 1807 pending resolutions against him in respect of his Indian administration. Those resolutions were defeated by large majorities.

In 1805 Cornwallis was reappointed Governor-General of India by Pitt, this time to curb the expansionist activity of Lord Wellesley. He arrived in India in July 1805, but died in October of a fever. He was succeeded by Sir George Barlow as provisional governor-general and Gilbert Elliot-Murray, Lord Minto, was appointed in 1806. During his time in India he expanded the British presence in the area to the Moluccas, Java, and other Dutch possessions during the Napoleonic Wars.

Through the influence of the Prince-Regent, Francis Rawdon-Hastings, Earl of Moira was appointed Governor-General of India in 1812, arriving in 1813. The Company was in the throes of another cash-flow crisis. Moira's answer was to export Kashmir wool from Tibet to Britain. Of course the problem that the Nepalese government would not allow the Company to trade with the fabled Tibet through Nepal, was surmountable when there was a large army unoccupied. The evidence does not support the claim that Moira invaded Nepal principally for commercial reasons. It was ostensibly a strategic decision. He was wary of the Hindu revival and solidarity among the Marathas, the Sikhs, and the Gurkhas amid the decaying Mughal Empire. He was hatching pre-emptive schemes of conquest against the Marathas in central India, and he needed to cripple Nepal first, in order to avoid having to fight on two fronts. The "illegal" occupation by the Nepalese from 1804 till 1812 of the Terai of Butwal, which was under British protection, was the immediate reason which led to the Anglo-Nepal war in 1814.

The British with Indian *sepoys* were not used to fighting in the mountainous conditions of Nepal so, although they vastly outnumbered the Nepalese, there were no great victories. Battles were closely fought but the British gradually overcame Nepalese positions through numbers and superior weapons. A treaty was signed in 1815 ceding to the British, territory which proved difficult to govern and was returned in 1816. Despite the British merchants' direct access to the wool growing areas after the war, the hopes of shawl wool trade were never realised. The British merchants found that they were too late. The shawl wool market was strictly closed and closely guarded. It was monopolised by traders from Kashmir and Ladakh who would not deal with the Company. About 5,000 Nepalese Gurkha men entered British service in 1815, most of whom were Kumaonis, Garhwalis and other Himalayan hill men. These groups, eventually lumped together under the term *Gurkha*, became the backbone of British Indian forces for over a century.

Lord Moira was more successful in the Third Anglo-Maratha War in 1817. The operations began with action against Pindaris, a band of Muslim and Maratha from central India which led Maratha forces to rise against the Company. By the end of the war, all of the Maratha powers had surrendered to the British. Shinde and the Pashtun Amir Khan were subdued by the use of diplomacy and pressure, which resulted in the Treaty of Gwailor. The *Peshwa* (foremost minister) surrendered in June 1818 and was sent off to Bithur near Kanpur under the terms of the treaty signed in 1818.

Moira confirmed the purchase of Singapore by Sir Stamford Raffles for the Company in 1819. Moira clashed with the Board of the Company over pay for army officers and was removed. Moira was succeeded by William Amherst, Earl Amherst in 1823. Amherst was an inexperienced governor who was, at least in the early days of his tenure in Calcutta, influenced heavily by senior military officers in Bengal. When a territorial dispute that he inherited involving the Anglo-Burmese border on the Naaf River spilled over into violence in 1823, Amherst ordered the troops in, to save face at a time of Burmese territorial aggression. The war was to take two years, with 15,000 killed on the British side and cost 13 million pounds, contributing to an economic crisis in India. It was only due to the efforts of powerful friends that he was not replaced until 1828.

Amherst was replaced by Lord William Bentinck who engaged in an extensive range of cost-cutting measures, earning the lasting enmity of many military men whose wages were cut. Reforming the court system, he made English, rather than Persian, the language of the higher courts and encouraged western-style education for Indians in order to provide more educated Indians for service in the British bureaucracy. Bentinck returned to the UK in 1835 to be succeeded by George Eden, Earl of Auckland in 1836.

As a legislator, Auckland dedicated himself especially to the improvement of native schools and the expansion of the commercial industry of India. The Russian empire was slowly extending its dominions into central Asia, and this was seen as an encroachment south that might prove fatal for the British Company rule in India. British fears of a Russian invasion of India took one step closer to becoming a reality when negotiations between the Afghans and Russians broke down in 1838. Russia, wanting to increase its presence in South and Central Asia, had formed an alliance with Persia which had territorial disputes with Afghanistan.

Auckland's plan was to drive away the besiegers of Herat and install a ruler in Afghanistan who was pro-British, in place of the current Afghan ruler. An army of 21,000 British and Indian troops set out from Punjab in 1838.

A surprise attack succeeded in the capture of Ghazni which provided a well supplied base. A decisive victory over Afghan troops led to the instalment of the British choice of Shuja Shah Durrani in Kabul. The majority of the British troops returned to India, but it soon became clear that Shuja's rule could only be maintained with the presence of a great number of British forces. The Afghans resented the British presence and the rule of Shah Shuja. This led to years of attacks on British forces by disaffected tribes against British occupation, including the 1842 massacre of General Elphinstone's retreating army of around 16,500.

Lord Auckland suffered a stroke and was replaced as Governor-General by Edward Law, Earl of Ellenborough, who was under instructions to bring the war to an end. He ordered the forces at Kandahar and Jalalabad to leave Afghanistan after inflicting reprisals and securing the release of prisoners taken during the earlier retreat from Kabul. The combined British forces defeated all opposition before taking Kabul in September. A month later, having rescued the prisoners and demolished the city's main bazaar as an act of retaliation for the destruction of Elphinstone's column, they withdrew from Afghanistan through the Khyber Pass in 1842.

Tensions between the Company and the local religious and cultural groups grew in the 19th century as the Protestant revival grew in Great Britain. These tensions erupted at the Indian Rebellion of 1857. The Rebellion began in May 1857 as a mutiny of sepoys of the East India Company's army in the town of Meerut, and soon escalated into other mutinies and civilian rebellions largely in the upper Gangetic plain and central India, with the major hostilities confined to present-day Uttar Pradesh, Bihar, northern Madhya Pradesh, and the Delhi region. The rebellion posed a considerable threat to Company power in that region, and was contained only with the fall of Gwalior in June 1858. The Mutiny was a result of various grievances. However the flashpoint was reached when the soldiers were asked to bite off the paper cartridges for their rifles, which they believed were greased with animal fat, namely beef and pork, against religious beliefs.

Governmental responsibilities were transferred to the Crown by the Government of India Act 1858. The Company's 24,000-man military force had also been transferred to the authority of the Crown (subsequently being incorporated into the Indian Army).

China/Hong Kong

The Qing government of China had become open to foreign trade in the 1680s, restricted to thirteen factories on the harbour of Canton during the trading season. In 1711 the Company was given permission by the Chinese Kangxi Emperor to enter Canton (Guangzhou) to trade tea for silver.

By 1817, the British decided that counter-trading in a narcotic drug, Indian opium, was a way to reduce the silver trade deficit. The Qing Administration originally tolerated opium importation, because it created an indirect tax on Chinese subjects, while allowing the British to double tea exports from China to England—which profited the monopoly for tea exports of the Qing imperial treasury and its agents. In 1820 the Qing government attempted to end the opium trade, but its efforts were complicated by local officials (including the Viceroy of Canton), who profited greatly from the bribes and taxes. A turning point came in 1834. Free trade reformers in England succeeded in ending the monopoly of the British East India Company, leaving trade in the hands of private entrepreneurs. Americans introduced opium from Turkey, which was of lower quality but cheaper. Competition drove down the price of opium and increased sales. In 1839 Governor of Canton, Lin Zexu, banned the sale of opium, demanded that all opium be surrendered to the Chinese authorities. After an incident in Kowloon, the British brought in the military.

The First Opium War of 1839-42 was regarded by British observers at the time as a praiseworthy last resort effort to correct the attitude of the Chinese towards legitimate trade. The war was a shock to the Chinese who lacked the modern technology of their adversaries. At the start of the war Hong Kong was seized as a future naval base and trade centre. Woosung, Shanghai and Chinkiang were shelled then taken by landing forces. A stunned Chinese government capitulated with the Treaty of Nanking which confirmed British possession of Hong Kong and opened a number of cities to British commerce. British consulates were opened and a British naval base established in Shanghai. France and the United States quickly gained similar privileges.

Britain used its naval domination to suppress piracy in Chinese waters to safeguard commerce. Head-money was paid to the crews of warships of up to £20 per head. Naturally the interference with its citizens by a foreign nation upset the Chinese government. An incident when Cantonese soldiers boarded a British registered vessel, prompted the consul John Bowring to use his powers to summon a flotilla to shell Canton. This basically started the Second Opium War 1856-58 settled by the 1858 Treaty of Tientsin which gained further concessions for the foreigners and legalised the opium trade.

The Company had lost Indian power in 1858 and the British government had taken control in China. An imperious legate like Lord Elgin was likely to exploit weakness so used disputes over treaty clauses to push for more control. An Anglo-Indian and French army landed in north China to march on Peking (Beijing). Looting was endemic when the imperial palaces of Peking were abandoned by Emperor Hsien-feng and his court in 1860. The summer palaces were burned down on orders from Elgin.

The Chinese customs service had passed into foreign control in 1853 as an emergency measure when Taiping insurgents threatened Shanghai. By 1873 customs were managed by Sir Robert Hart with a European staff of whom more than half were British. This guaranteed the Chinese government a reliable source of revenue and was a safeguard for foreign capitalists.

The sudden and complete collapse of China in the Sino-Japanese War 1894-95 enticed foreign nations to plunder. Japan demanded Formosa (Taiwan), the Liaotung Peninsula with a large monetary indemnity. The Europeans protested the Peninsula and in return the Chinese government granted France mineral rights in Yunnan, Kwangsi and Kwantung; Hankow was delivered to Germany. Russia was allowed a controlling stake in the Chinese Eastern Railway. In 1897 Germany was granted the monopoly of mines and railways in Shantung, and occupied Kiachow which was turned into a naval base. Russia slipped into Port Arthur in 1898 after she had helped evict the Japanese. Britain leased Wei-heiwei on the north coast as a naval base.

By the end of 1898 the nascent resistance against foreign penetration had emerged into the *I-ho chuan* (Righteous and Harmonious Fists) or *Boxers* who hated anything alien. They were initially anti-Manchu but gradually won supporters in court. The sympathetic governor of Shansi, Yu-hsien, incorporated the Boxers into the local militia before pointing them at foreign missionaries and converts.

The Dowager Empress, Tzu-hsi, formed an ambivalent alliance with the Boxers in an effort to deflect popular anger away from the ruling Dynasty. The Boxer rebellion had already drawn foreign warships to the Gulf of Chihli which apparently stimulated the Empress in 1900 to commit imperial troops to join 30,000 Boxers in an attack on the walled legation quarter in Peking (Beijing). The

Boxers boasted magical powers that made them immune from bullets, so tended to fight with swords and spears. The sparsely defended legations held out until 18,000 foreign troops arrived.

Russia took advantage of the unrest to commit 200,000 troops to Manchuria and to transfer warships to Port Arthur. Japan contested the Russian claims to Manchuria and Korea. This was basically the trigger for the formation of the Anglo-Japanese Alliance in 1902 which allowed Japan to go to war with Russia without fear of French intervention. In 1904 Japanese warships made a pre-emptive strike against the Russian squadron in Port Arthur. The subsequent land and sea actions overturned Russia power in the Far East. Japan, an Asian power, had defeated a European force to prove that European forces were not invincible. The precedent was set for the pre-emptive strike on Pearl Harbour decades later.

Burma (Myanmar)

Burma (Myanmar) lost Arakan, Manipur, Assam and Tenasserim to the British in the First Anglo-Burmese War (1824–1826). In 1852, the British easily seized Lower Burma in the Second Anglo-Burmese War. King Mindon tried to modernise the kingdom, and in 1875 narrowly avoided annexation by ceding the Karenni States. The British, alarmed by the consolidation of French Indo-China, annexed the remainder of the country in the Third Anglo-Burmese War in 1885. With the fall of Mandalay, all of Burma came under British rule, being annexed in January 1886. Rangoon became the capital of British Burma and an important port between Calcutta and Singapore.

Malaya

In 1771 a British firm operating in Madras, Jourdain, Sullivan and de Souza, sent Francis Light, a captain in the service of the East India Company, to meet the Sultan of Kedah to open the state's market for trading. The Sultan agreed to allow the firm to establish a trading post if the British agreed to protect Kedah from external threats. The Company would not agree to military aid. In 1772 the Company ordered Light to take over the island of Penang but, when the Company once again would not agree to aid, the new Sultan ordered him to leave in 1788. The British forced the Sultan to sign an agreement that gave the British the right to occupy Penang in return for annual rent of 6000 Spanish pesos.

In 1824 the British and the Dutch signed a treaty known as the Anglo-Dutch Treaty of 1824. The treaty, among other things, legally transferred Malacca to British administration. The treaty also officially divided the Malay world into two separate entities and laid the basis for the current Indonesian-Malaysian boundary. In 1826 the administration of Penang, Malacca and Singapore was established as the Straits Settlements with Penang as capital. In 1836 the capital was moved to Singapore.

Britain accepted Siamese sovereignty of the northern Malay states, especially Kedah, Terengganu, Kelantan and Pattani in return for Siam accepting British ownership of Penang and adjoining Prai province. Informal empire in Malaya depended on the cooperation of local princes who were expected to keep the peace.

Along with Perak, Selangor, another Malay state just south of Perak, had considerable deposits of tin around Hulu Selangor in the north, Hulu Klang in the central area and Lukut near Negeri Sembilan to the south. Around 1840, under the leadership of Raja Jumaat from Riau, tin mining became a huge enterprise. By the 1850s the area emerged as one of the most modern settlements on the Malay Peninsula apart from the Straits Settlements.

Until 1867 the Straits Settlements were answerable to the East India Company in Calcutta. Following dissolution of the Company in 1858 and, after intense lobbying by the Settlements' administrators, the colony was placed directly under power of the Colonial Office in London as a crown colony. After 1870, the maintenance of empire proved beyond the capacity of the local princes and the area fell into near anarchy. The main problem was the Chinese who had been imported to provide labour to tin mining in Selangor and Perak. The Chinese were connected to individual mutually hostile secret societies which sparked a civil war 1867-74.

In 1873, a ship from Penang was attacked by pirates near Selangor. A court was assembled and suspected pirates were sentenced to death. The Sultan expressed concern and requested assistance from Sir Andrew Clarke. Frank Swettenham was appointed to serve as the Sultan's advisor. Approximately a year later, a lawyer from Singapore named J.G. Davidson was appointed as British Resident in Selangor. Britain assumed formal protection of Perak, Selangor, Negri Sembilan and Pahang.

As Governor of the Straits Settlements, Sir Andrew Clarke signed the Treaty of Pangkor in 1874, which established indirect British rule over the Malay States. In that same year, Clarke successfully enforced a check on the abuse of coolies with support of the prominent Chinese leaders and European merchants. Clarke achieved fame through his negotiations in regard to Sungei Ujong in Malaya, sorting out the differences between different leaders in Negeri Sembilan.

To streamline the administration of the Malay states and especially to protect and further develop the lucrative trade in tin-mining and rubber, in 1895 Britain sought to consolidate and centralise control by federating the four contiguous states of Selangor, Perak, Negeri Sembilan and Pahang into a new entity, the Federated Malay States, with Kuala Lumpur as its capital. Although the sultans had less power than their counterparts in the Unfederated Malay States, the new entity enjoyed a much higher degree of modernisation.

A new treaty now known as the Bangkok Treaty of 1909 was signed between the two powers. In the new agreement, Siam agreed to give up its claim over Kedah, Perlis, Terengganu and Kelantan, while Pattani remained Siamese territory. Malay rulers did not acknowledge the agreement, but were too weak to resist British influence. In Kedah after the Bangkok Treaty, George Maxwell was posted by the British in Kedah as the sultan's advisor. The British effectively took over economic planning and execution.

Independent Johore, meanwhile, had to surrender Singapore to the British earlier on and despite the Sultan's political effort was forced to accept an advisor in 1914, becoming the last Malay state to lose her sovereignty.

Singapore

In 1819 Thomas Stamford Raffles arrived at the neglected island of Singapore to sign a treaty with the Sultan of Johore on behalf of the British East India Company to develop the southern part of the island as a trading post. In 1824 the entire island became a British possession under a further treaty. In 1826, it became part of the Straits Settlements, under the jurisdiction of British India.

Singapore became the capital of the Straits Settlements in 1836. By 1860, the population exceeded 80,000, with over half of the population being Chinese. Many immigrants came to work at rubber plantations, and after the 1870s the island became a global centre for rubber exports. Independent Johore had to surrender Singapore to the British.

Cocos

A Scottish sea captain, John Clunies-Ross, went to live on the Cocos (Keeling) Islands in 1827. He established a trading post and coconut plantations where he became "king" who coined his own currency. The islands were annexed by the

British Empire in 1857 with John Clunies-Ross II as Superintendent. In 1867 the islands were administered by the Straits Settlements. In 1886 Queen Victoria granted the islands in perpetuity to the Clunies-Ross family.

Sarawak

James Brooke, invalided out of the East India Company army, sailed a well-armed schooner to North Borneo. 1839-1841 Brooke made himself useful to Hasim Jeal, regent of Brunei who was attempting to dominate the province of Sarawak. Brooke, as Rajah of Sarawak, laid the foundations for stable government and subdued pirates. The British government approved Brooke as Rajah, and accepted his tiny state of Sarawak as part of empire.

Economics

In 1591 the merchants of London petitioned Queen Elizabeth I for a licence to trade in the East Indies and chose James Lancaster to lead three vessels to the Spice Islands of modern Indonesia. The trip was a disaster when only 25 men of 198 survived scurvy and natural accidents on the remaining ship to return to London. Unfortunately those sailors who had escaped scurvy on the long voyage were faced with the plague that was decimating London (30,000 killed). The East Indies would have been written off, but the merchants learned of a Dutch expedition.

England had been recognised as an international force since Henry VIII but internal religious and parliamentary unrest had prevented any sustained dominance. When King James I was petitioned on a need for the monopoly on East Indies trading in the face of opposition from the monopolistic Dutch East India Company (VOC), James granted the East India Company (EIC) monopoly forever or until trade was not profitable to the realm. The EIC introduced a class of Freeman of the Company which proved attractive to many nobles as a secret society with an oath and an annual feast. The Company imports of spices and cotton goods in the eighteenth century led to exports of mainly silver bullion. The English East India Company was prevented by the Dutch East India Company from complete success in Asia.

By the time of the First Anglo-Dutch War, goldsmiths had modelled their activities on the Bank of Amsterdam. Indeed much of England's goldsmiths' deposits were banked with the Bank of Amsterdam. After Charles II restoration in 1660, goldsmiths used the Government Exchequer for their short term deposits.

By the early 17th century, coffee houses were established in London which became the hot-houses of capitalism. When land came to be registered, mortgages could be negotiated in coffee houses that provided mercantile capital. In 1662 Charles II's Portuguese queen, Catherine of Braganza, introduced the act of drinking tea, which quickly spread throughout court and country and to the English *bourgeoisie*. In London, coffee houses introduced the new drink of tea (*tee*) mainly for the fashionably rich. The tea had been imported to Portugal from its possessions in Asia as well as through the trade merchants maintained with China and Japan. The British East India Company, which had been supplied with tea at the Dutch factory of Batavia, imported it directly from China from 1669.

With the expansion of Commonwealth ships for the Anglo-Dutch War, England was able to take some islands of the Caribbean, such as Jamaica in 1655. At first privateering against the Spanish was the attraction of the islands but soon English traders noticed the potential of growing sugar. The pirate Henry Morgan became a knighted sugar baron.

In the middle decades of the seventeenth century, the European economic crisis came to an end. After a period of transition, a new equilibrium appeared throughout Europe. The price of grain ceased rising, fell sharply, and then began to find a level. Food and energy came down, manufactures went up, and the general price level began to fluctuate on a fixed and level plain. Wages rose. Rents and interest fell. The distribution of wealth and income became a little more equal. Population, production, and productivity grew slowly. The maximum lawful rate of interest in England fell from 10 to 6 percent in the seventeenth century.

By mid century, sugar, produced by three-quarters of a million slaves and indentured Irish in the Caribbean, had become the single most valuable import to Britain, the profits of which had been translated into grandiose country estates and elegant town houses. Ships left the port of Liverpool with Indian calicoes and gold from the great banking houses to travel to West Africa where slaves were purchased, to be transported to the Caribbean where they were sold and the proceeds invested in sugar, molasses and treacle for transport back to Liverpool. These triangular voyages were immensely profitable to all involved except for the unfortunate slaves.

The 1650s also marked the start of a change in pattern in English exports with round trip shipping from London to Boston to Barbados to London. Instead of the traditional main export of fine woollen cloth, manufactured goods were sent to America, food and tobacco were shipped to Barbados to be replaced by sugar to England. This trans-Atlantic commerce increased under the Commonwealth and the Royal Navy commenced to be used as a guard against pirates.

Coffee houses were the preserve of middle and upper-class men; women drank tea in their own homes, but as yet tea was still too expensive to be widespread among the working classes. In part, its high price was due to a punitive system of taxation. The first tax on tea in the leaf, introduced in 1689, was so high at 25p in the pound weight that it almost stopped sales. It was reduced to 5p in the pound in 1692. By the eighteenth century many Britons wanted to drink tea but could not afford the high prices, and their enthusiasm for the drink was matched by the enthusiasm of criminal gangs to smuggle it in. What began as a small time illegal trade, selling a few pounds of tea to personal contacts, developed by the late eighteenth century into an astonishing organised crime network, perhaps importing as much as 7 million pounds weight annually, compared to a legal import of 5 million pounds. By 1784, the government realised that enough was enough, and that heavy taxation was creating more problems than it was worth. The new Prime Minister, William Pitt the Younger, slashed the tax from 119 per cent to 12.5 per cent. Suddenly legal tea was affordable, and smuggling stopped virtually overnight.

Sir John Banks became a Director and later, as Governor of the East Indian Company in 1672, he arranged a contract which included a loan of £20,000 and £30,000 worth of saltpetre (primary ingredient of gunpowder) for the king. Outstanding debts were also agreed and the Company was permitted to export 250 tons of saltpetre. So urgent was the need to supply the armed forces in the United Kingdom, America, and elsewhere that the authorities sometimes turned a blind eye on the untaxed sales.

The new Dutch regime of King William III in England imported Dutch innovations in public finance to England, the most important of which was the funded public debt, in which certain revenues (of the also newly introduced excises after the Dutch model) were dedicated to the amortisation and service of the public debt, while the responsibility for the English debt shifted from the monarch personally, to Parliament.

The problems of maritime losses had grown due to war and longer voyages. Insurance was introduced when c.1688 a financier Edward Lloyd opened a London coffee shop where insurance could be bought and sold. By 1700 Lloyd was publishing a shipping list tabulating all the details pertinent to a ship's voyage. Most importantly, Lloyd rated the hull and equipment with a code that allowed assessment of a ship's capability.

In May 1769 the stock of the East India Company peaked. In the ensuing three years the government was compelled to take an increasing role in the Company, through the Loan Bill and in the Regulating Act, which introduced the British government for the first time into a direct participation in the Company's Indian affairs.

By 1770 military and administrative costs of the EIC mounted beyond control in British-administered regions in Bengal due to the ensuing drop in labour productivity. At the same time, there was commercial stagnation and trade depression throughout Europe. The directors of the company attempted to avert bankruptcy by appealing to Parliament for financial help. This led to the passing of the Tea Act in 1773, which gave the Company greater autonomy in running its trade in the American colonies, and allowed it an exemption from tea import duties which its colonial competitors were required to pay. The British government granted the company a monopoly on the importation and sale of tea in the colonies. The colonists had never accepted the constitutionality of the duty on tea, and the Tea Act rekindled their opposition to it. Their resistance culminated in the Boston Tea Party on December 16, 1773, in which colonists boarded East India Company ships and dumped their loads of tea overboard. Tea became a major cause for the loss of American colonies.

The government also adopted the Regulating Act of 1773. Among other things the legislation raised the minimum shareholding necessary to vote from £500 to £1000 and restricted the term of Directors to four years. The intent was to stabilize the Board and decrease the power of shareholders. The power of Chairman increased and a Member of Parliament was preferred so that the government would be aware of activities.

Revenue had replaced commerce as the Company's first concern. Tax rolls replaced business ledgers. Arsenals replaced warehouses. The East India Company was controlled by the government with the object of collecting taxes through the means of a standing army. Adam Smith denounced the Company as a bloodstained monopoly: "burdensome", "useless" and responsible for grotesque massacres in Bengal. The government subjected the Company to ever-tighter supervision, partly because it resented bailing it out, partly because it was troubled by the argument that a company had no business in running a continent. In 1813 it removed its monopoly of trade with India. In 1833 it removed its monopoly of trade with China and banned it from trading in India entirely. In 1858, the year after the Indian mutiny vindicated the Company's critics, the government took over all administrative duties in India. It paid its last dividend in 1873 and was finally put out of its misery in 1874.

The Company had cost the British government a great deal of money. However in exchange Britain received an Empire.

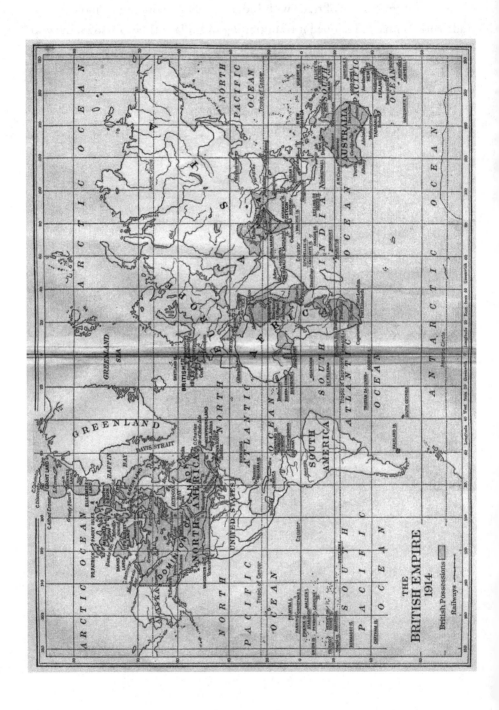

THE
BRITISH EMPIRE
1914

British Possessions
Railways

CHAPTER 5

The Constitutional Monarchy of British Royal Navy Dominance to British Empire 1700-1920AD

Chronology

1689	England	William III and Mary II joint monarchs
1694	**England**	**William III sole monarch; Bank of England incorporated**
1695		**100 year hot-dry peak**
1701		War of Spanish Succession
1702	England	Queen Anne
1707	**Britain**	**Act of Union of England and Scotland**
1714	Britain	**George I**
1715		100 year cold-wet peak
1715	Britain	Sir Robert Walpole, Whig Chancellor of Exchequer
1717	**Britain**	**Gold Standard adopted**
1719	France	Stock market collapse – Mississippi Bubble
1720	**Britain**	**Stock market collapse - South Sea Bubble**
1721	Britain	Sir Robert Walpole effectively Whig Prime Minister
1727	Britain	**George II**
1742	Britain	Henry Pelham, Whig Prime Minister
1745	Scotland	Jacobite uprising
1752	Britain	Gregorian Calendar adopted
1754	Britain	Thomas Pelham, Whig Prime Minister
1756	Europe	Alliance with Prussia against Austria
1760	Britain	**George III**
1762	Britain	John Stuart, Tory Prime Minister
1763	Britain	George Grenville, Whig Prime Minister
1765		**100 year cold-dry peak**
1765	Britain	Charles Watson-Wentworth, Whig Prime Minister
1766	Britain	William Pitt the Elder, Whig Prime Minister
1768	Britain	Augustus FitzRoy, Whig Prime Minister

1770	Britain	Frederick North, Tory Prime Minister
1773	Britain	Tea Act passed
1774	America	First Continental Congress
1776	**America**	**Declaration of Independence - American Revolution**
1782	Britain	Charles Watson-Wentworth, Whig Prime Minister
1782	Britain	William Petty-Fitzmaurice, Whig Prime Minister
1783	Britain	William Cavendish-Bentinck, Whig Prime Minister
1783	Britain	William Pitt the Younger, Tory Prime Minister
1784	Britain	India Act
1798	Egypt	Naval Battle of the Nile – victory to Admiral Nelson
1801	Britain	Henry Addington, Tory Prime Minister
1803	**Europe**	**War with France under Napoleon Bonaparte**
1804	Britain	William Pitt the Younger, Tory Prime Minister
1806	Britain	William Wyndham Grenville, Whig Prime Minister
1805		100 year warm-wet peak
1805	Spain	Naval Battle of Trafalgar – victory to Admiral Nelson
1807	Britain	Slave trade abolished
1807	Britain	William Cavendish-Bentinck, Tory Prime Minister
1809	Britain	Spencer Perceval, Tory Prime Minister
1811	**Britain**	**Regency Act - Prince of Wales George as Regent**
1812	Britain	Robert Banks Jenkinson, Tory Prime Minister
1812	America	War of 1812 with the United States of America
1815	Europe	Battle of Waterloo – victory to Britain, General Wellesley
1815	Britain	Corn Law
1819	Britain	Peterloo Massacre followed by repressive legislation
1820	Britain	**George IV**
1825		**100 year hot-dry peak**
1825	**Britain**	**Latin America Crisis**
1827	Britain	George Canning, Tory Prime Minister
1827	Britain	Frederick John Robinson, Tory Prime Minister
1828	Britain	Arthur Wellesley, Tory Prime Minister
1829	Britain	Catholic Relief Act
1830		100 year cold-wet peak
1830	Britain	**William IV**
1830	Britain	Charles Grey, Whig Prime Minister
1832	Britain	Reform Act
1832	Britain	formation of Conservative Party
1834	Britain	William Lamb, Whig Prime Minister
1834	Britain	Arthur Wellesley, Tory Prime Minister
1834	Britain	Sir Robert Peel, Conservative Prime Minister
1835	Britain	William Lamb, Whig Prime Minister

1837	Britain	**Queen Victoria**
1839	China	First Opium War
1841	Britain	Peel, Conservative Prime Minister
1842	China	Treaty of Nanking
1846	Britain	Bill of Repeal (Corn Laws)
1849	Britain	Lord John Russell, Whig Prime Minister
1849	Britain	Navigation Acts repealed opening free trade
1850	Britain	Foreign Secretary Palmerston commences gunboat diplomacy
1852	Britain	Edward Smith-Stanley (Derby), Conservative Prime Minister
1852	Britain	George Hamilton-Gordon (Aberdeen), Peelite Prime Minister
1853	Russia	Crimean War
1854	Crimea	Battle of Balaclava – charge of the Light Brigade
1855	Britain	Henry John Temple (Palmerston), Whig Prime Minister
1856	China	Second Opium War
1857	India	Sepoy Mutiny - Indian Rebellion
1857	**World**	**Global financial crisis**
1858	Britain	India Act
1858	Britain	Derby, Conservative Prime Minister
1859	Britain	formation of Liberal Party
1859	Britain	Palmerston, Liberal Prime Minister
1861	America	American Civil War
1865	Britain	Russell, Liberal Prime Minister
1865		**100 year cold-dry peak**
1866	Britain	Derby, Conservative Prime Minister
1868	Britain	Benjamin Disraeli, Conservative Prime Minister
1868	Britain	Gladstone, Liberal Prime Minister
1870-1	Europe	Franco-Prussian War
1874	Britain	Disraeli, Conservative Prime Minister
1880	Britain	Gladstone, Liberal Prime Minister
1885	Britain	Robert Gascoyne-Cecil (Salisbury), Conservative Prime Minister
1886	Britain	Gladstone, Liberal Prime Minister
1886	Britain	Salisbury, Conservative Prime Minister
1892	Britain	Gladstone, Liberal Prime Minister
1894	Britain	Archibald Primrose (Roseberry), Liberal Prime Minister
1895	Britain	Salisbury, Conservative Prime Minister
1897	Britain	Queen Victoria Diamond Jubilee
1901	Britain	**Edward VII**
1902	Britain	Arthur Balfour, Conservative Prime Minister
1905	Britain	Sir Henry Campbell-Bannerman, Liberal Prime Minister
1908	Britain	Herbert Henry Asquith, Liberal Prime Minister

1910	Britain	**George V**
1914	Europe	World War I
1916	Britain	David Lloyd George, Liberal Prime Minister
1925		100 year warm-wet peak

Chronology of English Maritime Dominance

I believe that political unrest in England had basically settled when William III and Mary II of England were crowned joint monarchs in April 1689. Parliament enacted the Bill of Rights 1689. Also in 1689 the Directors of East India Company passed a resolution about local government in India following improvements to Bombay and founding Calcutta. William approved the Charter of Incorporation of the Company of the Bank of England in 1694 which was to lead to improvements in commercial development. Half the initial proceeds went to improve the Royal Navy. Thus I believe that England/Britain enabled world dominance from 1694 by utilising a well-financed Royal Navy.

The eighteenth century saw the implementation of executive authority in the hands of the king's ministers, even though the king still had considerable influence. The Revolutionary Settlement Acts transformed the constitution, shifting the balance of power from the Sovereign to Parliament. For want of money, sovereigns had to summon Parliament annually and could no longer dissolve or prorogue it without its advice and consent. Parliament became a permanent feature of political life. The House of Commons had an influence over ministers, particularly members with landed interests. As the economy developed, there was increased lobbying from the commercial interests of merchants, shippers and financiers from the City of London as well as from plantation owners and those with India interests, including army officers. Parliament and the king were well aware of the propensity of the territories of Empire to stimulate trade and manufacture.

Political parties labeled "Whig" (*parliamentarian*) and "Tory"(*royalist*) had been in use in England since around 1681. Under William and Mary, Whigs became defenders of the new order and Tories adherents of the displaced Stuart dynasty. Under the Hanoverians the Whigs developed into a party associated with financial and mercantile interests of the City of London, and the Tories were identified with the land-owning class. The opposition of the two parties to each other encouraged lively parliaments that had much influence over the reigning monarchs from William III c.1700. The Whig Sir Robert Walpole took much control of the Hanoverian government from 1721 to commence parliamentary control of the kingdom.

The Royal Navy developed from 1707 into a well financed force in conjunction with the Dutch that dominated the navies of France and Spain. Despite losses in the Caribbean Battle of Cartagena de Indias, the Royal Navy returned to dominance in the 1740s to gain territory and prevent a French invasion of England in 1744.

I have estimated that the rise of Britain as a dominant culture commenced in 1745 enhanced by commencement of the EIC military dominance in India from 1757.

The combined forces of the American Continental Navy with France, Spain and Holland were too much for the Royal Navy during the Revolutionary War. The loss of the American colonies was to a degree offset by gains made in India by the East India Company.

British naval ascendancy rebounded in the 1780s so that the Royal Navy became once again dominant during the Napoleonic Wars. The innovative tactics by Admiral Jervis and Commodore Nelson against the Spanish at the Battle of Cape St. Vincent in 1797 commenced the Royal Navy recovery in the Mediterranean. This was followed by the victory of Vice Admiral Nelson over the French at the Battle of the Nile in 1798, which caused the French retreat from Egypt.

The combined Franco-Spanish fleet which had been gathered was smashed by Nelson in the Battle of Trafalgar (1805). This victory marked the culmination of decades of developing British naval dominance, and left the Navy in a position of uncontested hegemony at sea which endured until the early years of the 20th century.

The 1832 Parliamentary Reform Act created a middle class electorate. I place 1850 as the peak of British dominance even though the Empire would continue for another century. Once the Corn Law was repealed in 1846 the political, social and economic scenes in Britain became liberal and towards free trade. In such an atmosphere, the priority in society was to concentrate on producing industrial wealth, without any emphasis on military capability. The financial wealth of Empire had become the guiding force of British society and the model for future dominant cultures. The dominant policy was to keep the world safe for British business. It is extremely difficult for a liberal society to maintain dominance over other nations, and gunboat diplomacy had its limits. Even so, Foreign Secretary Lord Palmerston sent battleships to Greece in 1850 to place an embargo on Greek shipping to impress the government to consider compensation to British subjects. The Crimean War 1853-1856 demonstrated that any military dominance by Britain was restricted to the Royal Navy, and also raised the importance of the middle class in political forces. I have reached the opinion that the British Empire reached a peak of dominance c.1850 mainly due to internal political activity before the Crimean War.

Governmental responsibilities and costs of the East India Company were transferred to the Crown by the Government of India Act 1858. The Company's 24,000-man military force had also been transferred to the authority of the Crown (subsequently being incorporated into the Indian Army). The British government became direct rulers of the Indian sub-continent and Asian nations.

The positive effect of the Crimean War was that Britain addressed its attitudes to military governance. That all military honours should be given to the aristocratic leading officers without recognition to the fighting men who died in their thousands, was recognised as obsolete, especially as in the Crimea, much victory belonged to smaller units of soldiers. Queen Victoria rewarded the bravery of the fighting men with the award to sixty-two veterans (including privates, gunners, sappers, seamen and boatswains) of the first Victoria Cross medals. The idea of a heroine was borne when the bravery of Florence Nightingale was recognised for providing nursing services at the front. Politicians recognised the involvement of the middle class support for the war by adopting many middle class values in future decades.

The Reform and Redistribution Acts of 1867 and 1884-5 extended the vote to most urban and rural working men. I do not criticise the expansion of democracy *per se*, but I will state that a large government democratic base of uneducated people makes the maintenance of an internationally dominant culture difficult. A majority of lower class voters tend to find the benefits of a welfare state attractive, and a political party with socialist leanings will have a tendency to ignore budgetary restraints in favour of populist policy. Welfare states find it difficult to finance competent military forces.

The British welfare state had its beginnings under the Liberal Party of Campbell-Bannerman in 1906. The Liberal Party retained power as a minority government until during World War I in 1916. The subsequent Coalition government under Liberal David Lloyd George contained many Conservatives.

The parlous debt position of Britain in the face of the industrial and military might of the USA meant, in my opinion, that the British Empire was no longer a dominant culture in 1920

Climate/Geographic Access to Resources

Naval operations in European waters focused on the acquisition of a Mediterranean base, contributing to a long-lasting alliance with Portugal in 1703 and the capture of Gibraltar (1704) and Minorca (1708), which were both retained by Britain after the War of Spanish Succession. Naval operations also enabled the conquest of the French colonies in Nova Scotia and Newfoundland. In the mid eighteenth century, the Navy conducted amphibious campaigns leading to the conquest of French Canada, French colonies in the Caribbean and West Africa, and small islands off the French coast, while operations in the Indian Ocean contributed to the destruction of French power in India.

The British forces captured Havana, Cuba in 1762 together with the Spanish fleet as well as Manila in the Philippines. In 1763 France and Spain restored all their conquests to Britain and Portugal. Britain restored Manila and Havana to Spain, and Guadeloupe, Martinique, Saint Lucia, Gorée, and the Indian factories to France. In return, France ceded Canada, Dominica, Grenada, Saint Vincent and the Grenadines, and Tobago to Britain. France also ceded the eastern half of French Louisiana to Britain; that is, the area from the Mississippi River to the Appalachian Mountains. Spain ceded Florida to Britain. France had already secretly given Louisiana to Spain in the Treaty of Fontainebleau (1762). In addition, while France regained its factories in India, France recognised British clients as the rulers of key Indian native states, and pledged not to send troops to Bengal. Britain agreed to demolish its fortifications in British Honduras (now Belize).

At the Peace of Paris 1783 Britain lost her thirteen American colonies and the area south of Great Lakes and St. Lawrence River. The area east of the Mississippi River (East Florida and West Florida) went to Spain. Spain also reacquired Minorca in the Mediterranean. France was ceded Tobago in the Caribbean and Senegal in Africa.

A penal colony was founded in New South Wales, Australia in 1788 which led to exploration of the large continent. In 1840 the Treaty of Waitangi was signed between the British and various Maori chiefs, bringing New Zealand into the British Empire.

During the early 1800s, the Navy conducted amphibious operations which captured most of the French Caribbean islands and the Dutch colonies at the Cape of Good Hope and Ceylon and in the Dutch East Indies, but all of these gains except Ceylon and Trinidad were returned following the Peace of Amiens in 1802, which briefly halted the fighting

At the Congress of Vienna 1815, Guadeloupe and Reunion were returned to the French and the Netherlands regained Java and Surinam. Britain retained Malta, the Ionian Islands, Trinidad, Tobago, St. Lucia, Cape Colony and Mauritius.

There was a period of almost continual warfare in the nineteenth century which resulted in the expansion of Empire in Africa. Between 1817 and 1878 the tribes of the Eastern Cape were conquered before Zululand was subdued. The army in India fought campaigns in Burma (1824, 1853), Afghanistan (1838-42, 1878-80), conquered the Sind (1843) and the Punjab (1845-6). India became official British territory in 1858. By 1874, the functions of the East India Company were absorbed into the official government machinery of British India and its private presidency armies had been nationalised by the British Crown.

Hong Kong became a colony of the British Empire after the First Opium War (1839–42) followed by Peninsula in 1860 and then the Chinese New Territories was put under lease in 1898. Hawaii was ceded to the British in 1843 and Fiji in 1874.

Leaders Dominated by Parliament in War and Defence

England had succession worries after 1689 because King William and Queen Mary had no children. Mary's sister, Princess Anne was in line to the throne but her children had all died in childhood. Parliament passed an Act of Settlement 1701 in which the Crown would be inherited by a distant relative, Sophie of Hanover, and her Protestant heirs if the then current lineage ended. The Act extended to England and Ireland, but not Scotland whose Estates had not been consulted.

Scotland at the time was reeling from the failure to become a world trading nation from establishment of a colony on the Isthmus of Panama. The undertaking at Darien was badly managed from the outset and was doomed to failure due to its tropical environment and by lack of demand for trade goods. Disease and lack of food was a problem even before a siege by the Spanish in 1700. The Darien

Company had been backed by around a quarter of the Scottish money supply, so that its collapse left many nobles and landowners almost completely ruined.

William III died in 1702 of complications following a fall from his horse. Queen Anne ascended the thrones of England, Scotland and Ireland in March 1702. War with France had been basically in effect since 1689 and would continue until 1783. Anne continued to prosecute English interests against France in the War of Spanish Succession. English warfare was financed through taxation and the national debt made possible by the Bank of England. The crown was under the guidance of ministers, Godolphin and Marlborough. John Churchill, Duke of Marlborough led combined English, Dutch and German forces in the Low Countries. Admiral Sir Clowdisley Shovell's Royal Navy Fleet cruised on the western Mediterranean. A small squadron under Admiral John Benbow cruised in the West Indies.

The Whigs and Tories political parties' bitter opposition to one another had not waned. As a committed Anglican, Queen Anne was inclined to favour moderate Tories who had developed a party in favour of the Anglican Church, and landed interests of the country gentry. The Whigs were aligned with the burgeoning commercial interests and Protestant Dissenters. The Whigs supported the War of Spanish Succession and became more influential after the Duke of Marlborough won a great victory at the Battle of Blenheim 1704. This resulted in a number of Tories, who opposed the land war with France, being removed from office.

Later, Anne followed the policy of William III in balancing the parties. Anne's ministry led by Lord Godolphin and the Duke of Marlborough became less moderate in 1706 and forced her to dismiss moderate Robert Harley, Speaker of the House of Commons, from her ministry.

One of the key policies of Anne was political integration of England and Scotland and she was successful in stimulating both parliaments into discussion in 1705. Both countries appointed thirty-one Commissioners which conducted negotiations in 1706. Tories were not in favour of Union and only one Commissioner was Tory. The English purpose was to ensure that Scotland did not choose a monarch different from the one who occupied the English throne. In Scotland many proponents thought that Union would assist Scotland recover from the results of the Darien crisis. Some Commissioners believed that they would receive compensation for losses in the Darien Scheme and others were indirectly bribed. Scottish public opinion was decidedly against Union even as it passed through their Parliament. Democracy was extremely limited in this age. On May 1 1707 under the Act of Union, England and Scotland were united as a single sovereign state, the Kingdom of Great Britain.

In 1709 the Whigs chose to attack the ultra-Tory High Church preacher, Dr. Henry Sacheverell, and had him impeached in the 1710 House of Lords. The trial was full of rhetoric which was used as propaganda on both sides. When Sacheverell received only a token sentence, the public reacted with bonfires of congratulation. The Tories won the next election under leader Robert Harley.

The Kingdom of Great Britain inherited the war and in 1708 Rear-Admiral Sir Charles Wager destroyed a Spanish bullion fleet which hampered the Franco-Spanish war effort. The Tory government adopted a strategy to make amphibious attacks on French settlements in Nova Scotia and Newfoundland. The ambitious attack on Quebec in 1711 failed because of careless planning and difficulties navigating the St. Lawrence River. Peace was made in 1714 in which France ostensibly recognised Spanish independence. Britain gained Gibraltar, Minorca and Nova Scotia which recognised the power of the Royal Navy 124 ship force.

When Queen Anne died in 1714 the middle-aged George, Elector of Hanover, was made King of England as agreed in 1701. He was not a popular choice and was even welcomed with riots. King George I took the demonstrations personally and blamed the Tories, with their Jacobite supporters. The 1715 election produced the Whig parliament that George desired.

The Tories responded by adopting Jacobite policies, in particular a return of the Stuarts in the form of Catholic James Edward, grandson of James VII of Scotland. James arrived in Scotland in 1714 to rally a small number of supporters, but retreated to France after six weeks. A Spanish armada carrying troops set off from Cadiz in 1719 but ran into *Protestant* winds and were unable to land.

The Whig Member of the Privy Council, Sir Robert Walpole, was made First Lord of the Treasury and Chancellor of the Exchequer in 1715. In the evolution of Parliament, the Lord Treasurer assumed a leading position among Ministers effectively being Prime Minister. Factional politics caused Walpole to resign from Cabinet in 1717 at a time when the King had argued with the Prince of Wales. Walpole then brought about a royal reconciliation in 1720 so was again brought into Cabinet, just in time for the South Sea Bubble (see Economics below). The collapse of the financial Bubble left the country drowning in worthless financial paper.

Walpole was in fact lucky in his personal stock dealings after early profit-taking, in that his attempt to rebuy at the peak was thwarted by a mail delay. He managed the country's crisis on the basis that he knew government finance was sound even though individuals had lost fortunes. Walpole spoke in Parliament to quieten the fear of further collapse. Walpole gained political prestige when he managed the investigation into the Bubble, allowing senior Whigs to escape punishment. The stock of the South Sea Company was divided between the Bank of England and East India Company. The indebted Company itself managed part of the National Debt until the 1850s.

Historians credit Walpole as the first British Prime Minister. He was a believer in lavish entertainment to consolidate influence and became supreme in the art of Crown patronage. His country residence Houghton Hall was used to entertain the landed oligarchy and governing Tory caste of the country. With his brother-in-law Lord Townshend as Lord President of the Council, Walpole's political machine gained advantage at the time when George I effectively lost some power. The policy of Walpole's government was to keep Britain from war and thus not raise taxes. The internal policy was to keep law and order with the imposition of harsh punishments for any larceny by the villagers reduced to living on wage labour.

Prison was a growth sector under Walpole where private wardenship was quite lucrative because of payments necessary for decent food and accommodation. The prison hulks in various ports became overcrowded so the state authorised payments to merchants to take convicts to America. The Transportation Act 1718 allowed courts to sentence convicts to seven years transportation. Most were shipped to New England. Some were sold as slaves to Southern States.

Refugees from the countryside fled to London which was a prosperous international city. It was necessary for the social standing of politicians and landed gentry to be seen to live well in London. By the 1730s there were 500 coffee houses and scores of clubs in which all classes could conduct their politics and business and learn the news of the day. Specialist coffee houses existed where merchants could conduct shipping business such as Edward Lloyd's which led to the rise of the insurer Lloyds of London. Tea and chocolate were also available. Tea drinking was popular at court and took hold in London in the 1720s. Concurrent with the popularity of coffee and tea, sugar was introduced to the English palate to sweeten the beverages. Upper class consumption commenced to trickle down to the lower classes. The sweet British palate was established.

When George II came to the throne in 1727 on the death of his father, he retained both Walpole and Townshend who commenced to clash on policies of foreign affairs. In the wake of the Townshend retirement in 1730, Walpole concluded the Treaty of Vienna that created the Anglo-Austrian Alliance. He used his influence to prevent Hanoverian George II from entering a European conflict in 1733 when the War of the Polish Succession broke out.

Walpole tried to offset the revenue lost to smuggling by introducing an excise tax on tobacco and wine in 1733, payable at warehouses rather than at port. This raised the opposition of merchants who influenced Whig politicians. Walpole withdrew his Excise Bill but dismissed many Whigs who dared to oppose it. He thus lost a considerable element of the Whig Party to the opposition, including one hundred *Patriot* Whigs. The general election of 1734 produced a reduced Whig majority in parliament. Walpole was still in charge but his loss in popularity curbed his political authority. After Queen Caroline died in 1737, the Prince of Wales, Frederick Louis became politically involved with a number of Walpole's opponents, including the *Patriot* Whig, William Pitt *the Elder*.

In 1739 Walpole's anti-war policy caused problems when the Spain claimed the right to board British vessels to ensure that trade was not being carried out with Spanish colonies. The King, Commons and even part of Walpole's Cabinet faction were in favour of war with Spain. Walpole reluctantly agreed to the War of Jenkin's Ear (claim by a merchant of injury by a Spanish cutlass), really to ensure that Spain did not renege on the lucrative *asiento* to allow slaves to be sold in South America.

In the 1741 election, the Whigs again attained a majority but there were many Whigs against the aging Prime Minister. In 1742 the naval disaster at Cartegena prompted the resignation of Walpole who was elevated to the House of Lords as Earl of Orford. He was succeeded by his enemy, Spencer Compton, Lord Wilmington, who immediately commenced an enquiry into Walpole's government. By mid 1742 the War of Austrian Succession had broken out in Europe. With Walpole went peace.

Without knowing it at the time, Walpole had followed the theory that Adam Smith later produced in his 1776 book "*The Wealth of Nations*". Smith indicated that the best government was that which got out of the way and permitted the invisible hand of the market to do its work. The market which provided Walpole's prosperity was that of sugar which had developed Britain's sweet tooth in tea, coffee, cocoa, and other sweet victuals. The expansion of bitter tea consumption in particular increased sugar consumption. Consumption of sugar, obtained mainly from the colonies in the West Indies, grew by five times between 1710 and 1770. As well as popular consumption, the English sugar barons were conspicuous consumers of all luxuries. Tea-drinking also spurred the search for a European imitation of Chinese porcelain, first successfully produced in England at the Chelsea porcelain manufactory, established around 1743-45 and quickly imitated. At this time there does not appear to have been any government direction towards Empire.

Lord Wilmington died in 1743 to be succeeded by Henry Pelham as First Lord of the Treasury and Chancellor of the Exchequer. He was an advocate of peace, so was reluctantly involved in the War of Austrian Succession because of Britain's treaty with Austria. Britain's main involvement was in America and India. The war was expensive because of the manpower involved in Flanders and the need to defend George II's province of Hanover.

In 1745 the Jacobite rising broke out in Scotland to support Prince Charles Stuart in his claim to succeed his grandfather James II as King of England. The government was divided between complacency and panic. The panic came from the view that *Bonny Prince Charlie* would not have made an attempt without assurance of a supporting invasion by France and/or Spain. In fact, due to the army in Europe, Britain did not have enough troops domestically to resist any invasion.

After successes in Scotland the Jacobites marched south where they expected a mass uprising by English Jacobites. The Catholic uprising did not occur and there was no sign of the French. The brother of Pelham, Duke of Newcastle as Secretary of State, managed to rally southern militias and regular forces sufficient to encourage the Jacobites to withdraw to Scotland. Finally at Culloden, under the youngest son of George II, William Duke of Cumberland, the British outnumbered the rebels in a quick final battle. The English endeavoured to destroy the Highland culture which was blamed for the uprising. *Bonny Prince Charlie* fled overseas, but, no longer welcome in France, was exiled to Rome. The fleeing Scots became active in the British colonies.

The Royal Navy was despatched to assist the East India Company's campaign on French enclaves on the India Coromandel Coast. In 1745 HMS Deptford and Preston took three French vessels returning from China through the Sunda Straits. In America the war opened with a successful attack on Cape Breton Island and the capture of Fort Louisburg in 1745. The Royal Navy at last decided to blockade Atlantic ports, which was extremely expensive in terms of material and men. In 1747 the British under Sir George Anson introduced a new naval battle technique of attacking line astern which resulted in a number of victories.

In 1747 Frederick, Prince of Wales, rejoined the political opposition. In response George II called an election. The Whig government increased its majority and the group of country gentlemen called Tories continued their decline. By 1747 thirty years of Whig oligarchy and systemic corruption had weakened party ties so that there were nearly as many Whigs in opposition to the ministry as there were Tories.

Pelham's elder brother Thomas, Duke of Newcastle, had commanded foreign policy as Secretary of State for a quarter century. He negotiated peace with France at the Treaty of Aix-la-Chapelle 1748 which lost Louisburg in exchange for Madras and French withdrawal from the Low Countries. In 1749 Parliament passed the Consolidation Act to reorganise the Royal Navy. Frederick, Prince of Wales, died in 1751, allowing his teenage son George William to become heir apparent to the throne. Britain adopted the Gregorian Calendar in 1752.

Henry Pelham died in 1754 and was succeeded by Newcastle as Prime Minister. The 1754 election produced another large Whig majority. Newcastle slighted the active parliamentary speakers William Pitt and Henry Fox when seeking someone to represent the government in the House of Commons. He chose Sir Thomas Robinson whom he could dominate, which resulted in increased criticism of the government by Pitt and Fox. Pitt was a hyperactive manic depressive whose oratory stirred both parliament and public listeners.

Newcastle, the Prime Minister, had hoped to isolate France by surrounding it with favourable allies so was surprised in 1756 when Austria abandoned its twenty-five year alliance with Britain. Frederick II of Prussia quickly made an alliance with Britain against countries conspiring against him. Britain was still committed to defend the King's home territory of Hanover.

The British Royal Navy was already dominant, and Prussia had the most powerful land forces in Europe during the Seven Years War. This allowed Britain to focus its military forces in the fight against French incursions in the colonies that had burst into warfare in America and India. The French opened the war in Europe with an attack on Minorca in 1756 nearly two years after fighting had broken out in the American Ohio Country. Frederick II of Prussia crossed the border of Saxony and forced the surrender in 1756 of the Saxon army, which was incorporated into Prussian forces. The following year Frederick marched into Bohemia to lay siege to Prague. The Austrian counter-attack produced Frederick's first defeat. He was forced to leave Bohemia to defend Prussia from Russia, and the French were approaching from the west. Frederick *the Great* proved one of Europe's finest generals when he first defeated the French and then routed a numerically larger force of Austrians.

Newcastle took the blame in 1756 for the poor start to the War, and was replaced by William Cavendish, Duke of Devonshire. The administration was largely run by Newcastle's rival, William Pitt, who was able to raise money to send troops to America. The administration lost the support of George II and was replaced in 1757 by the second Newcastle Whig Ministry. An agreement was reached for separation of powers by rivals. Newcastle provided the parliamentary strength but it was Secretary of State, William Pitt, who ran the war. Newcastle's strategy had been for British involvement on the Continent, but William Pitt was more concerned with a strategy of global naval domination that was the birth of Empire.

Under Admiral Anson, now First Lord of the Admiralty, new ships were built and old ones refitted. In 1757 there were ninety ships of the line and 150 support vessels. A problem was manning the ships which was solved by reintroducing the press-gang. In 1757 a ruthless press-gang impressed 3000 men in New York, up to a quarter of the male population. Considerable efforts were made to improve pay and conditions for Royal Navy sailors to make conscription easier.

Unfortunately the Hanoverian army under the English Duke of Cumberland was defeated and forced to surrender following a French invasion of Hanover. The Convention of Klosterzeven removed Hanover and Brunswick from the war, so Frederick of Prussia requested British assistance. In fact Prussia was able to dominate Europe without much help from the British who had two regiments in North America. Britain's King George II revoked the Treaty of Klosterzeven to allow Hanover to re-enter the war. The new commander of Hanoverian forces, Duke Ferdinand of Brunswick, drove the French back across the Rhine River. In India, Clive restored British power in Bengal.

British naval dominance allowed Louisburg to be recaptured in 1758. At the request of an American merchant, Pitt authorised an attack against the French port of Saint Louis in Senegal, West Africa. The mission was so lucrative that Pitt sent out further expeditions to capture other slave ports, Goree and Gambia. At the suggestion of a Jamaican sugar planter, Pitt planned expeditions to French islands in the Caribbean. The attack on Martinique failed but Guadeloupe was captured in 1759.

Pitt tried to repair some of the damage to colonial feelings, caused earlier by Braddock and Loudon, by winning friends in American assemblies to fight the land war in the American way. The old aristocratic generals were recalled and young officers were promoted. Quebec City was captured by General James Wolfe in 1759.

In 1758, under Pitt, the British concluded the Anglo-Prussian Convention with Frederick, in which they committed to pay him an annual subsidy of £670,000 and dispatched troops to reinforce the Hanoverian army. The Prussians suffered a series of defeats in 1759 including a disastrous Battle of Kunersdorf. The French planned to invade the militia-defended British Isles in 1759 however naval victories by the Royal Navy at Lagos and Quiberon Bay prevented any such action. The Hanoverians continued their successes against the French which prevented them from sending troops against the Prussians who were embattled by the Austrians and Russians.

George II died in 1760 to be succeeded by his grandson, the twenty-two year old George III who did not agree with Pitt's alliance with Newcastle and British interference in Germany. He lobbied for his old tutor, John Stuart, Earl of Bute, to be given the post of Secretary of State for the Northern Department so that he could support withdrawal from Germany. Pitt was able to increase troops for Hanover.

The war extended to the east in 1762 after Spain declared war against Britain, followed by Portugal against her neighbour. Spain, aided by the French, invaded Portugal but was stalled by British/Portuguese forces. The Prussians were on the edge of collapse in 1762 when Russia's Empress Elizabeth died. Her successor Peter III withdrew Russian armies and mediated a Prussian truce with Sweden. The British naval blockade of French ports had sapped the morale of the French, who took another hit with the fall of the French forces at Newfoundland.

In 1763 further political changes again influenced the war. Bute and Newcastle had refused to support Pitt's moves against Spain which forced Pitt's resignation. Pitt's brother-in-law, George Grenville, was given the post of Leader of the House of Commons. The new British Prime Minister Lord Bute withdrew British subsidies to Frederick, and Catherine *the Great* overthrew Peter III to bring Russia back into the war. However Austria was facing a financial crisis that made it disposed towards a peace. The Treaty of Hubertusburg in 1763 ended the war in central Europe, and the Treaty of Paris 1763, the Seven Years War.

Bute, a poor speaker, lost the confidence of George III in 1763, particularly after introducing a very unpopular Cider Tax. Pitt blamed him for the terms of the peace most favourable to France. After the Peace of Paris was signed, Bute resigned in favour of Grenville after Henry Fox had rejected the job. Grenville inherited an economy with debt from the war but an economy downscaled in peace. There had been a banking crash in Amsterdam that affected the associated English money markets. Harvests were poor and prices high. Not surprisingly Grenville turned to America to raise finance by imposing a tax on French molasses used to produce colonial rum (Sugar Act 1764), and to back it up with quasi-military customs enforcement.

The erudite American smugglers commenced to agitate that Britain was introducing a Star Chamber equivalent to misuse and abuse of power by the English monarchy and courts. Even more outrageous to Americans was the introduction of Grenville's 1765 Stamp Act which required documents and newspapers to be printed on paper from London bearing an embossed revenue stamp that had to be paid for in English currency. This Act was met by rioting throughout the colonies of America. One of four Lords to vote against taxing the Americans was Charles Cornwallis, Marquess Cornwallis, later forced to surrender at Yorktown. The government asserted the right of Britain to make laws for the colonies which were economic satellites of the mother country. The cost of militarily removing the French menace to their welfare had to be retrieved.

George III made various attempts to get William Pitt to form a ministry to oust Grenville, but in the end was forced to dismiss Grenville in favour of the leader of the Rockingham Whigs, Charles Watson-Wentworth, Marquess of Rockingham. Rockingham won a repeal of the unenforceable Stamp Act in 1766, however he also passed the Declaratory Act 1766 which asserted the right to legislate for the American colonies. The English parliamentarians had no real idea of the democratic principles operating in the colonies that produced debates in town halls of Philadelphia and Boston. Boston was more literate than London with 70% of male citizens able to read political information.

Internal dissent in 1766 led to the resignation of Rockingham in favour of William Pitt who chose the office of Lord Privy Seal and elevation to the House of Lords as Earl of Chatham. He made Charles Townshend, Chancellor of the Exchequer, and William Petty, Earl of Shelburne, Secretary of State. Shelburne had a conciliatory policy towards America but this was undermined when Townshend passed the Revenue Act of 1767 to generate revenue in the American colonies after repeal of the Stamp Act. The Revenue Act was passed in conjunction with the Indemnity Act 1767 which was intended to make the tea of the monopoly British East India Company more competitive than smuggled Dutch tea. The Indemnity Act repealed taxes on tea imported to England to allow the tea to be re-exported to the colonies. The English tax cut would be partially covered by the Revenue Act taxes on tea in the colonies.

The Revenue and Indemnity Acts stirred the Americans into action. The Massachusetts House of Representatives petitioned George III to repeal the Revenue Act, which inspired the other colonial assemblies to follow suit. The appointee to the new post of Colonial Secretary, Wills Hill, Viscount Hillsborough, was also President of the Board of Trade who opposed any concessions to the colonists. In 1768 he sent a letter to the colonial governors in America, instructing them to dissolve the colonial assemblies if they responded to the Massachusetts Circular Letter. When The Massachusetts House refused to rescind the letter, Hillsborough ordered the Governor to dissolve the legislature. In 1769 Boston organised a boycott of British imports, which was joined by merchants in other colonies. Before the boycott subsided in 1771 a mountain of tea grew in London warehouses.

The dissention in the multi-party Chatham ministry in 1768 led the aged William Pitt once again to resign, in favour of Augustus FitzRoy, Duke of Grafton, who had been effectively Prime Minister during Chatham's illness. Frederick North, Earl of Guilford, was Leader of the Commons and Chancellor of the Exchequer. Grafton struggled to contain challenges to Britain's Empire and was unable to rule cabinet. He was widely attacked for allowing France to annex Corsica, and stepped down in 1770 handing over power to Lord North. The political dissention did not allow attention to be paid to naval intelligence that rebuilding of French and Spanish navies had narrowed the gap with the Royal Navy. It was estimated that Britain's 126 ships of the line were nearly matched by 121 of the natural enemies'.

North formed a Tory government from aristocrats, many of whom were previously Whigs, and a number of the previous cabinet. Critics of British colonial rule became known as *Radical* Whigs or *Patriot* Whigs. North enjoyed a good relationship with George III. The French and Spanish were jealous of British dominance but could not yet challenge the Royal Navy. John Montagu, Earl of Sandwich was appointed First Lord of the Admiralty in 1771. The cabinet followed the Sandwich strategy of keeping the majority of the fleet in European waters and retaining only toeholds on the American coast.

The Customs Board in Boston requested naval and military support to enforce the Townshend acts, so a fifty gun warship arrived in Boston in 1768. After a ship belonging to John Hancock, a leading merchant and smuggler, was seized, the port erupted into riot. Hillsborough instructed Boston Governor Bernard to find evidence of treason in Boston under the Treason Act 1543. Hillsborough had already instructed Lieutenant-General Thomas Gage to send a force to Boston. Four regiments began unloading in Boston enabling the Customs Board to return, under military occupation.

North presented a motion to Parliament for partial repeal of the Revenue Act which was successful in 1770, but the duty on tea was maintained. The duty was affirmed when the Tea Act was passed in 1773 which also allowed the East India Company, then in dire financial straits, to export directly to America. Many colonists opposed the Act, not so much that it rescued the Company, but because it followed the principles of the Townshend Acts.

The East India Company was in arrears to the government and the Bank of England because it had not paid its monopoly fee since loss of tea's sales to America in 1768. Lord North passed the Regulating Act 1773 limiting dividends and the Company Court of Directors. It prohibited servants of the company from engaging in private trade and accepting bribes, which had already made many fortunes. The Governor of Bengal was made Governor-General with a four man Council assisting. British judges were to be sent to establish a Supreme Court at Calcutta.

After the Boston Massacre (five civilians) 1770 and the acquittal of the eight soldiers involved, middle class groups identifying themselves as *Sons of Liberty* became more active. In 1773, the *Sons of Liberty* issued and distributed a declaration in New York City called the *Association of the Sons of Liberty in New York*, which formally stated their opposition to the Tea Act and that anyone who assisted in the execution of the act was "*an enemy to the liberties of America*" and that "*whoever shall transgress any of these resolutions, we will not deal with, or employ, or have any connection with him*".

The Sons of Liberty took direct action to enforce their opposition to the Tea Act at the Boston Tea Party. Members of the group, wearing disguises meant to evoke the appearance of Native American Indians, poured several tons of tea into the Boston Harbor at the end of 1773 in protest of the Tea Act. The British government felt this action could not remain unpunished, and responded by closing the port of Boston and putting in place other laws known as the "Coercive Acts". Many colonists, particularly those outside Boston, were outraged by the destruction of public property. Those colonists who remained loyal to the British Crown called themselves Loyalists, "Tories", or "King's men."

The imposition of the Quartering Act which authorised the billeting of troops in occupied barns and buildings brought sympathy to Boston. The Virginian,

George Washington, wrote of his intense opposition to the Act, even though he criticised the Tea Party. In the following weeks the southern colonies united to send food to Boston which was essentially under military occupation and naval blockade.

Each colony had established a Provincial Congress or an equivalent governmental institution to govern itself, but still recognised the British Crown and their inclusion in the Empire. The British responded by sending combat troops to re-impose direct rule. The First Continental Congress was called in 1774 to try to unite the colonies in support of the basic British right that taxes should not be imposed without representation.

The looming battle between the government and America was obscured by the English recession of 1773-74 in the woollen, cotton, silk-weaving industries that forced men and women out of work. In the Scottish highlands and western isles there was a mass flight from lairds who demanded high rents on poor land. The Irish also suffered from rent-racking. This built a flood of emigration to the new lands released in America well south of the fractious New England. In 1774 the government passed the Quebec Act which defined the frontiers of Canada and detached the south from the North American colonies. Moreover it barred colonists and immigrants from the north western lands to which they had felt entitled.

In 1774 General Gage was appointed the military governor of the Province of Massachusetts Bay to implement the Coercive Acts. Britain passed the Conciliatory Resolution in February 1775, which ended taxation for any colony that satisfactorily provided for the imperial defense and the upkeep of imperial officers. This was too little too late. The First Continental Congress in 1774 included delegates from twelve colonies (not including Georgia) which met briefly to consider options, including an economic boycott of British trade; rights and grievances; and petitioned King George III for redress of those grievances. Gage's attempts to seize military stores of Patriot militias sparked the Battle of Lexington April 1775.

The Second Continental Congress met after the battle had begun, to request the King to intervene in Parliament on behalf of the colonies. After the Battle of Bunker Hill in June 1775, Congress formed the Continental Army under General George Washington. Continental Congress eventually received Parliament's Conciliatory Resolution in July 1775 and rejected it. Another petition was sent to London with the former governor of Pennsylvania but the King refused to see him.

George III declared the colonies to be in a state of *"open and avowed rebellion"*. The King had the same policy as later became common in modern America, in that he would not deal with rebels. On July 4, 1776 the Congress issued a Declaration of Independence which ceased all American efforts at reconciliation.

A number of early historians blamed George III for the American war, blaming his madness. In fact George's dementia did not occur until much later in his reign. Lord George Germain, Viscount Sackville was appointed Secretary of State for the American Department in 1775. Together with Lord North he made false assumptions of the forthcoming American war – that American forces were inferior to the British; that the war could be fought on similar lines to European wars; that a British victory would return the colonies' allegiance. The British did not contemplate guerrilla warfare by irregular forces that augmented regular forces. In 1776 Sackville worked with General Burgoyne to plan the Saratoga campaign, but his unclear orders to General Howe contributed to the campaign's failure. The tax on tea was repealed with the Taxation of Colonies Act 1778, part of another late Parliamentary attempt at conciliation that failed.

Shortage of troops for British forces necessitated the need for mercenaries. The Landgraf of Hessen-Kassel obliged by sending 19,000 mainly Hessian troops to serve with the British Army in North America. The Hessians, instilled with submission to German autocrats, were willing to fight for a monarchy against foes that British propaganda painted as vicious rebel Yankees.

North's arrogance about the dominance of the Royal Navy had not allowed Britain to make European alliances except for Prussia. Thus Britain was unprepared for the European acceptance of the new nation, the United States of America. It was natural in 1778 that Britain's perpetual enemy France would ally to the American rebels, and that Spain would follow (1779). No doubt the French encouraged the Dutch Republic to enter the war in 1780. Britain now faced a war on multiple continents without a single ally. The American allies had provided the rebels with weapons and ammunition well before their formal declaration of war. Empress Catherine II of Russia formed an alliance in 1780 to protect neutral shipping against Britain's search and seizure policy of neutral shipping for French contraband. This brought the Russian, Denmark-Norway navies into possible retaliation against the Royal Navy in Europe.

As late as the Siege of Charleston in 1780, Loyalists could still believe in eventual British victory, as British troops inflicted heavy defeats on the Continental forces at the Battle of Camden and the Battle of Guilford Court House. In late 1781, the news of Lord Cornwallis's surrender at the Siege of Yorktown reached London; Lord North's parliamentary support ebbed away and he resigned the following year following a motion of no confidence. The King drafted an abdication notice, which was never delivered, but finally accepted the defeat in North America, and authorised the negotiation of a peace. American Loyalists fled to Canada.

After North's resignation, William Petty, Earl of Shelburne, took office as Secretary of State under the Marquess of Rockingham. After Rockingham's death months later, Shelbourne was requested to form a government whose main duty was to secure peace in the American war. Shelburne brought into his cabinet as Chancellor of the Exchequer, William Pitt *the Younger*, the twenty-three year-old son of the previous Prime Minister. Shelburne agreed to generous borders in the Illinois Country, but rejected demands by Benjamin Franklin for the cession of Canada and other territories.

In 1782 Admiral Sir George Rodney was ordered to the West Indies with thirty-six ships of the line to counter a slightly smaller French squadron. The Battle of Saintes demonstrated the power of the new British weapon, the fearsome Carronade short cannon. Another innovation, copper hull sheathing, improved speed and manoeuvrability of the ships. The resultant victory saved the British West Indies.

The American war cost over 100,000 dead and wounded of all the participants. At the Peace of Paris 1783 Britain lost her thirteen colonies and the area south of Great Lakes and St. Lawrence River. The area east of the Mississippi River (East Florida and West Florida) went to Spain. Spain also reacquired Minorca in the Mediterranean. France was ceded Tobago in the Caribbean and Senegal in Africa. The Dutch Republic lost Negapatnam in India.

In England the 1760s and 1770s saw the introduction of wage saving machinery in the manufacture of cotton, iron, steel and pottery, as well as the first practical applications of James Watt's and Matthew Boulton's steam engines. The public was confident that Britain was moving ahead in trade and empire despite the war in America. However between 1778 and 1783 the British Empire had faced a huge crisis caused by the lack of allies. The navy was outnumbered and there was insipid political leadership. Britain was lucky that its enemies also suffered from poor leadership otherwise another empire would have been lost. As it was, the psychological shock to the country made it realise its vulnerability.

Charles Fox, who had earlier resigned from Shelburne's government, formed an opposition with Lord North which forced Shelburne out of office late in 1783.

Edmund Burke's bill to reform the East India Company failed in the Upper House. This was the trigger for George III to force Fox and North out of office end 1783. The King asked William Pitt *the Younger* to form a government, as the youngest Prime Minister of Great Britain. Pitt called himself an independent Whig but most considered him a Tory. The government was quickly defeated on a motion of no confidence but Pitt refused to resign. Pitt held the confidence of the King and had support in the Lords. An election was called in 1784 with a massive swing to Pitt.

His administration secure, Pitt could begin to enact his agenda. His first major piece of legislation as Prime Minister was the India Act 1784, intended to address the shortcomings of the 1773 Act, which re-organised the British East India Company and kept a watch over corruption. The India Act created a new Board of Control to oversee the affairs of the East India Company. It differed from Fox's failed India Bill 1783 and specified that the Board would be appointed by the King. The Act centralised British rule in India by reducing the power of the Governors of Bombay and Madras and by increasing that of the Governor-General, Lord Charles Cornwallis. The governor-general was given greater powers in matters of war, revenue and diplomacy.

A supplementary Act of 1786 enforced the demand of Cornwallis that the powers of Governor-General of India be enlarged to enable the offices of the Governor-General and Commander –in-Chief to be jointly held by the same official, and demarcated the borders between Crown and Company. Having temporarily achieved a state of truce with the Crown, the Company continued to expand its influence to nearby territories through threats and coercive actions. By the middle of the 19th century, the Company's rule extended across most of India, Burma (Myanmar), Malaya, Singapore, and British Hong Kong, so that a fifth of the world's population was under its trading influence.

Also in 1784, James Matra, Treasury officer and a junior officer on Captain James Cook's visit to Australia, put forward to cabinet "*A Proposal for Establishing a Settlement in New South Wales*" which included convicts as settlers. The Government also incorporated into the colonisation plan, the project for settling Norfolk Island, with its attractions of timber and flax, proposed by Sir Joseph Banks's Royal Society colleagues, Sir John Call and Sir George Young. In 1787 the first fleet of eleven ships with over a thousand settlers (including 778 convicts) set sail for Botany Bay under Captain Arthur Phillip. When Botany Bay proved unsuitable for settlement, the fleet moved to neighbouring Port Jackson where a settlement was established at Sydney Cove.

The important domestic issue with which Pitt had to concern himself was the national debt, which had increased dramatically due to the rebellion of the American colonies. Pitt sought to eliminate the national debt by imposing new taxes. Pitt also introduced measures to reduce smuggling and fraud.

The volume of Anglo-American trade actually increased after 1783, particularly imports of raw cotton for the new machine-operated Lancashire mills. In 1779 Samuel Compton had combined the spinning jenny and the water-frame into one machine called the mule. The mule could produce 300 times as much yarn as a person on a spinning wheel. These machines produced more yarn than weavers could handle until 1787, when Edmund Cartwright invented the power loom. The Industrial Revolution had flowered.

Pitt sought European alliances to restrict French influence, forming the Triple Alliance with Prussia and the United Provinces in 1788. In 1790, Pitt took advantage of the alliance to force Spain to give up its claim to exclusive control over the western coast of North and South America.

In 1788, Pitt faced a major crisis when King George III fell victim to a mysterious illness, a form of mental disorder that incapacitated him. If the sovereign was incapable of fulfilling his constitutional duties, Parliament would need to appoint a regent to rule in his place. All factions agreed the only viable candidate was the King's eldest son, George, Prince of Wales. The Prince, however, was a supporter of Charles Fox; so had he come to power, he would almost surely have dismissed Pitt. However, he did not have such an opportunity, as Parliament spent months debating legal technicalities relating to the Regency. Fortunately for Pitt, the King recovered early in 1789, just after a Regency Bill had been introduced and passed in the House of Commons.

The general elections of 1790 resulted in a majority for the government, so Pitt continued as Prime Minister. In 1791, he proceeded to address one of the problems facing the growing British Empire: the future of British Canada. By the Constitutional Act of 1791, the province of Quebec was divided into two separate provinces: the predominantly French Lower Canada and the predominantly English Loyalist Upper Canada.

In 1793 revolutionary France declared war on Great Britain which allowed Pitt's government to increase taxes, and raise armies. Many, particularly Jacobites, in Britain favoured the basic principle of equal rights broadcast by the French Revolution, which needed to be suppressed to maintain British unity. Pitt passed repressive legislation against parliamentary reformers. In 1794 the privilege of the writ of *habeas corpus* was suspended. Holland requested urgent military assistance from Pitt against the French in 1794 without success. The Dutch put this down to allowing the Dutch maritime competition in the West Indies to decline in favour of British trade.

Problems manning the Royal Navy led Pitt to introduce the Quota System 1795 in addition to the existing system of Impressment. Britain only had a small standing army and thus contributed to the war effort mainly by sea power and by supplying funds to other land coalition members facing France. The First Coalition to oppose revolutionary France, which included Austria, Prussia, and Spain, broke up in 1795 when Prussia and Spain made separate peace with France.

In 1797 the Pitt government was forced to protect gold reserves by preventing individuals from exchanging paper money for two decades. Nearly two hundred years later, the indebted American Nixon government was forced to take the same action due to Vietnam War finance that in my opinion led to the peak of American dominance. Pitt introduced Britain's first income tax which never really went away (except 1816-1842). Never-the-less government debt spiralled upwards, covered by the national debt which went over 150% of GNP in 1797.

The French were stalled by a naval blockade on Atlantic and Mediterranean seaboards. Seaborne offensives on the French West Indies' colonies were successful and highly profitable. The cost was a high mortality rate of 70% in soldiers and sailors, exacerbated by malaria and alcoholism. Despite the protests of planters, negro slaves were recruited to increase the ranks of the West India Regiment. By 1801 the French, Dutch and Spanish possessions were under British control. As well, Britain obtained Malta, Minorca and Dutch colonies in the East Indies, Trincomalee (Sri Lanka) and Cape Town (South Africa).

In 1798, the Irish attempted a rebellion in the hope that the French would assist them overthrow the British Protestant monarchy. Pitt thought that the Irish problem could be solved by incorporating Ireland into a union. The union was established through the Act of Union 1800. Pitt tried to grant concessions to Roman Catholics by abolishing political restrictions under which they had been forced to live since Cromwell. George III was strongly opposed to Catholic Emancipation which he believed would be against his coronation oath to protect the Church of England. Pitt resigned in 1801 to allow his childhood friend Henry Addington to form a new administration.

The French had discovered a way around their financial weakness by making the war pay for itself from forced contributions by the "liberated" peoples. The

Revolution had changed the French forces by rewarding non-aristocratic talent with promotion to commanders. British contribution to the forces of war in Europe was minimal but British finances subsidised the armies of Austria, Prussia and Russia. France obtained the Austrian Netherlands (Belgium) and the Rhineland. Napoleon's daring strategy was to attack Britain's finances by interrupting the commercial interests in the Middle East through capturing Egypt. The Royal Navy under Sir Horatio Nelson in 1798 destroyed Napoleon's fleet and transports which left the army isolated in Egypt. A British expeditionary force evicted the French in 1801. Napoleon had escaped earlier.

The Second Coalition, which included Austria, Russia, and the Ottoman Empire, was defeated by France in 1800. Only Great Britain was left fighting Napoleon Bonaparte, the First Consul of the French Republic. The harvest failures in 1799-1800 required importing grain from America. In 1801 Ireland theoretically joined the fight as the United Kingdom of Great Britain and Ireland.

Addington negotiated the Treaty of Amiens in 1802 allowing peace with France, not the least because Britain had reached a state close to financial collapse. By 1803 Addington had overhauled the income tax administration to allow finances to recover sufficiently to declare war on France when it became clear that the French were likely to invade Malta. However, it was Napoleon's plan to invade Britain, only thwarted by the Royal Navy in 1805.

Addington sought better relations with Russia, Austria and Prussia that allowed a Third Coalition shortly after he left office. Addington's greatest failing was his inability to manage a parliamentary majority, by cultivating the loyal support of MPs beyond his own circle and the friends of the King. Addington was driven from office by his old friend Pitt in opposition with Charles Fox and William Grenville.

Pitt returned to the premiership in 1804 without Fox who was opposed by the King. Many of Addington's supporters and Pitt's old colleagues joined the Opposition. In 1805 the Royal Navy under Admiral Nelson won a crushing victory in the Battle of Trafalgar to confirm the British naval supremacy, and which made an invasion of Britain impossible. The Coalition however was no match on land for Napoleon and was defeated at the Battle of Austerlitz. Pitt died in 1806 to be succeeded by his cousin William Grenville, Baron Grenville with a coalition which included the Whig Charles Fox as Foreign Secretary. King George's opposition to Fox was put aside for national interest in war.

Grenville's ministry was a national unity government known as the *Ministry of All the Talents*. It was not successful in bringing peace with France, but did abolish the slave trade in Britain in 1807. Grenville tried again to achieve Catholic Emancipation but timing during war with Catholic France practically guaranteed failure. Grenville was dismissed by King George in 1807 in favour of the second ministry of William Cavendish-Bentinck, Duke of Portland that included George Canning, Lord Castlereagh, Lord Hawkesbury, and Spencer Perceval.

Portland's second government saw the United Kingdom's complete isolation on the continent but also the beginning of recovery, with the start of the Peninsular War. In 1808 the British army under Lieutenant- General Sir Arthur Wellesley landed in Portugal, and France turned on its ally Spain to try to control the Iberian Peninsula. Wellesley's strategy was a war of attrition in which the better-fed army would succeed. The Royal Navy escorted convoys of merchantmen to ensure that the British army was well provisioned. The French army had a bad time living off the land. Wellesley repeatedly beat French armies which made Napoleon politically bankrupt. His desperation led to his invasion of Russia, the failure of which caused the disintegration of Napoleon's European *imperium* by 1812-13.

In late 1809, with Portland's health poor and the ministry rocked by the scandalous duel between Canning and Castlereagh, Portland resigned, dying shortly thereafter. The king accepted the Cabinet's recommendation of Spencer Perceval for his new Prime Minister. The new ministry was not expected to last. It was especially weak in the Commons, where Perceval had only one cabinet member – Home Secretary Richard Ryder – and had to rely on the support of backbenchers in debate. In the first week of the new Parliamentary session in January 1810 the Government lost four divisions. As Chancellor, Perceval continued to find the funds to finance Wellesley's campaign in the Iberian Peninsula, whilst contracting a lower debt than his predecessors or successors.

King George III had celebrated his Golden Jubilee in 1809 but by the following autumn he was showing signs of a return of the illness that had nearly led to Regency in 1788. The prospect of another Regency was not attractive to Perceval, as the Prince of Wales was known to favour Whigs and dislike Perceval. Twice Parliament was adjourned in November 1810, as doctors gave optimistic reports about the King's chances of a return to health. In December, select committees of the Lords and Commons heard evidence from the doctors, and Perceval finally wrote to the Prince of Wales on 19 December saying that he planned the next day to introduce a Regency Bill. As with Pitt's bill in 1788, there would be restrictions: the Regent's powers to create peers and award offices and pensions would be restricted for 12 months, the Queen would be responsible for the care of the King, and the King's private property would be looked after by trustees. The Prince of Wales, supported by the Opposition, objected to the restrictions, but Perceval steered the bill through Parliament.

The 1811 parliamentary session was largely taken up with problems in Ireland, economic depression and the bullion controversy in England (a Bill was passed to make bank notes legal tender), and military operations in the Peninsula. The restrictions on the Regency expired in 1812, the King was still showing no signs of recovery, and the Prince Regent decided, after an unsuccessful attempt to persuade Grey and Grenville to join the government, to retain Perceval and his ministers. Richard Wellesley, Marquess Wellesley, after intrigues with the Prince Regent, resigned as Foreign Secretary and was replaced by Lord Castlereagh.

The Opposition meanwhile was mounting an attack on the Orders in Council, which had caused a crisis in relations with America and were widely blamed for depression and unemployment in England. Rioting had broken out in the Midlands and North, and been harshly repressed. Henry Brougham's motion for a select committee was defeated in the Commons, but, under continuing pressure from manufacturers, the government agreed to set up a Committee of the Whole House to consider the Orders in Council and their impact on trade and manufacture. The committee began its examination of witnesses in early 1812. Percival was assassinated when he arrived to attend the Committee.

Robert Banks, Earl of Liverpool, succeeded Percival as Prime Minister. The cabinet proposed Liverpool as successor with Lord Castlereagh as leader in the Commons. But after an adverse vote in the Lower House, they subsequently gave both their resignations. The Prince Regent, however, found it impossible to form a different coalition and confirmed Liverpool as prime minister. Liverpool's government contained some of the future great leaders of Britain, such as Robert Stewart, Lord Castlereagh; George Canning; Arthur Wellesley; Robert Peel, and William Huskisson. Liverpool is considered a skilled politician, who held together the liberal and reactionary wings of the Tory party.

The fledgling United States declared war on Britain in 1812 for several reasons, primarily the impressment of American merchant seamen into the Royal Navy. The USA was suffering from trade restrictions caused by the French war, and British support of American native tribes against American expansion, possibly into Canada. Largely tied down by European needs, Britain operated defensive measures, including blockades of the Atlantic coast. Land and naval battles were fought on the American-Canadian border where Britain repelled American invasions. In 1814-15 Britain became more aggressive to succeed in burning the capitol Washington DC, but the Americans repulsed three invasions of New York, Baltimore and New Orleans. By 1814 both sides were weary of a costly war that offered victory to neither. The Treaty of Ghent was signed end 1814 which ended the war early in 1815. The War of 1812 was notable by American naval victories against the great Royal Navy.

Also in 1814, Arthur Wellesley, now Duke of Wellington, led his armies into southern France at a time when Austria, Prussia and Russia threatened eastern France. Napoleon abdicated but he returned from Elba a year later to again raise armies. Wellington and the Prussian general, Blucher, defeated the French at Waterloo in 1815. Napoleon was sent into exile at St. Helena.

After 1815 the British patriotism saw no bounds and assertive superiority founded the feeling that its system of government and the industry of its people reached the highest state yet realised by civilisation. In 1817 Liverpool's Foreign Secretary, Viscount Castlereagh, insisted that Britain's security required her to maintain *"a navy equal to the navies of any two powers that can be brought against us"*. Lord Castlereagh achieved the basis for many years of peace. This policy was followed throughout the nineteenth century.

Never-the-less Britain was ready to make concessions at the Congress of Vienna 1815 in order to confine France within its borders without damaging her national integrity. Guadeloupe and Reunion were returned to the French and the Netherlands regained Java and Surinam. Britain retained Malta, the Ionian Islands, Trinidad, Tobago, St. Lucia, Cape Colony and Mauritius.

Liverpool's chief economic problem during his time as Prime Minister was that of the nation's finances. The cost of war was debt which reached 226% of GDP in 1815 and reached a peak of 260% in 1821. The interest on the national debt, massively swollen by the enormous expenditure of the final war years, together with the war pensions, absorbed the greater part of normal government revenue. The refusal of the House of Commons in 1816 to continue the wartime income tax, left ministers with no immediate alternative but to go on with the ruinous system of borrowing to meet necessary annual expenditure. Liverpool eventually facilitated a return to the gold standard in 1819.

King George III who had been permanently demented since 1811 finally died in 1820. His Regent, Prince of Wales became George IV. George had been known for leading an extravagant lifestyle which had done much to define the Regency sub-period of the Georgian period of the Hanover kings. George IV had been separated from his wife Caroline since 1796 and refused to recognise her as Queen.

Because of a largely perceived threat to the government over the Corn Laws and Catholic emancipation, temporary legislation was introduced. Liverpool suspended Habeas Corpus in both Great Britain (1817) and Ireland (1822). Following the cavalry charge Peterloo Massacre in 1819, Liverpool's government imposed the repressive Six Acts legislation which limited, among other things, free speech and the right to gather for peaceful demonstration. In 1820, as a result of these measures, Liverpool and other cabinet ministers were almost assassinated in the Cato Street Conspiracy. Liverpool supported the repeal of the Combination Laws banning workers from combining into trade unions in 1824, although the powers of these unions were restricted in 1825 following strikes.

George Canning succeeded Liverpool as Prime Minister in 1827 but the Tory party was split between "High Tories", and the moderates supporting Canning who was forced to invite a number of Whigs to join his Cabinet. Canning fell ill and died in August 1827. His successor Frederick Robinson, Viscount Goderich, was unable to hold together Canning's fragile coalition and resigned after 144 days in office.

Field Marshal Arthur Wellesley, Duke of Wellington, was invited in 1828 by King George IV to form a Tory government. The first government suffered from resignation of four important ministers Lords Dudley and Palmerston, and Messrs Huskisson and Grant. These minsters were replaced by Lord Aberdeen, Foreign Secretary; Sir Henty Hardinge, Secretary at War; Sir George Murray, Secretary of State; William Vesey-Fitzgerald, President of Board of Trade. The Home Secretary was Robert Peel. Wellington's main problem was Catholic emancipation giving almost full civil rights to Catholics in the United Kingdom, against opposition from George IV. The Catholic Relief Act 1829 passed with a good majority and Wellington vowed to resign if assent was not given by the King.

Peel established the Metropolitan Police Force in 1829 with 1000 constables at Scotland Yard in London. He also reformed the criminal law, reducing the number of crimes punishable by death, and simplified it by repealing a large number of criminal statutes and consolidating their provisions into what are known as Peel's Acts. He reformed the gaol system, introducing payment for gaolers and education for the inmates.

King George IV died in 1830 to be succeeded by the third son of George III, as William IV. Wellington's government fell in 1830 following riots over the Reform Bill which he violently opposed in line with Tory policy. The Whig Charles Grey, Viscount Howick, formed a Whig government for the first time since 1777. His main task was to pass the Reform Bill which essentially had forced his predecessor's departure.

The Parliamentary Reform Act 1832 finally saw the reform of the House of Commons and led to the abolition of slavery throughout the British Empire in 1833. Under the Whigs and Radicals, the Reform Act broadened the voting franchise and ended the system of "rotten boroughs" and "pocket boroughs" (where elections were controlled by powerful families), and instead redistributed power on the basis of population. It added 217,000 voters to an electorate of 435,000 in England and Wales. Only the upper and middle classes voted, so this shifted power away from the landed aristocracy to the urban middle classes. After parliamentary investigations demonstrated the horrors of child labour, limited reforms were passed in 1833. The Whigs also passed the Poor Law Amendment Act 1834 that reformed the administration of relief to the poor.

The Reform Act strengthened the House of Commons by reducing the number of boroughs controlled by peers. Some aristocrats complained that, in the future, the government could compel them to pass any bill, simply by threatening to swamp the House of Lords with new peerages. The Reform Act did very little to appease the working class, since voters were required to possess property worth £10, a substantial sum at the time. This split the alliance between the working class and the middle class, giving rise to the Chartist Movement. The Chartist movement, which demanded universal suffrage for men, equally sized electoral districts, and voting by secret ballot, gained a widespread following. The Tories were united against further reform, and the Liberal Party (successor to the Whigs) did not seek a general revision of the electoral system until 1852. The 1850s saw Lord John Russell introduce a number of reform bills to correct defects the first act had left unaddressed. However, no proposal was successful until 1867, when Parliament adopted the Second Reform Act.

Howick resigned in 1834 allowing his Home Secretary, William Lamb, Viscount Melbourne to become Prime Minister. Melbourne was a conservative with the aristocratic vested interest in the status quo. He opposed the repeal of the Corn Laws arguing not only had Catholic emancipation failed, but also that the reform bill had not improved the condition of the people. King William

IV's opposition to the Whigs' reforming ways led him to dismiss Melbourne in November. He then gave the Tories under Sir Robert Peel an opportunity to form a government. Peel's failure to win a House of Commons majority in the resulting 1835 general election made it impossible for him to govern, and the Whigs returned to power under Melbourne. This was the last time a British monarch attempted to appoint a government against parliamentary majority. Around this time Tory Peel commenced using the term Conservative Party.

In 1836 Melbourne was blackmailed by the husband of Caroline Norton as having an affair. Melbourne was vindicated in court, but the scandal should have been enough to bring him down politically. The King and Wellington urged him to stay on as Prime Minister. William IV died in 1837 and was succeeded by his eighteen year-old niece Princess Victoria of Kent as Queen Victoria. Melbourne was mentor to the young Queen who was breaking away from the dominance of her mother, Duchess of Kent. Over the next four years Melbourne trained her in the art of politics and the two became friends.

The First Opium War between the East India Company and China commenced in 1839. The British government sent expeditionary forces from India, which ravaged the Chinese coast and dictated the terms of settlement. Melbourne resigned in 1839 but Sir Robert Peel placed conditions on his acceptance of government that were unacceptable to Victoria. Melbourne was persuaded to stay on as Prime Minister. He finally resigned permanently in 1841 after the Conservative victory in the General Election. The Treaty of Nanking 1842 not only opened the way for further opium trade, but ceded territory including Hong Kong, unilaterally fixed Chinese tariffs at a low rate, granted extraterritorial rights to foreigners in China.

China was not the only target of parliamentary approved efforts to break into Far Eastern markets. During the 1840s and 1850s anti-piracy operations influenced favourable treaties with Siam (Thailand) and Japan. The East India Company was able to exercise informal control over Malaya, Borneo and Sarawak to the advantage of British trade.

The Conservative, Sir Robert Peel was asked to form a government at a time of recession and a budget deficit run up by the Whigs. To raise revenue, Peel reintroduced income tax that raised more than expected, which allowed for the removal and reductions of tariffs. Peel was the subject of a failed assassination attempt in 1843. Peel recognised the changing social fabric of Britain when he introduced the Factory Act 1844 which restricted the hours that children and women could work in a factory, and introduced rudimentary safety standards for machinery.

The investment capital needed for the Industrial Revolution had come mostly from merchants engaged in domestic and foreign trade, from landowners who profited from their estates in Britain and plantations in the colonies, and from banks. Industrialists at that time were not a natural Conservative constituency, which remained the landed gentry. Peel then attacked this constituency when he moved to repeal the Corn Laws which he hoped would free food to relieve the Irish Famine. Although the Conservative Party refused to support the bill, Peel's Bill of Repeal 1846 passed in Commons with Whig and Radical support. Wellington persuaded the Lords to pass the bill. However at the same time Peel's Irish Coercion Bill failed in Commons so Peel resigned as Prime Minister. Free trade became a feature of British political life.

The Queen and Prince Consort were indignant at actions by Henry Temple, Viscount Palmerston, as Foreign Minister when he intervened in European affairs, often without knowledge of the cabinet. When Benjamin Disraeli and others took several nights in the House of Commons to impeach Palmerston's foreign policy, the foreign minister responded to a five-hour speech by Anstey with a five-hour speech of his own, the first of two great speeches in which he laid out a comprehensive defence of his foreign policy and of liberal interventionism more generally.

Peel's Whig successor in 1849, John Russell, Lord Russell, received more criticism than Peel on Irish policy. Parliament repealed the restrictive Navigation Acts as a prelude to freer trade. This was welcomed in Lancashire and by its thriving cotton industry which depended heavily on export markets and the supply of raw materials from the United States and elsewhere. Areas supporting heavy industry, such as iron, shipbuilding and engineering, also benefited and boosted their competitive ability internationally.

In 1850 Foreign Secretary Palmerston sent a Royal Navy squadron into the Aegean to blockade Piraeus in support of a private citizen's claims. In the subsequent debate Palmerston made the well known declaration that a British subject ought everywhere to be protected by the strong arm of the British government against injustice and wrong; comparing the reach of the British Empire to that of the ancient Roman Empire, in which a Roman citizen could walk the earth unmolested by any foreign power. This became known as *gunboat diplomacy*. Anti-piracy actions were part of the 1840s 1850s effort to break into Far Eastern markets. Britain built a large number of wooden steam-driven screw gunboats during the 1850s, some of which participated in the Crimean war, Second Opium War and Indian Mutiny.

Russell's premiership was frustrating, and, due to party disunity and infighting, he was unable to secure the success of many of the measures he was interested in passing. Russell saw conflict with his headstrong Foreign Secretary, Palmerston, whose belligerence and support for continental revolution he found embarrassing. Palmerston was forced to resign when he recognised Napoleon III's coup of 1851, without royal approval. The government also introduced a militia bill in the House of Commons, the vote on which was made a vote of confidence on the government. Palmerston succeeded in introducing an amendment to the militia bill which passed by eleven votes. Thus the majority vote in favour of the amendment to the militia bill caused the downfall of Russell's ministry in 1852 and a General Election.

The Conservative Edward Stanley, Earl of Derby, formed a minority government with so many new men in ministries that the government was known as the *"Who? Who?"* Ministry. Benjamin Disraeli was Chancellor of the Exchequer who had a great influence on cabinet. As with all minority governments, the Derby minority government had a difficult time governing. Their main preoccupation was avoiding any issue which might cause one of the small groups to go over to Whigs and cause a "no confidence" vote on the minority government. When Disraeli submitted his first Budget to Parliament in December 1852, the budget proved so unpopular with the Peelites (Conservative Free Traders), the Free Traders and the Irish Brigade that the budget was voted down in a "no confidence" vote. As a result the Derby minority government fell, making way for a Peelite-Whig coalition under George Gordon, Earl of Aberdeen.

The Peelite, Aberdeen, formed the government whose cabinet which contained Lord Palmerston and Lord John Russell, who were certain to differ on questions of foreign policy. One of the foreign policy issues on which Palmerston and Russell disagreed, was the type of relationship that Britain should have with France and especially France's ruler, Louis Bonaparte. Palmerston as Home Secretary could not direct foreign policy although he was still vocal in cabinet. Some British government officials felt that Louis Bonaparte was seeking foreign adventure in the spirit of his uncle—Napoleon I. Consequently, these officials felt that any close association with Louis Bonaparte would eventually lead Britain into another series of wars. As Prime Minister, the Earl of Aberdeen was one who feared France and Louis Bonaparte.

However, other British government officials were beginning to worry more about the rising political dominance of the Russian Empire in Eastern Europe and the corresponding decline of the Ottoman Empire. As Prime Minister, Aberdeen eventually led Britain into war on the side of the French/Ottomans against the Russian Empire in 1853. This war would eventually be called the Crimean War. The entire foreign policy negotiations surrounding the dismemberment of the Ottoman Empire, which would continue throughout the end of nineteenth century, would be referred to as the "Eastern Question" (possible interference with British trade in the Near East).

Aberdeen was really not in favour of Britain's entrance into the Crimean War. However, he was following the pressure that was being exerted on him from some members of his cabinet, including the belligerent Palmerston. In this rare instance Palmerston was actually being supported by John Russell, both of whom were in favour of a more aggressive policy against perceived Russian expansion. Since the 1830s *Russophobia* had infected opinions of the public who were used to British naval dominance which unfortunately suggested similar British military superiority.

The Russians occupied the Turkish satellite states of Wallachia and Moldavia in 1853 and deployed along the northern banks of the Danube River. The Ottoman Empire declared war on Russia. A Russian naval raid destroyed the Turkish fleet at Sinope. In 1854 following an ignored ultimatum, Britain and France declared war on Russia. British and French troops landed on the Crimean peninsula at Eupatoria north of Sevastopol. After an earlier battle the allies decided on a siege of Sevastopol. A Russian attack on the allied supply base at Balaclava in October 1854 was rebuffed. The Battle of Balaclava is noted for its famous (or rather infamous) charge of the Light Brigade, caused at least in part by poor command of the British commander, Lord Raglan. Russian forces tried to relieve the siege at Sevastopol and tried to defeat the Allied armies in the field in the Battle of Inkerman. However, this attempt failed and the Russians were rebuffed. Both sides dug in for the winter against which the British had no proper clothing.

Dissatisfaction as to the course of the war arose in England. As reports returned detailing the mismanagement of the conflict, Parliament began to investigate. In 1855, John Roebuck introduced a motion for the appointment of a select committee to enquire into the conduct of the war. The motion was passed with a large majority which Aberdeen treated as a motion of no confidence in his government. Aberdeen resigned. Queen Victoria asked Derby to form a government but Palmerston's intransigence did not allow it. The Queen reluctantly asked Palmerston to form a government.

In 1855 Tsar Nicholas I died and was succeeded by his son Alexander II who did not wish to make peace, but was convinced of the need to prevent war on the Russian homeland. The war continued when Palmerston thought peace terms were too soft on Russia. It was not until the fall of Sevastopol in late 1855 that peace was formally discussed. An armistice was signed in 1856 leading to a peace treaty after a month's negotiations. The Black Sea was to be a demilitarised zone.

In 1856 a British army landed in Persia to persuade Shah Nasr-ud-Din to relinquish his claim to the fortress on the Afghan-Persian border, Herat. Despite resistance from Russia, the Shah gave way, so that a Russia gateway to India was closed. However Russia continued to advance east towards the northern border of Afghanistan with occupation between 1864 and 1868 of Khiva, Tashkent and Samarkand.

Aggressive action in 1856 by British consul Parkes at Canton (Guangzhou) sparked reprisal action by Chinese Commissioner Ye who placed a bounty on English heads. In London, the Attorney-General had no doubt that Parkes had acted in breach of international law. Palmerston, however, backed Parkes on the principle that distant subordinates' actions should not be second-guessed. The government's policy was subsequently strongly attacked in the Commons on high moral grounds by Richard Cobden and William Gladstone during a censure debate. Palmerston replied to claim that if the motion of censure was carried it would signal that the House had voted to *"abandon a large community of British subjects at the extreme end of the globe to a set of barbarians - a set of kidnapping, murdering, poisoning barbarians"*. The Censure motion was carried by a small majority so Palmerston requested to the Queen that Parliament be dissolved for a general election. Regardless of the debate, the situation in China escalated into the Second Opium War.

Palmerston was re-elected with an increased majority so parliament decided to seek redress from China. The Qing government was already occupied with the Taiping Rebellion so was not in a sound position to confront the East India Company and Britain militarily. Britain sought an alliance from France, the United States and Russia. Guangzhou was occupied by the British and French with their modern weapons against Chinese near-medieval firearms.

After a Treaty of Tientsin 1858, most favourable to the alliance, militant Chinese ministers prevailed on the Xianfeng Emperor to resist encroachment from the West. In 1859 a large British naval force was prevented from accompanying Anglo-French envoys to Peking (Beijing) and withdrew after heavy fighting. In 1860 a very heavy Anglo-French force captured Yantai and Dalian before landing at Beitang for the march to Peking. The Chinese forces were annihilated and the foreigners entered Peking where summer palaces were burned. The 1858 Treaty of Tianjin was finally ratified in 1860. Britain obtained Kowloon (next to Hong Kong) and the legalisation of opium.

In June, news came to Britain of the Indian Rebellion of 1857. Palmerston sent Sir Colin Campbell and reinforcements to India. Palmerston also agreed to transfer the authority of the British East India Company to the Crown. Edward Smith-Stanley, Earl of Derby formed another minority government in 1858, upon the demise of Lord Palmerston's first ministry, with Benjamin Disraeli again at the Exchequer and Leader of the Commons. The Sepoy Mutiny rebellion saw the end of the East India Company's rule in India. In August, by the Government of India Act 1858, the company was formally dissolved and its ruling powers over India were transferred to the British Crown for the first time. Once again, the British government was short-lived, collapsing after only a year.

After the Italian republican Felice Orsini tried to assassinate the French emperor with a bomb made in Britain, the French were outraged. Palmerston introduced a Conspiracy to Murder Bill which made it a felony to plot in Britain to murder someone abroad. At first reading, the Conservatives voted for it but at second reading they voted against it. Palmerston lost by nineteen votes. Therefore, in 1858 he was forced to resign. Parliament was dissolved in 1859 and a General Election ensued which the Whigs won.

Palmerston rejected an offer from Disraeli to become Conservative leader but attended the meeting where the Liberal Party was formed. The Queen asked Lord Granville to form a government but although Palmerston agreed to serve under him, Russell did not. The Queen asked Palmerston to become Prime Minister. Russell and Gladstone agreed to serve under him. Palmerston's last premiership saw attention paid to criminal and company law in passing the Offences against the Person Act 1861 and the Companies Act 1862. Although Gladstone was Chancellor of the Exchequer he was often at odds with his leader, particularly over voting reform and the cost of dockyard defence.

Britain had taken the lead in the eclipse of the Chinese Emperor in 1860, but its partner, France, was already infiltrating Indo-China. Russia had its eyes on Korea and territory along China's northern borders. Britain showed no interest in annexing territory in China apart from Hong Kong and adjoining Kowloon, possibly recognising the immediate past problems with India. British commerce had a near monopoly of Chinese markets and a stranglehold on Chinese border customs.

Palmerston favoured the Confederacy in the American Civil War but understood that this was not in Britain's economic interest because corn was more important than cotton. When a US Navy warship stopped a British steamer to seize two Confederate envoys en route to Europe, Gladstone was enraged. He internally threatened war with the Union if the envoys were not released and sent additional troops to Canada. A Confederate ship, CSS Alabama, was built in Britain and it was suggested by a law officer that it be detained as breaching Britain's neutrality. The "Alabama" had already put to sea for its raiding cruise which captured or destroyed many Union ships. After the war the US claimed damages against Britain which Palmerston refused to pay. After Palmerston's death in 1865, Gladstone agreed to pay $15,500,000 as damages.

After many years of protestant missionary fervour which favoured humanitarian treatment of subdued races, the Indian Mutiny tended to change public opinion of the "noble savage". Insurrection by black people in Jamaica in 1865 ended in martial law being declared by Governor Eyre, which led to many deaths. The debate over Eyre's actions marked a start to openly racist sentiment in elements of the nation.

Palmerston had won the general election of 1865 and immediately had to deal with Fenian violence in Ireland which he believed was caused by America. The eighty year old Palmerston was leaning towards an alliance with France and Prussia against threats from the USA and Russia when he died. The Foreign Secretary, John Russell, by then Earl Russell, became Prime Minister. In 1866 party disunity brought down his government, and Russell went into retirement.

Edward, Lord Stanley, Earl of Derby, returned the Conservatives to power with Disraeli again a leading figure. The administration's success was the Reform Act 1867 which expanded voter suffrage. Disraeli was an imperialist who believed that Britain should retain strong global power. Also in 1867 he encouraged the Anglo-India army in to an Abyssinian expedition to free hostages from Emperor Theodore.

In 1868 Derby retired from political life, allowing Disraeli to succeed him briefly before losing that year's election. The Liberal, William Gladstone assumed government in 1868, committed to low public spending and electoral reform and with an unfocused imperial policy. With the Irish Church Act 1869 Gladstone disestablished the Church of Ireland and with the Ballot Act 1872 introduced secret voting. He introduced reforms to the British Army, Civil Service and local government; and made peacetime flogging illegal. Unions were slowly liberalised through the Trade Union Act 1871. Despite Gladstone's peace pretensions, Britain had little influence on Europe and was unable to prevent the Franco-Prussian War in 1870. Gladstone unexpectedly dissolved parliament in 1874 and called a general election which he lost.

The Conservative liberal Disraeli became Prime Minister with a cabinet of six peers and six commoners. The Conservatives had campaigned on patriotic principles to arouse national pride in the working-class electorate. The party stood for patriotism, the monarchy and empire. Disraeli's new government enacted many domestic reforms including legislation which made inexpensive loans available to towns and cities to construct working-class housing. The Conspiracy and Protection of Property Act 1875 was meant to protect workers who were also allowed to picket and sue employers. Trade unions were legitimised.

In 1875 Disraeli approved the purchase of the majority of shares in the Suez Canal which the majority of British ships to the Far East used as India's lifeline. Economically Britain could afford the expense because it had reduced its public debt/GNP ratio to 58% from the precarious peak of 260% in 1821. It was Disraeli who reluctantly introduced the Royal Titles Act 1876 which allowed Queen Victoria to style herself as Empress of India. It was of course only coincidence that, also in 1876, Queen Victoria created Disraeli as Earl of Beaconsfield necessitating him to move from Commons to Lords.

Reports of atrocities to Christians in Bulgaria emboldened a retired Gladstone into writing anti-Turkish pamphlets to stir up the Liberals against Disraeli who favoured continued alliance with the Ottomans against Russia. The Russo-Turkish War commenced in 1877 when British interests were divided. In 1878 the Ottoman Emperor appealed to Britain to save Constantinople which caused the government to seek £6million to prepare for war. Gladstone had re-entered politics but less than half of the Liberal party voted with him. The Treaty of San Stefano 1878 was unacceptable to the British because it would create a Russian state in Europe. The Treaty of Berlin 1878 ratified what was negotiated behind the scenes with Russia modifying Bulgaria, Turkey maintaining the safeguards for the Dardanelles, and Turkey ceding Cyprus to Britain where naval ships could be based. Disraeli returned to England as a hero for peace.

The fickle nature of working-class democracy was demonstrated in 1879 when sentiment moved against Disraeli over the wars in the Transvaal, Zululand and Afghanistan. The rash of wars inspired Gladstone to tour Britain denouncing policies that were damaging Britain's reputation for fair play and justice. The Liberal victory in the 1880 election was a sign to Gladstone that the country needed to return to its old values of moral strength as a global power that could simply influence other powers without warfare. Other powers must have noticed because there was a surge of annexations in Africa, the Far East and the Pacific by Germany, Italy, the United States and Japan. Gladstone was already caught in the Boer War which commenced in December 1880, but he negotiated a peace in March 1881.

Britain was caught in a trade war exacerbated by the worldwide economic recession beginning in 1873. At the time, the episode 1873-1879 was labelled the *Great Depression* and held that designation until the Great Depression of the 1930s. The period provoked a protectionist response in many nations. The French, German, Italian, Russian and United States reacted by dropping free trade in favour of protection. As trade barriers were erected, British exports tumbled, yet the Liberals retained their belief in free trade. Between 1880 and 1910 Britain's portion of the world's trade fell from 23% to 17%. Britain's balance of payments remained reasonably strong on the back of banking, shipping, insurance and investments.

Gladstone's Liberal cabinet ordered the bombing of Alexandria in 1882 which commenced the Anglo-Egyptian War and the occupation of Egypt. The invasion was probably to protect the Suez Canal, although others theorised that it was to protect British investments in Egypt and thus improve Liberal political advantage. The 1884 Reform Act extended the voting franchise to agricultural labourers which added six million to the electoral rolls. The murder of General Gordon in Khartoum was sheeted home to Gladstone because it was believed that he had neglected military affairs. Gladstone resigned as Prime Minister and declined the Queen's offer of an earldom.

The Conservatives won the 1885 election with a minority government under aristocratic Robert Gascoyne-Cecil, Marquis of Salisbury, and Viscount Cranborne. In July 1885 the Housing of the Working Classes Bill was introduced amid criticism of State socialism but the Act was narrowly passed. The split of the Liberals over Irish Home Rule enabled Salisbury to return to power with a majority in 1886. The faction against Home Rule broke away from the Liberals to form the Liberal Unionists Party. Racism soon became an issue after Salisbury's comments that the losing Liberal opponent to the Unionist's Bruce in the Holborn by-election 1888 was *"a black man"*. In fact the *"black man"* was an Indian Dadabhai Nairoji, who finally won a seat for the Liberals in 1892.

Salisbury saw the need for maintaining control of the seas and passed the Naval Defence Act 1889 which facilitated £20million on the Royal Navy over four years. This was the biggest ever expansion of the navy in peacetime: ten new battleships, thirty-eight new cruisers, eighteen new torpedo boats and four new fast gunboats. The aim was to raise the Royal Navy again to strength equivalent to the next two biggest navies of the world, then France and Russia. However the implementation was opposed by Gladstone in the next government.

The Liberals won the 1892 election with a minority government under Gladstone who reintroduced the Home Rule Bill that had previously lost him government. The Bill passed Commons but failed in the Lords. Gladstone resigned in March 1894 and died four years later. Archibald Primrose, Earl of Rosebery, succeeded Gladstone as Prime Minister largely because Queen Victoria disliked most of the other leading Liberals. Rosebery was of the imperialist faction which favoured policies such as expansion of the fleet but failed to attract support in the Commons. The Unionist factions of the Conservative Party stopped the Liberals domestic legislation in the Lords. Rosebery offered the resignations' of his cabinet in 1895 to the Queen who chose the Conservative Unionist leader Lord Salisbury to form a government. The Unionists won heavily in the 1895 general election.

Salisbury as Prime Minister also served as Foreign Secretary with a policy of *"Splendid Isolation"* which was basically Britain's aloof stance from European affairs. Leading Liberal Unionist Joseph Chamberlain sought and accepted the post of Secretary of State for the Colonies. Chamberlain's goal was to expand the British Empire and reorder imperial trade and resources; to foster closer relations between Britain and the settler colonies, with the objective of reforming the empire as a federation of Anglo-Saxon nations.

The 1897 Diamond Jubilee of Queen Victoria coincided with public admiration for the Anglo-Saxon empire assisted by the popular press, so that the Boer War was simply considered the natural extension of Empire in competition with the imperial reach of France, Italy, Russia and Germany. Public schools since the 1880s had inspired their pupils towards public service in government and the armed services which allowed ready officer recruits for the Boer War. It was the public schools which impressed their students to speak "standard English" to try to eradicate regional accents. *Oxbridge* (Oxford/Cambridge) became the standard educated accent for London and the Queen's English of Empire. Britain entered the twentieth century as the greatest unquestioned imperial power in terms of territory and population. Thousands, including the Anglo-Saxon colonies in Australia and New Zealand came forward in the imperial spirit to volunteer for military service in South Africa.

In 1892 the Russians had joined the French in the Mediterranean which threatened the Suez Canal, and thus India. A naval race developed, with Britain competing against France and Russia in building battleships. In 1898 Britain possessed 52 battleships with 12 under construction; France and Russia had 39 with 18 on the blocks. These figures did not take into account Germany which had 17 battleships and 5 under construction.

In 1898, after losing primacy in China to territorial demands from France, Germany and Russia, Salisbury's government announced that it had no territorial claims to China. Britain leased Wei-heiwei on the north coast of China as a naval base. Salisbury felt that defending Britain's commercial empire in China against rival imperial claims, would stretch military resources too thin. The movement of warships from the home and Mediterranean fleets already depleted resources, but Britain could not allow Germany, Russia and France to act without a counter.

Joseph Chamberlain, Secretary of State for the Colonies, advocated investment in the tropics of Africa, the West Indies and other underdeveloped possessions. In 1899 Britain set out to complete its takeover of the future South Africa, which it had begun in 1814 with the annexation of the Cape Colony, by invading the gold-rich Afrikaner republics of Transvaal and the neighbouring Orange Free State. The chartered British South Africa Company had already seized the land to the north, renamed Rhodesia after its head, the Cape tycoon Cecil Rhodes. War with the Transvaal became inevitable, and the Second Boer War commenced in 1899.

The general election of 1900 was strongly influenced by the war so became known as the Khaki Election. Chamberlain dominated the election and ensured that the Boer War was the main issue. The Conservative Party government of Lord Salisbury was returned to office with an increased majority over the Liberal Party. Twenty-six year old Winston Churchill successfully gained the seat of Oldham as a Conservative. Also in 1900 the Labour Representation Committee was formed by the Trade Union Congress to combine left-wing organisations into a single body which would establish a Labour group in parliament. During the last two years of his ministry, from the autumn of 1900 until the summer of 1902, old age and ill health forced Salisbury to give up the Foreign Office, though he continued as Prime Minister.

Since 1895 the Australian colonies had worked on a Constitution that would allow an Australian Federation of the six colonies. In 1900 Chamberlain managed the Commonwealth of Australia Constitution Act through the House of Commons, in the hope that the new federation would adopt a positive attitude towards imperial trade and the Boer War. The Act came into force in January 1901, but there were already contingents in Africa from the separate colonies, with New South Wales sending the first in 1899 closely followed by the other states. For logistic reasons these troops were called the 1st Australian Regiment.

Queen Victoria died in January 1901 after a 63year reign and her imperial heritage was continued by her eldest son as King Edward VII. The Treaty of Vereeniging ended the Boer War in May 1902. The British had put nearly 450,000 troops into the field and had spent nearly £200 million. A royal commission was convened to hear evidence over how the war was conducted. What was revealed was a lack of an army intelligence system, mismanaged hospitals, and the rejection of thousands of young working-class volunteers because of physical debility. The results appeared to confirm critics' opinions that the nation was in decline.

In July 1902 Salisbury resigned due to ill health, and was succeeded by his nephew, Arthur Balfour, Earl of Balfour. Chamberlain remained Colonial Secretary which was unofficially titled *"First Minister of the Empire"*. Although popular, Chamberlain had problems being in the minority Liberal Unionists. A notable achievement of Balfour's government was the establishment of the Committee on Imperial Defence.

After invasion of Manchuria by Russia, Britain was forced to seek the 1902 Anglo-Japanese Alliance which would be triggered if either country was attacked by two or more countries. This was an admission by Britain that it could no longer retain dominance in China on its own. Japan defeated Russian claims to Manchuria and Korea. After the failure of the Germans to agree to an Anglo-German Treaty in 1902, Balfour and his Foreign Secretary, Lord Lansdowne presided over a dramatic improvement in relations with France, culminating in the *Entente Cordiale* of 1904. In 1904 Admiral Sir John Fisher became First Sea Lord and became a driving force for the development of a new Dreadnought class of battleship. He also produced plans for a new high speed battle cruiser.

In the face of increasing German and US economic power, Chamberlain crusaded for tariff reform. The threat of higher prices for food imports split the government. Chamberlain resigned in 1903 to vocally support tariff reform in the electorate. Balfour tried to maintain a balancing act between reformers and free traders, but eventually resigned in December 1905. In the 1906 election the Conservatives were defeated by the Liberals in a virtual landslide under Sir Henry Campbell-Bannerman. The Labour Representative Council won 29 seats, whose parliamentarians decided to adopt the name Labour Party.

Under Campbell-Bannerman, the Liberal government appeared to introduce progressive liberalism, which introduced more relaxed laws for trade unions, free school meals, unemployment and sickness pay, and medical insurance. The welfare state had its beginnings under Campbell-Bannerman. It was typical of the left-wing attitude that Hardie, a Labour Party MP denounced the Boer War as capitalist aggression against a race of farmers. Campbell-Bannerman resigned due to ill-health in 1908 to be succeeded by his Chancellor of the Exchequer, Herbert Asquith.

There was apprehension about German armament plans which was probably behind the *Entente* with Russia in 1907. The first new battleship, HMS Dreadnaught, was commissioned end 1906 as the first of number of the Dreadnought Class ships in the naval arms race with Germany. The Asquith government continued the arms race as well as the welfare state under Chancellor David Lloyd George. Winston Churchill, who had switched to the Liberals, pushed against sweatshop conditions in the workplace. The Conservatives still had power in the Lords and refused to pass a number of Bills, including the Licensing Bill 1908. Most importantly the Conservatives planned to oppose the *"People's Budget"* which increased taxes on the rich and tariff reform to pay for battleships and welfare programs. Class warfare was conducted in the daily press before the Lords rejected the budget in 1909 to cause a general election in 1910.

The election was dominated by talk that a returned Liberal government would create sufficient peers to gain control of the House of Lords (this was rejected King Edward VII). The 1910 election resulted in a hung parliament under a minority Liberal government supported by Irish Nationalists. The Budget – for which the Liberals had obtained the slim electoral mandate – was passed by both Commons and Lords in April. The Commons passed resolutions which would form the basis for the Parliament Act: to remove the power of the Lords to veto money bills, to reduce their veto of other bills to a power to delay for up to two years (the Bill would become law if passed a third time by the Commons), and also to reduce the term of Parliament from seven years to five. In the debate Asquith hinted that he would ask the King to create peers. King Edward died in May 1910 to be succeeded by George V as King of the United Kingdom and British Dominions, and Emperor of India. A constitutional conference on parliamentary reforms broke down in November 1910 and the Liberals requested dissolution which the king granted.

The general election of 1910 returned another minority Liberal government supported by MP's from Ireland. The Parliament Act 1911 essentially broke the power of the House of Lords as a major base of political power. Although opposed to women's suffrage, Asquith believed it was up to the House of Commons to decide. During his premiership, three Conciliation Bills were brought forth which would have extended the right to vote of a limited number of women, however these foundered due to lack of parliamentary time and other delaying tactics. The price of Irish support in 1910 was the Third Irish Home Rule Bill, which Asquith delivered in legislation in 1912. Asquith's efforts over Irish Home Rule nearly provoked a civil war in Ireland over the province of Ulster, only averted by the outbreak of a European war. It became apparent after the near civil war in Ireland that the military was out of favour with the more socialist factions in parliament. This did not bode well for future military activity.

In 1912 the Asquith Cabinet was informed that a decision had been taken in 1906 about secret operations with the French in the event of war with Germany. They were advised that secret plans were well advanced to send a 160,000 expeditionary force to the Franco-Belgian frontier if France were attacked by Germany. This was no doubt a surprise because all the public plans and spending had been about naval superiority. The British army was equipped for small colonial wars and not for continental struggles.

The Great War (only called World War I in 1939) was triggered by the assassination of Archduke Franz Ferdinand of Austria which invoked alliances of major powers into conflict. Austria-Hungary attacked Serbia which was defended by Russia. As Austria's ally, Germany was led by the Prussian General Staff into the Schlieffen Plan which called on a western strike via Belgium against France. The secret treaty with France meant that Britain declared war on Germany, sustained by the knowledge of imperial support by the dominions of Canada, Australia, New Zealand and South Africa ("*if the old country is at war, so are we*").

The population of the United Kingdom put aside its political differences to respond to the raising of a volunteer army in alliance with France in August 1914, following the German invasion of Belgium. The Defence of the Realm Act gave the government wide-ranging powers during the war period, such as the power to requisition buildings or land needed for the war effort, or to make regulations creating criminal offences. The dominant figures in the management of the war were Winston Churchill (First Lord of the Admiralty) and Field-Marshal Lord Kitchener, who had taken over the War Office from Prime Minister Asquith.

Asquith's wartime cabinet was brought down in May 1915, due in particular to a crisis and the failed Gallipoli Campaign in the Dardanelles. The Australian and New Zealand Army Corps (ANZAC) had been particularly devastated by losses from an ill conceived operation, poorly administered by British command. The political support from Australia and New Zealand still continued, but there was much questioning by the dominions of British military control competence in subsequent battles in France. Colonial conscription became necessary to provide the numbers required to fight a war of attrition.

Asquith proceeded to form a new coalition government, with the majority of the cabinet coming from his own Liberal party and the Unionist (Conservative) party brought in to shore up the government. Former Conservative leader A.J.Balfour was given the Admiralty, replacing Churchill. Kitchener, popular with the public, was stripped of his powers over munitions (given to a new ministry under Lloyd George). By autumn 1915 Asquith's Coalition was close to breaking up over conscription forced by lack of volunteers due to horrendous losses in France. In January 1916, conscription was introduced. Conscription put into uniform nearly every physically fit man, six million out of ten million eligible. Of these about 750,000 lost their lives and 1,700,000 were wounded.

By late 1916 the war had not gone well under Asquith. There was no movement on the Western Front, despite millions of casualties. The Allied attacks on Turkey through Gallipoli and Mesopotamia had been both total disasters. Russia and Italy were proving to be weak allies, and the Treasury was running out of money to buy war supplies in the United States.

This coalition government lasted until 1916, when the Unionists became dissatisfied with Asquith and the Liberals' conduct of affairs, particularly over the Battle of the Somme. The government collapsed as a result of the political manoeuvrings of Andrew Bonar Law (leader of the Conservatives), Sir Edward Carson (leader of the Ulster Unionists), and David Lloyd George (then a minister in the cabinet). The Liberal, Lloyd George, enjoyed wide support and duly formed a new coalition government. Asquith was still the party head but he and his followers moved to the opposition benches in Parliament. Lloyd George immediately transformed the British war effort, taking firm control of both military and domestic policy. The largely Unionist small War Cabinet took complete charge of the national war effort. Lloyd George wanted to make the destruction of Turkey a major British war aim, and two days after taking office told Robertson that he wanted a major victory, preferably the capture of Jerusalem, to impress British public opinion.

Lloyd George engaged almost constantly in intrigues calculated to reduce the power of the generals, including trying to subordinate British forces in France to the French General Nivelle who was critical of British General Haig. Lloyd George plotted with part of the War Cabinet which was then opposed by missing members, Robertson and Lord Derby (Minister for War). Amid prospects of the government falling, Cabinet opinion turned in favour of Haig. Lloyd George lost any remaining respect of the senior military.

In January 1917, the Kaiser signed the order for unrestricted German submarine warfare to resume. At first, the British Admiralty failed to respond effectively to the German offensive but in early 1917 nearly 90% of Britain's merchant shipping tonnage was brought under state control whilst remaining privately owned. Merchant shipping was concentrated on the transatlantic route where it could more easily be protected. Lloyd George had raised the matter of convoys at the War Committee in November 1916, only to be told by the admirals present, including Jellicoe, that convoys presented too large a target, and that merchant ship masters lacked the discipline to "keep station" in a convoy. Carson (First Lord of the Admiralty) and Admirals Jellicoe and Duff agreed to "conduct experiments". However, convoys were not in general use until August 1917, by which time the rate of shipping losses was already in decline after peaking in April.

In April 1917, the United States Congress declared war on Germany and entered the War in May 1917, at least in part due to Germany's resumption of submarine warfare against US merchant ships trading with France and Britain. In the early stages the importance of America was its productive strength, boosted by the billions of dollars in Allied war orders. It produced half of the worlds food exports which could be sent to Britain and Europe.

Tsar Nicholas II had abdicated in March 1917 and by November the Bolshevik Party had gained control of Russian government. In December the Russian government commenced an armistice and negotiation with the Germans. In the face of a German invasion against an ineffective army, the Bolsheviks acceded to the Treaty of Brest-Litovsk in March 1918. The Germans had already commenced to move troops to the Western front for a spring offensive. They then had more soldiers on the Western Front than the allies and had calculated that US troops would take much time in arriving. The Allied armies fell back 40 miles in confusion, and facing defeat, London realised it needed more troops to fight a mobile war. Lloyd George somehow found a half million soldiers and rushed them to France.

The United States had a small army, but, after the passage of the Selective Service Act, it drafted 2.8 million men and by summer 1918 was sending 10,000 fresh soldiers to France every day. General John J. Pershing, American Expeditionary Forces (AEF) commander, refused to break up U.S. units to be used as reinforcements for British Empire and French units. Many American commanders used the same flawed tactics which the British and French had abandoned early in the war, and so not all American offensives were particularly effective. However, the manpower and morale boost to the seasoned troops gave the allies a decisive edge over the Germans. Victory over Germany was achieved on November 11, 1918 after German morale had collapsed on both the Western and Home Fronts.

In the election of December 1918 Lloyd George led a coalition of Conservatives and his own faction of Liberals to a landslide victory. The Conservatives had control within the coalition of more than two-thirds of its seats. Asquith's independent Liberals were crushed and emerged with only 33 seats, although they were still the official opposition as the two Liberal factions combined had more seats than Labour. The question of the secret treaty with France was never answered.

Lloyd George represented Britain at the Versailles Peace Conference, and, on the whole, stood on the side of generosity and moderation. He did not want to utterly destroy the German economy and political system. Although criticised by many, including John Maynard Keynes, Lloyd George was probably vindicated by history when the massive reparations forced on Germany led to World War II.

Britain, France and Italy imposed severe economic penalties on Germany in the Treaty of Versailles. The United States Senate did not ratify the Treaty; instead, the United States signed separate peace treaties with Germany and her allies. The US Senate also refused to enter the newly created League of Nations on President Wilson's terms, and Wilson rejected the Senate's compromise proposal.

The Great War was a major economic catastrophe as Britain went from being the world's largest overseas investor to being its biggest debtor, with interest payments consuming around 40 percent of the national budget. Inflation more than doubled between 1914 and its peak in 1920, while the value of the Pound Sterling fell by 61.2 percent. The Debt/GDP ratio grew from 25.83% in 1913 to 154% in 1921.

As well, the economically weakened Britain was beset with widespread social unrest in Ireland, Egypt, India, West Indies, Iraq and Palestine. The home front was not safe due to trade union militancy and strikes. The government chose to blame the Communist menace (*the Red Menace*) stemming from Russia as the cause for this unrest. It was more likely that the war had left established law and order weakened and vulnerable to the epidemic of protest and disorder that appeared in 1919 when risk of war had faded. In this book, the unrest is simply attributed to the natural cyclical decline of the British Empire

The Colonial British Empire 1700-1900AD

Leaders in War and Defence in America and the West Indies

There were slave revolts in the Caribbean even though there was little chance of success. Antigua in the 1720s and 1730s, and Jamaica in mid century flared into ferocious violence before being put down. In the 1720s, a number of Native American groups began to migrate to the Ohio Country from the East, driven by pressure from encroaching colonists.

Between 1710 and 1730 the population of Pennsylvania grew from 24,500 to 85,700, mostly Scots-Irish from Northern Ireland. By 1776 it is estimated that almost half the Ulster population crossed the Atlantic and that one in seven American colonists were Scots-Irish. At first the Scots-Irish from Ulster headed for New England where their violence made them unwelcome. They were encouraged to head south to Philadelphia and its river, the Delaware, which at first welcomed them because of their frontier toughness as an asset to native Indian aggression. Unfortunately their habit of squatting on any vacant land they fancied caused problems, so they were encouraged to move inland through German immigrant country. Those who did not settle, spread south towards the hills of Appalachia where they were well suited to the harsh pioneering life. The language of the Scots-Irish was instrumental in the developing American English dialect. Linguists say the famous southern expression "*you-all*" is a Scots-Irish translation of the plural "*yous*".

Already since the 1740s, the French in the Caribbean had challenged the British in the sugar empire. The plantations in St. Dominique were supplied by French slave ships and were evidently more productive than the British. French sugar undercut British prices in Europe. As well, the French encouraged British American ships to smuggle French rum and molasses to America which undercut British West Indies produce. The British parliament tried to limit French incursions with the Treaty of Aix-la-Chapelle 1748 which swapped strategic outposts in India and Canada.

The French strategy in America was to link their colonies of New France (Canada) to Louisiana by a chain of roads, navigated rivers, portage trails and forts. Key to this strategy was the broad stretch of territory known as the "Ohio Country" which was peopled by various Native American tribes. Fort building was an effort to maintain territory that became the frontier when Britain and France declared war in 1744. The British colonists' war effort was fragmented because they were disunited. The New Englanders sent volunteers to the siege of Louisburg and hoped that success would provide land in New France. At the end of the war the situation reverted to fort holding.

The British Virginians, who claimed the hinterland of America as part of their 1609 charter, formed the Virginian Ohio Company in 1747 to survey and lay claim to trans-Appalachian lands. The mid-Atlantic colonies of New York, New Jersey, Pennsylvania, Delaware and Maryland were opposed to the French and their Native American (Indian) allies moving south from Canada. The Native American Iroquois League claimed the region by right of conquest.

The Indians were unable to understand the European principle of land ownership. The Indian concept was that they had been given land by the Great Spirit as a right as long as they cultivated and hunted on it. When a tribe sold land it believed that it still had the right to cultivate and hunt. When they were excluded from what they considered their rights by settlers, they were confused and angry. Alcohol was used by land speculators to deceive the native owners. The anger would lead to war.

After initially remaining neutral, the Ohio Country Indians largely sided with the French. Armed with supplies and guns from the French, they raided via the Kittanning Path against British settlers east of the Alleghenies. In 1753, a lanky six foot two twenty-one year-old Virginian major, George Washington, was dispatched to carry a letter to the French to cease and desist from garrisoning territories belonging to King George. The subsequent 1754 expedition by

Lieutenant-Colonel Washington to attack the French ended in disaster due to rain damaged ammunition at Fort Necessity.

Representatives from the colonies met at Albany in 1755 in an effort to create a common front against the French and the Iroquois. The meeting appealed to the British government which decided to send troops. The colonists were not aware of any obligation to the home government that they had created, which would cause future problems. British General Edward Braddock had two regiments of foot, artillery and some Virginian militiamen. Braddock had no experience of partisan warfare in rough country and paid little attention to the militia who had experienced Indian fighting. En route to Fort Duquesne a third of his army was lost when it was ambushed by a French-Indian detachment so Braddock retired to his base at Fort Cumberland.

After the Indians destroyed Fort Granville in the summer of 1756, the colonial governor John Penn ordered Lt. Colonel John Armstrong to destroy the Shawnee villages west of the Alleghenies. Meanwhile other British and colonial forces drove the French from Fort Duquesne and built Fort Pitt, the origin of the city of Pittsburgh, Pennsylvania. This was the start of the actual first world war, the Seven Years War which was fought in Europe, America and Asia.

The British saw the allegiance of the French Arcadians of Nova Scotia to the French and Indian Confederacy as a threat. Governor Charles Lawrence decided to deport all Arcadians to remove that threat after the Battle of Beausejour in 1755. In the first wave of expulsions, Arcadians were deported to other British colonies. During the second wave, after the fall of Louisburg in 1758, they were deported from Northern Arcadia and Canada to England and France, from where they migrated to Louisiana.

American feelings towards Britain were not assisted by the new commander of British forces, General John Campbell, Earl of Loudoun, whose aristocratic contempt for colonials was not hidden. He would not allow independent colonial commands despite their local knowledge and ability to gain Indian allies. He ranked American officers below their British counterparts, and introduced the lash to colonial volunteers. He did however have experience against guerrilla fighting during the Jacobite Rebellion, so he trained his army as Ranger huntsmen and mobile light infantrymen. Pitt sent the energetic officers, Major-General Jeffrey Amherst and Brigadier James Wolfe, to assist in this new form of fighting.

Pitt's goal was the complete extinction of French power in North America which required the conquest of New France. Three armies invaded New France in 1758, under General Lord Abercromby, which advanced on Forts William, Henry and Ticonderoga. Brigadier John Forbes followed in Braddock's steps to take Fort Duquesne. The third and largest army under Amherst was to make a seaborne attack on Louisburg and if possible down the St Lawrence River to Quebec. Abercromby was repelled from Ticonderoga, but Forbes occupied Fort Duquesne. Unfortunately Louisburg stalled in siege despite Wolfe's fine action with the advance guard.

In 1759 the forces of General James Wolfe defeated the French at the Plains of Abraham outside Quebec after a three month siege. The French counter-offensive in 1760 saw some success but failed to retake Quebec due to lack of naval support, blocked by the British. After the capitulation of Montreal, in 1760, the Indian Seven Nations of Canada resigned from the war and negotiated the Treaty of Kahnawake with the British. The Seven Years War finished in North America with the defeat of French forces at Newfoundland in 1762.

In the 1763 Treaty of Paris, France ceded control of the entire Ohio region to Great Britain, without consulting its native allies, who still believed they had territorial claims. Colonies such as Pennsylvania and Virginia claimed some of the westward lands by their original charters. Land speculation boomed between 1763 and 1774 as investors and land companies sought to carve empires from the territories beyond the Appalachians. Immigrants, particularly Irish and Scots, poured into America. Two thousand pioneers passed annually down the Shenandoah Valley in western Virginia on the way towards the backcountry of Carolina.

When the British quarrel with American colonists turned to war in 1776, the Royal navy had suffered from peacetime neglect. It basically surrendered command of the sea when France entered the war in 1778. Britain had not previously fought major land battles 3000 miles away from its home base, and lack of command at sea was a major factor in defeat. In the 1781 encounter off the Chesapeake, French numerical superiority kept the British force at bay so assisted in Cornwallis' surrender at Yorktown.

The Anglo-French War sparked by the French Revolution caused attacks on the West Indies against French, Dutch and Spanish possessions. Heavy losses of soldiers and sailors forced Britain to recruit negro slaves to keep numbers up of the West India Regiment. By 1801 Britain had acquired Tobago, Martinique,

Guadeloupe, St. Lucia from the French; Curacao, Demerara and Essequibo from Holland; and Trinidad from Spain.

The West Indies were forced to emancipate their slaves in 1833, and then by 1846, by Britain's Sugar Duties Act had to compete with sugar imported from slave-operated plantations of Cuba and Brazil. Not surprisingly the economy of the British West Indies collapsed.

Canada

Mainland Nova Scotia came under British rule with the 1713 Treaty of Utrecht; the Treaty of Paris (1763) ceded Canada and most of New France to Britain after the Seven Years' War. The Royal Proclamation of 1763 created the Province of Quebec out of New France, and annexed Cape Breton Island to Nova Scotia. St. John's Island (now Prince Edward Island) became a separate colony in 1769. To avert conflict in Quebec, the British passed the Quebec Act of 1774, expanding Quebec's territory to the Great Lakes and Ohio Valley.

The 1783 Treaty of Paris recognised American independence and ceded territories south of the Great Lakes to the United States of America. To accommodate English-speaking Loyalists in Quebec, the Constitutional Act of 1791 divided the province into French-speaking Lower Canada (later Quebec) and English-speaking Upper Canada (later Ontario), granting each its own elected legislative assembly.

The Canadas were the main front in the War of 1812 between the United States and Britain. Following the war, large-scale immigration to Canada from Britain and Ireland began in 1815. Between 1825 and 1846, 626,628 European immigrants reportedly landed at Canadian ports. These included Irish immigrants escaping the Great Irish Famine as well as Gaelic-speaking Scots displaced by the Highland Clearances. Between one-quarter and one-third of all Europeans who immigrated to Canada before 1891 died of infectious diseases.

The desire for responsible government resulted in abortive Rebellions of 1837. The Durham Report subsequently recommended responsible government and the assimilation of French Canadians into English culture. The Act of Union 1840 merged the Canadas into a united Province of Canada. Responsible government was established for all British North American provinces by 1849. The signing of the Oregon Treaty by Britain and the United States in 1846 ended the Oregon boundary dispute, extending the border westward along the 49th parallel. This paved the way for British colonies on Vancouver Island (1849) and in British Columbia (1858).

In 1841 the British government instituted a single legislature composed of, an assembly, council, and governor general; the 84 members of the lower chamber were equally divided amongst the two former provinces, though Lower Canada had a higher population. From 1841 to 1844, parliament sat in Kingston; from 1844 until the 1849 fire that destroyed the building, the legislature was in Montreal. After a few years of alternating between Toronto and Quebec City, in 1866, the legislature was finally moved to Ottawa, Queen Victoria having chosen that city as Canada's capital in 1857.

The 1867 Constitution Act officially proclaimed Canadian Confederation, initially with four provinces –Ontario, Quebec, Nova Scotia, and New Brunswick. Canada assumed control of Rupert's Land and the North-Western Territory to form the Northwest Territories, where the Métis' grievances ignited the Red River Rebellion and the creation of the province of Manitoba in 1870. British Columbia and Vancouver Island (which had been united in 1866) joined the Confederation in 1871, while Prince Edward Island joined in 1873.

The Dominion of Canada became a constitutional monarchy under the Constitution Act with the executive formally called the *Queen-in-Council*, the legislature the *Queen-in-Parliament*, and the courts as the *Queen on the Bench*. The British North America Act limited the powers of the provinces, providing that all subjects not explicitly delegated to them by that document remain within the authority of the federal parliament, while simultaneously giving the provinces unique powers in certain agreed-upon areas of funding. The Conservative Party won the first election of 1867 under Sir John Macdonald.

To open the West, the government sponsored the construction of three transcontinental railways (including the Canadian Pacific Railway), opened the prairies to settlement with the Dominion Lands Act, and established the North-West Mounted Police to assert its authority over this territory. In 1898, during the Klondike Gold Rush in the Northwest Territories, the Canadian government created the Yukon Territory. Continental European immigrants settled the prairies, and Alberta and Saskatchewan became provinces in 1905.

Canada had offered troops in the Boer War despite considerable misgivings among the Canadian community. Because Britain still maintained control of Canada's foreign affairs under the Confederation Act, its declaration of war in

1914 automatically brought Canada into World War I. Volunteers sent to the Western Front later became part of the Canadian Corps.

The Conscription Crisis of 1917 erupted when conservative Prime Minister Borden brought in compulsory military service over the vehement objections of French-speaking Quebecers. The Conscription Crisis of 1917, coupled with disputes over French language schools outside Quebec, deeply alienated Francophone Canadians and temporarily split the Liberal Party. Borden's Unionist government included many Anglophone Liberals, and it swept to a landslide victory in the 1917 elections. In 1919, Canada joined the League of Nations independently of Britain. The 1931 Statute of Westminster affirmed Canada's independence.

Fiji

The United Kingdom declined its first opportunity to annex Fiji in 1852. *Tui Vitu* Cakobau offered to cede to the British, but was considered only a chief among equals. A constitutional monarchy was established with the government in 1871 dominated by European settlers. The collapse of the new regime drove Cakobau to make another offer of cessation in 1872 which the British accepted.

Hawaii

The British explorer Captain James Cook visited Hawaii in 1778 which he named the Sandwich Islands. Cook had not been given a mandate to annex those islands whose natives cultivated their land, but as trade with them developed, Britain's naval presence increased. The European visitors brought disease which decimated the native population. By 1820, Eurasian diseases, famine, and wars among the chiefs killed more than half of the native Hawaiian population. During the 1850s, measles killed a fifth of Hawaii's people.

A Spanish threat to annex lands in the Pacific was answered by partial mobilisation of the British fleet which caused a backdown. By 1800 the Pacific was a British pond.

King Kamehameha became dominant in the islands in 1810 to commence a powerful dynasty. American missionaries converted many natives to Christianity, including King Kamehameha III. When King Kamehameha V died in 1874 the resultant election led to riots and the landing of US and British troops. The House of Kalākaua assumed the monarchy.

In 1887, Kalākaua was forced to sign the 1887 Constitution of the Kingdom of Hawaii, which stripped the king of much of his authority. There was a property qualification for voting, which disenfranchised most Hawaiians and immigrant labourers, and favoured the wealthier white immigrant community. In 1893, a group of mostly Euro-American business leaders and residents formed a Committee of Safety to overthrow the Kingdom and seek annexation by the United States. After negotiations, in June 1897, US Secretary of State agreed to a treaty of annexation with representatives of the Republic of Hawaii.

Australia

The Royal Society (of London for Improving Natural Knowledge) was founded in 1660 as a scientific advisor to the British government. Although bipartisan, the Royal Society had a number of aristocratic Members of Parliament by the Chatham Ministry under President James Douglas, Earl of Morton. Almost unnoticed during American troubles, Prime Minister Pitt allowed a joint Royal Society/Royal Navy voyage to the Pacific Ocean to observe the transit of Venus, and explore the seas for the surmised *Terra Australis Incognita* or "unknown southern land". It is possible that the exploration was sparked by the proposal that Britain found a colony of banished convicts in the South Sea (or in Terra Australis) to enable the mother country to exploit the riches of those regions, which had been put forward in 1766 by John Callander in *Terra Australia Cognita*.

The Society was represented by Joseph Banks, an advisor to George III, and the captain of the ship, HMS Bark Endeavour, was Lieutenant James Cook. The voyage observed the 1769 transit of Venus from Tahiti then claimed a number of Pacific islands for Great Britain. Cook circumnavigated New Zealand and mapped the east coast of Australia to make landfall in Botany Bay in 1770 where Banks discovered new flora. Endeavour returned to England in 1772.

Cook carried with him the mandate to declare British sovereignty over any territory which he found to be unpopulated or whose inhabitants were manifestly making no use of their land. Cook declared Australia *terra nullius* (land of no-one) and annexed it in 1770. The natives, aborigines, were nomads who did not till the soil, and lacked any apparent social organisation or religion. Cook and his contemporaries never subscribed to the notion of the noble savage.

Sir Joseph Banks in 1779 urged the government to use one of Australia's harbours, Botany Bay, as a penal settlement at the time when the American unrest was causing the halt of the flow of convicts to America. In 1786 the British cabinet finally agreed to a colony in New South Wales. The first flotilla, under Captain Phillip, anchored off Botany Bay in 1788, but quickly shifted to the better harbour nearby, which was named Sydney after the Colonial Secretary.

From the beginning there were three types of colonists – officials and guards, free settlers, and convicts. Unfortunately the latter, who were supposed to provide the muscle for supporting agronomy, were mainly urban recidivists without experience of farming. In the new environment, the administration worked on the basis that the able should be able to feed themselves, and those who were unable could starve. Discipline was rigorously enforced, and escape was perilous. After 1791 those convicts who ended their sentence were offered land in the hope that they might become self-supporting, and barriers were raised to stop return to Britain.

In 1792 Governor Phillip returned to England leaving Major Francis Grose in control. He abolished civilian courts and transferred the magistrates under the authority of Captain Foveaux. Grose relaxed Phillip's prohibition on trading of rum (any distilled beverage). The colony was short of coin so rum became currency particularly when the New South Wales Corps used its power to buy imported rum to exchange it for goods and labour. Thus the Corps became known as the Rum Corps.

Some former convicts with land grants became successful and an open elite. The real elite apart from officials were the officers of the New South Wales Corps who were scoundrels allowed by Grose to fill their pockets at the expense of the colony. The Corps farmers were provided with convict labour and could sell produce to the government store at good profits.

Grose's replacement, Captain William Paterson, tried to reign in the Corps. He was unsuccessful, as was Governor John Hunter from 1795. One of the Corps leaders, Lieutenant John Macarthur strongly opposed Hunter on behalf of the Corps, even writing to Britain accusing Hunter of ineffectiveness and trading rum. Hunter was recalled. Paterson, now Lieutenant Colonel, returned in 1799 with orders to stamp out trading in rum but soon ran afoul of Macarthur.

The late 1790s and early 1800s saw the arrival of a new kind of convict – political offenders and Irish nationalists. This resulted in a short-lived insurrection in 1804. In 1800, the founder of Norfolk Island colony, Captain Phillip King, returned to Australia as Governor of New South Wales. In 1801 King slighted Macarthur who tried to organise a petty social boycott which resulted in a duel between Paterson and Macarthur. Macarthur was arrested and sent to England with a lengthy despatch on his shortcomings. The despatch vanished and the English courts refused to hear the case. Macarthur resigned his commission rather than accept a posting to Norfolk Island. He returned in 1805 as a civilian, still with much power due to his cronies in the Rum Corps.

Macarthur had gained friends at the Colonial Office, which allowed him to claim 5000acres of prime land which he named Camden Park. He had already been improving his flock of sheep at Elizabeth Farm by importing Merinos from the Dutch Cape Colony and the Royal flock at Kew.

King raised some powers against rum trading but was resisted by the Corps. He had been lobbying for a replacement and Governor William Bligh arrived in 1805. Bligh determined to break the Corps and especially John Macarthur who in retaliation organised the Rum Rebellion, the only successful armed takeover of government in Australian history. Bligh was arrested by the Corps and deposed. Foveaux returned to Sydney to become acting Lieutenant Governor. Macarthur was sent to England for trial and Bligh given a ship on which to return to England. The Colonial Office decided that naval governors were untenable so sent Major-General Lachlan Macquarie to take over as Governor in 1810. The NSW Corps (102nd Regiment) was to be replaced by the 73rd Regiment of Foot. Macarthur was to be tried in Sydney, but after eight years in exile, was never tried.

Governor Macquarie was able to control the rum trade better, introducing and enforcing a licensing system. However, he was still forced to pay for public works projects in rum due to the lack of currency. The construction of Sydney Hospital was entirely funded by granting a monopoly on the import of rum to the contractors and using troops to prohibit the landing of rum anywhere but at the hospital dock. In 1813 Macquarie bought Spanish dollars from America and punched-out the centre, to make the Holey dollar, worth five shillings. The centre or dump was used as a fifteen penny piece. In 1819 the British government authorised the commercial distillation of spirit so that trafficking in rum ceased to be a problem.

In 1808 Macarthur had sent his son Edward to England to keep his friend apprised of the Macarthur version of Australian events, and take the first bale of Australian wool. Due to the Napoleonic War the wool was in demand and sold for a record price. The export of wool made Macarthur the richest man in New South Wales. By 1821 there were 290,000 sheep in Australia and within twenty years raw wool exports topped ten million pounds annually. Wool became the equivalent to tobacco of Virginia and sugar of the West Indies.

Between 1819 and 1825 British subsidies were allocated to encourage pauper emigration. In 1834 the Poor Law included provisions for assisting poor emigrants. However most emigrants were not state-funded since it was promoted that anyone who was thrifty and industrious would prosper in the colonies.

In 1803 a British settlement was established in Van Diemen's Land (Tasmania) and it became a separate colony in 1825. The United Kingdom claimed the western part of Western Australia (Swan River Colony) in 1828. Separate colonies were carved from New South Wales – South Australia 1836; Victoria 1851; Queensland 1859. The Northern Territory was excised from South Australia in 1911. The Federal Capital Territory (later renamed the Australian Capital Territory) was formed in 1911 as the location for the future federal capital of Canberra.

A gold-rush began in Australia in the early 1850s and the Eureka Rebellion against mining licence fees in 1854 was an early example of civil disobedience. There was racial friction in Australia following the import of Chinese labourers after the gold-rush. The trade union movement agitated against further Chinese immigration on the grounds that it would drive down wages. This resulted in the Immigration Restriction Act 1901 known more popularly as the "White Australia" policy.

Between 1855 and 1890, the six colonies individually gained responsible government, managing most of their own affairs while remaining part of the British Empire. The Colonial Office in London retained control of some matters, notably foreign affairs, defence, and international shipping. As part of the British Empire, the Australian colonies offered troops for the war in South Africa. They included the official contingents dispatched by each of the six colonial governments, Australians who were already in southern Africa working as gold-miners enlisting in British or Cape Colony regiments such as the Bushveldt Carbineers, men who made their own way to participate, and others who joined privately raised units such as Doyle's Australian Scouts.

In 1901, federation of the colonies was achieved after a decade of planning, consultation and voting. One of the key architects of Australia's Constitution, Edmund Barton became the new nation's first Prime Minister at a grand ceremony in Centennial Park, Sydney, in January 1901. The Commonwealth of Australia was established and it became a dominion of the British Empire in 1907.

Without an aristocracy to hinder reform and with a large population from the working class, social reforms were more easily achieved than in Britain. As industrialisation and agricultural wealth grew, there developed a wealthy upper class with conservative views that formed conservative political parties. The working men tended to form labour unions with socialist tendencies that provided the basis of the Australian Labour Party. On the fringes were small clamorous groups with more radical views. The democratic governments of Australia oscillated between policies determined by the main political parties.

In 1914, Australia joined Britain in fighting World War I, with parliamentary support from both the outgoing Commonwealth Liberal Party and the incoming Australian Labor Party. Shortly after the outbreak of war—following a request by the British government, the Australian Naval and Military Expeditionary Force (AN&MEF) was formed. The objectives of the force were the German stations at Yap in the Caroline Islands, Nauru and at Rabaul, New Britain. During the Battle of Bita Paka near Rabaul the first Australians of WWI were killed.

It was decided to keep the volunteers of the First Australian Imperial Force (AIF) in Egypt, away from the European winter, for training and to guard the Suez Canal. Later in November, Winston Churchill, in his capacity as First Lord of the Admiralty, put forward his first plans for a naval attack on the Dardanelles. A plan for an attack and invasion of the Gallipoli peninsula was eventually approved by the British cabinet in January 1915. It was decided that the Australian and New Zealand troops would take part in the operation.

After the failure of naval attacks, it was decided that ground forces were necessary to eliminate the Turkish mobile artillery and allow minesweepers to clear the waters for larger vessels. The ANZAC forces were part of the invasion of Gallipoli strongly defended by the Turkish army. After eight months of bloody fighting it was decided to evacuate the entire force from the Gallipoli peninsula. Many Australians regard the defeat of the Australian and New Zealand Army Corps (ANZACs) at Gallipoli as the birth of the nation—its first major military action as a nation, albeit under British Command.

After the Gallipoli Campaign, Australian troops returned to Egypt and the AIF underwent a major expansion, which involved the raising of another three infantry divisions and the establishment of the ANZAC Mounted Division. In 1916 the infantry was moved to France where it was deployed on the Western Front. The cavalry was used to fight in Palestine where they were successful in a number of battles. Australians took part in many of the major battles fought on the Western Front in France. Of about 416,000 who served, about 60,000 were killed and another 152,000 were wounded.

After the losses in Gallipoli, the First AIF experienced a shortage of soldiers as the number of men volunteering to fight overseas declined and the casualty rate increased. At the time, military service within the Commonwealth of Australia and its territories was compulsory for Australian men, but that requirement did not extend to conflict outside of Australia. In 1916, Prime Minister Hughes called a plebiscite to determine public support for extending conscription to include military service outside the Commonwealth for the duration of the war. The referendum, held in 1916, narrowly rejected the proposal. A second plebiscite, held a year later, also failed.

The last of the main transports conveying Australian troops left England in December 1919, arriving back in Australia in early 1920. A year later, in 1921, the AIF was officially disbanded. The process of repatriation did not end there, though. Upon their return to Australia the effort shifted towards placing the returned soldiers into employment, or education and taking care of those that were too badly injured to work. In order to meet these needs the Commonwealth established the Repatriation Department, tasked with managing the placement of returned soldiers into employment, training, education, housing. Eventually this also included the colossal task of managing the provision of war pensions, managing repatriation hospitals and convalescent homes and administering the Soldier Settlement Scheme.

Although previously, Australian foreign interests had been largely handled by Britain, as a combatant, Australia sent its own delegation to the Paris Peace Conference in 1919, while it also began to take a more assertive role in regional affairs in the Pacific. At the peace conference Prime Minister Hughes pushed aggressively for reparations and an Australian mandate over German New Guinea; a stance which conflicted with the liberal internationalist inspired Fourteen Points put forward by American President Woodrow Wilson. Regardless, following the war, there was little real change in Imperial relations and Dominion affairs and, as a result, the war arguably did not lead to any significant change in Australia's perception of its role in the world.

New Zealand

The first Europeans known to have reached New Zealand were Dutch explorer Abel Tasman and his crew in 1642. Europeans did not revisit New Zealand until

1769 when British RN explorer Captain James Cook mapped almost the entire coastline. Following Cook, New Zealand was visited by numerous European and North American whaling, sealing and trading ships. They traded food, metal tools, weapons and other goods for timber, food, artefacts and water.

In 1788 Arthur Phillip assumed the position of Governor of New South Wales and claimed New Zealand as part of New South Wales. The introduction of the potato and the musket transformed the native Māori agriculture and warfare. Potatoes provided a reliable food surplus, which enabled longer and more sustained military campaigns. The resulting inter-tribal Musket Wars encompassed over 600 battles between 1801 and 1840. The British Government appointed James Busby as British Resident to New Zealand in 1832.

In 1835 the nebulous United Tribes of New Zealand sent a Declaration of the Independence to King William IV of the United Kingdom asking for protection. Ongoing unrest and the dubious legal standing of the Declaration of Independence prompted the Colonial Office to send Captain Hobson to claim sovereignty for the British Crown and negotiate a treaty with the Māori. The Treaty of Waitangi was first signed in the Bay of Islands in 1840. In response to the commercially run New Zealand Company's attempts to establish an independent settlement in Wellington and French settlers "purchasing" land in Akaroa, Hobson declared British sovereignty over all of New Zealand. With the signing of the Treaty and declaration of sovereignty, the number of immigrants, particularly from the United Kingdom, began to increase.

New Zealand, originally part of the colony of New South Wales, became a separate Colony of New Zealand in 1841. The colony gained a representative government in 1852 and the first New Zealand Parliament met in 1854. In 1856 the colony effectively became self-governing, gaining responsibility over all domestic matters other than native policy. (Control over native policy was granted in the mid-1860s.) Following concerns that the South Island might form a separate colony, Premier Alfred Domett moved a resolution to transfer the capital from Auckland to a locality near the Cook Strait. Wellington was chosen for its harbour and central location, with parliament officially sitting there for the first time in 1865.

In 1907, at the request of the New Zealand Parliament, King Edward VII proclaimed New Zealand a dominion within the British Empire, reflecting its self-governing status. New Zealand was involved in world affairs, fighting alongside the British Empire in the First World War.

South Africa

The Portuguese discovered the southern- most cape in South Africa in 1488 which was named *Cabo das Tormentas* (Cape of Storms). In 1652 the Dutch East India Company established a refreshment station with Calvinist settlers at the Cape of Good Hope in what would become Cape Town. The Dutch transported slaves from Indonesia, Madagascar, and India as labour for the colonists in Cape Town. The Colony began properly in 1671 with the first purchase of land from the *Khoikhoi* natives (*Hottentots*) outside the fort Castle of Good Hope. In 1685 French Protestant Huguenot refugees from the revocation of the Edict of Nantes arrived as immigrants.

The Dutch East India Company stopped the colony's policy of open immigration, monopolised trade, combined the administrative, legislative and judicial powers into one body, told the farmers what crops to grow, demanded a large percentage of every farmer's harvest, and generally harassed them. This tended to discourage further development of industry and enterprise. From these roots sprung a dislike of orderly government, and libertarian view-point that has characterised the "*boers*" or Dutch farmers for many generations. Seeking largely to escape the oppression of the Dutch East India Company, the farmers trekked farther and farther from the seat of government.

The Netherlands fell to the French army under the leadership of Napoléon Bonaparte in 1795. Reacting to the weakness of the Dutch East India Company holdings, a British army under General Sir James Henry Craig set out for Cape Town in order to secure the colony for the Stadtholder Prince William V of Orange against the French. The governor of Cape Town refused at first to obey any instructions from the Prince, but after the British threatened to use force, he capitulated. The *Boers* of the independent government of Graaff Reinet did not surrender until an army had been sent against them and in 1799, and again in 1801 when they rose in revolt. In February 1803, as a result of the Peace of Amiens, the colony came under the control of the Batavian Republic. The British reoccupied the colony in 1806 to keep Napoleon Bonaparte out of the Cape and this was formally ceded by the Dutch Government in 1814.

Britain had to manage the Cape to provide support for the Royal Navy. It had inherited a mixed population of whites of Dutch and French ancestry who called themselves Boers, black slaves of the Boers, *Khoikhois* (Hottentots) and *Xhosa*

The British started to settle the eastern border of the colony, with the arrival in Port Elizabeth of the 1820 Settlers. They also began to introduce the first rudimentary rights for the Cape's black African population and, in 1833, abolished slavery. The resentment that the Dutch farmers felt against this social change, as well as the imposition of English language and culture, caused them to trek inland *en masse*. This was known as the Great Trek, and the migrating Afrikaaners settled inland, forming the *"Boer republics"* of Transvaal and the Orange Free State. British immigration continued in the Cape, even as many of the Afrikaaners continued to trek inland, and the ending of the British East India Company's monopoly on trade led to economic growth.

At first the Cape government feared that the mass exodus would lead to widespread war once the Boers collided with the expanding native Ndebele and Zulu states which lay in their path. In 1842 the new Boer republic of Natalia was annexed as a protective measure. In fact the well armed Boers could take care of themselves. Victory over the Ndebele and Zulus in the late 1830s led to the occupation of areas that became Transvaal and Orange Free State republics. In 1854 Britain recognised their independence.

Peace and prosperity led to a desire for political independence. In 1854, the Cape Colony elected its first parliament, on the basis of the multi-racial Cape Qualified Franchise. Cape residents qualified as voters based on a universal minimum level of property ownership, regardless of race. A Boer complaint was that the British had failed to deal with the Xhosa or Kaffirs on the Cape's eastern frontier. Regular guerrilla wars had been fought as the Xhosa defended their lands against the encroaching whites. In 1850-53 British soldiers carried out a scorched earth policy which starved the Ngquika Xhosa. Resistance was strong and the British brought in German mercenaries who were given land in exchange for defending fortified villages against the Xhosa.

The discovery of diamonds in Griqualand, which was annexed as a crown colony in 1871, greatly stimulated investment and immigrants. Digging for diamonds and laying railway tracks were labour intensive requiring only an unskilled workforce. Black migrant workers, particularly Pedi from Transvaal and Basotho then used their wages to buy obsolete muskets and breechloaders. The Zulus had for some time been assembling an arsenal. The need for white supremacy became urgent by the mid-1870s.

Executive power remained completely in the hands of the British Governor and the colony was stricken with tensions between its eastern and western halves.

In 1875 Prime Minister Benjamin Disraeli's Colonial Secretary, Lord Carnarvon, in an attempt to extend British influence, approached the Orange Free State and the Transvaal Republic and tried to organise a federation of the British and Boer territories to be modelled after the 1867 federation of French and English provinces of Canada, however the Boer leaders turned him down. The successive British annexations, and in particular the annexation of West Griqualand, caused a climate of simmering unease for the Boer republics.

In 1872, after a long political battle, the Cape Colony achieved "Responsible Government" under its first Prime Minister, John Molteno. Henceforth, an elected Prime Minister and his cabinet had total responsibility for the affairs of the country.

A period of strong economic growth and social development ensued, and the eastern-western division was largely laid to rest. The system of multi-racial franchise also began a slow and fragile growth in political inclusiveness. A sequence of native rebellions and wars evidenced the push against white power. Local British forces with the new Martini-Henry rifles and Gatling guns could handle Cape unrest. The Boers were in trouble particularly in Transvaal. In 1877, the Cape expanded by annexing Griqualand West and Griqualand East. Also in 1877 Sir Theophilus Shepstone, the British Secretary for Native Affairs in Natal, annexed the South African Republic (Transvaal Republic), for Britain using a special warrant.

Upon taking his throne, Zulu King Cetshwayo had expanded his army and reintroduced many of the paramilitary practices of the famous Shaka, king of the Zulus. He had also started equipping his *impis* with firearms although this was a gradual process and the majority had only shields, clubs (*knobkerries*) and spears (throwing spears and the famous *assegais*). Over 40,000 strong, disciplined, motivated and confident Zulu warriors were a formidable force on their own home ground, their lack of modern weaponry notwithstanding. The Transvaal Boers became more and more concerned, but King Cetshwayo's policy was to maintain good relations with the British in Natal in an effort to counter the Boer threat.

The Transvaal Boers led by Paul Kruger (the future Transvaal President) thereafter elected to deal first with the perceived Zulu threat to the status quo, and local issues, before directly opposing the British annexation. Disraeli's Tory administration in London did not want a war with the Zulus. Sir Bartle Frere however, had been sent to the Cape Colony as governor and high commissioner in 1877 with the brief of creating a Confederation of South Africa from the various British colonies, Boer Republics and native states. He concluded that the powerful Zulu kingdom stood in the way of this, and so was receptive to British Natal resident, Sir Theophilus Shepstone's, arguments that King Cetshwayo and his Zulu army posed a challenge to the colonial powers peaceful occupation of the region. In January 1879, the British under Lord Chelmsford invaded Zululand with about 7,000 regular troops, a similar number of black African levies and a thousand white volunteers. The Zulu capital at Ulundi was captured in July 1879. The British consolidated their power over Natal, the Zulu kingdom and Transvaal. The British conquered the Pedi of Sekhukhune but had trouble with the Basotho, who fought as rifle-armed cavalry. Basutoland became a British protectorate governed by local native chiefs.

Transvaal formally declared independence in late 1880 and their militia besieged British army garrisons all over the Transvaal. The three main engagements of the first Boer War were all within about sixteen miles of each other, centred on the Battles of Laing's Nek (January 1881), Ingogo River (February 1881) and the rout at Majuba Hill (February 1881). These battles were the outcome of Major General Sir George Pomeroy Colley's attempts to relieve the besieged forts. Hostilities continued until March 1881, when a truce was declared. In the final peace treaty, the Pretoria Convention, negotiated by a three-man Royal Commission, the British agreed to complete Boer self-government in the Transvaal under British suzerainty, the Boers accepting the Queen's nominal rule and British control over external relations, African affairs and native districts.

The discovery of diamonds around Kimberley in 1868 and gold in the Transvaal 1886 led a return to instability, particularly because they fuelled the rise to power of the ambitious colonialist Cecil Rhodes. Other potential imperial colonisers included Portugal, which already controlled West (modern day Angola) and East Africa (modern day Mozambique), Germany (modern day Namibia), and further north, Belgium (modern day Democratic Republic of the Congo) and France (West and Equatorial Africa, and Madagascar).

Rhodes had made himself a multi-millionaire by accumulation of diamond-mining concessions. By 1891 he had secured a monopoly over the Kimberly diamond fields for his Rhodes De Beers Consolidated Company and had extensive investments on the Rand. Rhodes used Bechuanaland as a spring board to enter Zambesia (modern Zimbabwe and Zambia) through his British South Africa Company.

The Ndebele king, Lobengula, bad been bribed to grant mineral and settlement rights but was unprepared to see settlers arrive armed with machine guns and artillery. He ordered his *impis* to attack villages near British settlements. The Company used the belligerence to commence the Matabele War 1893-4 which was one-sided because the traditional Ndebele frontal attacks were no match for machine guns. Ndebele resistance did not end with the demise of Lobengula's state and further uprising in 1896 resulted in settlers' deaths. The British retaliated in Zimbabwe (Rhodesia). The war lasted until 1897 when the last guerrilla forces were hunted down. Rhodes had successfully fought for his dream of an Anglo-Saxon English speaking state in Rhodesia. The Anglo-German agreement of 1890 affirmed British claims to Uganda and what is now Kenya, and German to Tanganyika.

On becoming the Cape's Prime Minister, Rhodes instigated a rapid expansion of British influence into the hinterland. In particular, he sought to engineer the conquest of the Transvaal in 1880. Transvaal had become a pawn in international power politics as the Boer population was courted by Germany. German political interest and investment strengthened the Transvaal's sense of independence from Britain and Cape Town. The completion of the Delagoa Railway gave the Transvaal free access to the sea where German shipping was welcome. There had been a rapid explosion of expatriate migrant workers (*uitlanders*) during the initial exploitation of the Witwatersrand gold fields in the Transvaal. The British government pushed for political rights for the almost entirely British *uitlanders*.

Rhodes tried to organise a revolution. Rhodes' private army surrendered after the Jameson Raid 1895, and the ringleaders were sent back to Britain by Transvaal President Kruger for trial. Rhodes withdrew from public life when his ill-fated Jameson Raid failed and brought down his government. The German Kaiser sent an ill-judged telegram of congratulation with a pledge of support to Kruger.

From 1896 to the outbreak of the Second Boer War in 1896, Britain posed as the champion of democratic rights and defender of Britain's historic influence in southern Africa. War broke out when the breakdown of negotiations over the *uitlanders'* franchise encouraged an offensive by the Transvaal to secure Cape and Natal railways to prevent British reinforcements. Loss of ground and three defeats by the Boers stunned the British public because of the threat to Empire. In the winter of 1899-1900 the Boer High Command failed to follow up its advantages, which allowed a new commander Field Marshal Lord Roberts to develop a new strategy with British and Australian forces.

Roberts launched his main attack in 1900 and although hampered by a long supply route, managed to outflank the Boers defending Magersfontein. In February, a cavalry division launched a major attack to relieve Kimberley. Although encountering severe fire, a massed cavalry charge split the Boer defences, opening the way for Major General John French to enter Kimberley that evening, ending its 124 days' siege. At the Battle of Paardeberg, Roberts then surrounded the retreating Boer army. In Natal, after a siege lasting 118 days, the Relief of Ladysmith was affected, the day after Cronje surrendered. Roberts then advanced into the Orange Free State from the west, putting the Boers to flight at the Battle of Poplar Grove and capturing Bloemfontein, the capital, unopposed. The Orange Free State was annexed and renamed the Orange River Colony. The Boers abandoned Pretoria, capital of Transvaal without a fight.

President Kruger, and what remained of the Transvaal government, had retreated to eastern Transvaal. Despite the loss of their two capital cities and half of their army, the Boer commanders adopted guerrilla warfare tactics, primarily conducting raids against infrastructure, resource and supply targets, all aimed at disrupting the operational capacity of the British army. The British were forced to quickly revise their tactics. They concentrated on restricting the freedom of movement of the Boer commandos and depriving them of local support. The railway lines had provided vital lines of communication and supply, as the British had advanced across South Africa. The British also implemented a "scorched earth" policy under which they targeted everything within the controlled areas that could give sustenance to the Boer guerrillas with a view to making it harder and harder for the Boers to survive.

The Boers and the British both feared the consequences of arming Africans. The memories of the Zulu and other tribal conflicts were still fresh, and they recognised that whoever won would have to deal with the consequences of a mass militarisation of the tribes. There was therefore an unwritten agreement that this war would be a *"white man's war."*

The last of the Boers surrendered in May, 1902 and the war ended with the Treaty of Vereeniging signed on 31 May 1902. The treaty ended the existence of the South African Republic and the Orange Free State as independent Boer republics and placed them within the British Empire. The Union of South Africa was established as a member of the Commonwealth in 1910. It proved a key ally to Britain as a Dominion of the British Empire during World War I.

Egypt

Egypt was invaded by the French forces of Napoleon I in 1798. After the French were defeated by the British, Muhammad Ali established a dynasty that was to rule Egypt until the revolution of 1952. The dynasty became a British puppet. Khedive Muhammad Ali annexed Northern Sudan (1820–1824), Syria (1833), and parts of Arabia and Anatolia; but in 1841 the European powers, fearful lest he topple the Ottoman Empire itself, forced him to return most of his conquests to the Ottomans. His military ambition required him to modernise the country: he built industries, a system of canals for irrigation and transport, and reformed the civil service.

In 1854 and 1856 Ferdinand de Lesseps obtained a concession from Sa'id Pasha, the Khedive of Egypt and Sudan, to create a company to construct a canal open to ships of all nations. Muhammad Isma'il succeeded to government in 1863. The Suez Canal, built in partnership with the French, was completed in 1869. Its construction led to enormous debt to European banks, and caused popular discontent because of the onerous taxation it required. In 1875 Isma'il was forced to sell Egypt's share in the canal to the British Government. Within three years this led to the imposition of British and French controllers who sat in the Egyptian cabinet, and, "*with the financial power of the bondholders behind them, were the real power in the Government.*"

In 1882 Egypt appeared to be a flourishing state, but was in fact sliding into insolvency. A protest by unpaid army officers led to an army coup by Urabi Pasha, under an apparent national movement towards a government independent of the ruling British and French. Urabi took control of Alexandria, which triggered the arrival of a large British expeditionary force. France had already ruled out armed intervention. Urabi was captured and exiled. Free passage through the Suez Canal was the ostensible reason for the British occupation.

Possession of Egypt gave Britain responsibility for the Egyptian empire in the Sudan which was in rebellion under a messianic holy man who called himself the Mahdi. British forces were sent in 1884 where they were forced into conflict with religiously inspired *ansars* (dervishes). The British were supposed to withdraw under General Gordon, but Gordon singlehandedly reversed government policy when he prepared to defend Khartoum. The British government was then forced to send a relieving army in 1885 under General Wolseley which was attacked en route by a larger force of dervishes who were driven off. Khartoum had fallen and

Gordon speared to death. The British government promised a campaign to recover Khartoum and punish the Sudanese but a Russian incursion into Afghanistan caused troops to be withdrawn.

The Mahdi died, probably from typhus, and the government of the Sudan passed to Khalifah Abdullah bin Muhammad. After the Islamic militant state was routed in the Battle of Toski 1889, there was no threat to Egypt.

French interest in the area prompted the British to sanction reconquest of the Sudan in 1896. The slow advance southward was led by Sir Herbert Kitchener who treated the war as a crusade for civilisation and vengeance for the death of Gordon. Public interest in 1897-8 allowed an increase to troops ahead of a decisive battle against the large Khalifah's army. In 1898, after the Battle of Omdurman, British and Egyptian flags were flown in Khartoum.

An example of the failure to take lessons from history was the action of Field Marshall Lord Haig, Commander-in-Chief on the World War I Western Front 1915-1918. As Major Haig he had witnessed the devastating effect of rifle and machine-gun fire on the attacking *ansars*, yet this made no difference to his offensives in France where advancing British troops faced the same odds against German fire power.

Organised English Religion

In May 1532 the Church of England agreed to surrender its legislative independence and canon law to the authority of the monarch, Henry VIII. In 1559, Parliament recognised Queen Elizabeth as the Church's supreme governor, with a new Act of Supremacy that also repealed the remaining anti-Protestant legislation. With the Act of Toleration enacted in 1689, Nonconformists had freedom of worship. That is, those Protestants who dissented from the Church of England such as Baptists, Congregationalists and Quakers were allowed their own places of worship and their own teachers and preachers, subject to acceptance of certain oaths of allegiance. The British Monarch is formally Supreme Governor of the Church of England, but its spiritual leader is the Archbishop of Canterbury, who is regarded by convention as the head of the worldwide communion of Anglican Churches. In practice the Church of England is governed by the General Synod, under the authority of Parliament.

The early Puritan movement was Reformed or Calvinist and was a movement for reform in the Church of England. The Puritans objected to ornaments and ritual in the churches as idolatrous (vestments, surplices, organs, genuflection). The later Puritan movements were often referred to as Dissenters and Nonconformists and eventually led to the formation of various Reformed denominations. The most famous and well-known emigration to America was the retreat of the Puritan separatists from the Church of England, who fled first to Holland, and then later to America, to establish the English colonies of New England, which later became the basis for the United States.

After the Church of England became the specific English Church, the early years were difficult for English adherents of the Roman Catholic Church, although the persecution was not particularly violent. The civil rights of adherents to Roman Catholicism were severely curtailed, and there was no longer, as once in Stuart times, any Catholic presence at court, in public life, in the military or professions. Many of the Catholic nobles and gentry who had preserved on their lands among their tenants' small pockets of Catholicism, had followed James II into exile, and others at last conformed to Anglicanism, meaning that only very few Catholic communities as such, survived.

In the late 18th and early 19th century most restrictions on Catholic participation in public life were relaxed under acts such as the *Papists Act 1778* and *Roman Catholic Relief Act 1791*. By the date of Sir Francis Burdett's Catholic Relief Bill in 1825, Catholic emancipation looked a likely success. Indeed, the success of the bill in the Commons in April, followed by Robert Peel's tender of resignation, finally persuaded Liverpool that he should retire. Catholic emancipation however was not fully implemented until the major changes of the Catholic Relief Act of 1829 under the leadership of the Duke of Wellington and Sir Robert Peel.

In the 1840s and 1850s, especially during the Great Irish Famine, thousands of poor Irish Catholic people moved to England, establishing communities in cities and towns up and down the country such as London and Liverpool, thus giving Catholicism a huge numerical boost. In 1850, the Catholic Church in England and Wales re-established a hierarchy. The Catholic religion tended to become popular with the middle and lower classes, whereas the upper class stayed with the Church of England. By the nineteenth century, England no longer had the Church of England as the sole dominant religion but was tolerant of other religions.

A strong tradition of Methodism developed from the 18th century onwards. The Methodist revival was started in England by a group of men including John

Wesley and his younger brother Charles as a movement within the Church of England, but developed as a separate denomination after John Wesley's death. Presbyterian churches derive their name from the presbyterian form of church government, which is government by representative assemblies of elders. A number of Presbyterian churches were opened in England by Scottish immigrants.

The movement to end slavery in the British Empire coincided with the Christian missionary campaign "to save souls of the poor heathen". The British churches collected money from their parishioners so that intrepid missionaries could spread the word of God to races conquered by the military.

The Growth and Decline of the Economy

Mercantile problems of overdue debts, caused by delayed return of merchant voyages, were solved by the introduction of bills of credit in 1683. An organisation was set up to handle the financing of these bills in a tavern called the Nag's Head in Cateaten Street, London. After 1694 this became the Bank of England.

In 1694 King William III was again in need of funds to prosecute the war with France, and the Whig government supported his idea to create the Bank of England. The Charter of Incorporation of the Company of the Bank of England was signed on July 27, 1694. The Bank of England was allowed to issue notes against £1,200,000 which it advanced to the Government at 8% together with a service charge annuity of £4000. The generous terms indicates the low bargaining power of King William's government. The notes could be traded and essentially later redeemed for specie. Half the funds went to rebuilding the Royal Navy.

This in one fell swoop put the English public debt on the same footing of creditworthiness in the eyes of Dutch investors, as the Netherlands. In the following decades wealthy Dutch investors invested directly in British government bonds, and also in British joint-stock companies like the Bank of England, and the East India Company. This was facilitated after 1723 when such stocks, and certain government bonds, were traded jointly on the London and Amsterdam Stock Exchanges.

In the 1670s English merchants began to participate in the slave trade, needed to run the West Indies plantations. In 1713 the English received the right to supply slaves to the Spanish colonies. Slavery produced great profits for the sugar plantations which provided planter capital for the later Industrial Revolution.

English consumers received cheap sugar due to international competition and established the sweet taste of the English, particularly when tea imports grew under the East India Company. The mercantile marine grew from the increase in trade carried by English ships.

Early English exports were dominated by woollen textiles in all forms to southern Europe. Production of grain increased in the 1700s encouraged by the previous high prices and increased enclosures. Exports of grain rose dramatically from the 1670s but were still only a small proportion of the grain output which had reached a surplus. The Corn Laws brought protection to the producer when prices were low and encouraged exports by means of bounties.

An innovation to rival the Bank of England was a Land Bank attempted by Dr. Hugh Chamberlen who attempted in 1693 to interest the Scottish parliament in a scheme to create bills secured by an estate of land. After rejection of the scheme in Scotland, it was presented in a slightly different form to the English where it was adopted by the Tories in opposition to the Whig Bank of England scheme. The land bank was approved, despite bitter opposition from the Bank of England in 1696, but to the shame of its founder failed to receive the necessary subscriptions. Chamberlen retired to Holland in 1699.

In 1694 John Law, the son of an Edinburgh goldsmith, fled to Holland after a trial for the death of his opponent in a duel at London. He studied the workings of the Bank of Amsterdam, and in 1705 he submitted a scheme for a land bank to the Scottish parliament. The scheme, of extending the concept of commercial paper credit into the issue of paper money, was rejected, partly through the influence of another Scot, William Patterson (a founder of the Bank of England).

The public at the time was more concerned with the high price of silver which actually made the coins of the time worth more for their silver than the coined value. The Treasury proposed recalling the coins and reissuing coins at 20-25percent lower weight of silver. This was basically the same form of debasement that royalty had exercised for millennia. This time John Locke, advisor to Warden of the Mint Sir Isaac Newton, successfully lobbied that government tampering with coinage was as criminal as the actions of coin-clippers. Success by Locke meant hoarding of pure silver coins which caused prices and wages to collapse.

Two banks were established in Scotland by charter from the king; the Bank of Scotland 1695, and the Royal Bank of Scotland in 1727. The Scottish bankers invented *cash accounts* wherein they agreed to advance money against the security of a bond signed by three responsible persons. The holder of the *account* was not obliged to draw out money, and interest was commenced when funds are drawn. Money could be paid into the *account* which payments cancel the equivalent amount of debt to the bank and stop the interest on that amount. This was equivalent to a modern line of credit or over-draft, and was the forerunner to interest on cash deposits.

Although the Bank's notes were not at first legal tender, 1694 marks the commencement of the general acceptance of paper money by the public. The wealthy were able to make use of the new form of banknotes. In 1717 Britain adopted the Gold Standard by proclaiming a new ratio between gold and silver which drove silver out of use. The convenience of the Bank's notes spread throughout the kingdom, and up until 1796 the circulation was generally equal to the capital of the bank. <u>Many economists date 1700 as the start of the modern age of capitalism, as a system that demanded constant endless growth at least equivalent to the cost of debt.</u> The main reason for the prudent circulation of notes was that the then current *mercantile theory* was that land, bullion and coin were the only substantial measures of wealth. Paper was simply a more efficient measure of coin.

King George I recommended in 1717 that measures should be taken to reduce the National Debt which had increased sharply in the War of Spanish Succession. (Ratio debt/GNP was later estimated at 61.01% - *Source – Public Spending Chart for United Kingdom 1692-2011*). Although nowhere near the amount of French national debt, hopes were engendered in 1719 that an English scheme of debt reduction, more responsible than Laws' French Banque Generale scheme, would succeed.

The South Sea Company, founded in 1711, was a company of merchants holding monopolies of English trade with the immensely rich east coast of South America, and which had swapped shares for some discounted Government annuities. Fractious relations with Spain did not allow any exploitation of the South Seas trade monopoly, but the annuities had proved profitable. In January 1720 the South Sea company proposed to the government that national perpetual debt of £51.3m be liquidated by incorporating it with the Company's shares. The swap promised that the unwieldy form of perpetual debt could be transformed into more negotiable financial instruments that could reduce the debt to zero in less than 27 years.

Supporters of the South Sea scheme included politicians and courtiers who purchased shares of the Company in advance of expected government approval.

Such insider trading assisted in a rise in the share price which made the scheme more viable.

The Bank of England, another major chartered joint-stock company, counter-bid for the government stock takeover in an attempt to retain its primary role in English financial affairs. A higher offer, and what was later revealed as bribery and corruption, helped the South Sea Company to success in parliament over the Bank of England. Even while the matter was before parliament, stock fever had excited the public, which looked to trade in Exchange Alley, not only in South Sea stock but in a number of new dubious company floats.

The speculative rise of South Sea Company stock from £114 in December 1719 to £335 in April 1720, when the scheme was approved, was assisted by listing restrictions, inflow of funds from the Continent, and generous part-payment terms. In a similar manner to British privatisation nearly three centuries later, only one-tenth to one fifth of the inflated stock price needed to be paid on subscription, with the balance over three years. The public's appetite was whetted by the promise of great leveraged profits. The high stock prices made conversion of government debt into Company stock, more attractive.

While the South Sea Company stock was spiralling higher, the creation of other joint-stock ventures exploded. The new companies, nick-named "*bubbles*", had only the promise of extravagant projects, but were seized upon by the speculators in the hope that the new stock could be resold quickly at a profit. One company with the objective of "*carrying on an undertaking of great advantage, but nobody to know what it is*", sold 1000 shares to raise £2000 in five hours. The *bubble* then burst when the promoter disappeared the following day. The *bubbles* obviously worried the directors of the South Sea Company because, money, speculative or otherwise, was being drawn away from their scheme.

In June 1720 King George proclaimed "*bubble companies*" unlawful, and in July, the Bubble Act was passed, making companies without royal charter, illegal. That the South Sea Company was obviously legal, attracted switching into its stock, allowing a peak c. £950 in July. More importantly however, the public had been made aware that shares can fall, which caused a lull in speculative mania. As well, the loans that the South Sea Company had offered to allow purchase of its stock had become unsustainable by August. By September the value of the stock had fallen to £400. Prices again collapsed after news that Company directors had already sold near the market peak, and following denials of a Bank of England rescue.

A parliamentary enquiry was called in December 1720, but, as throughout history, most efforts of politicians were expended on fixing blame, rather than coping with crisis. The crisis deepened early in 1721 when it became common belief that leading goldsmiths and banks had loaned large sums of money secured with South Sea Company stock. Many bankers closed their doors to stop the demand for cash, and there was a run on the Bank of England itself. Without credit, company after company collapsed, despite apparently sound business prospects. It was over two years before stability returned to the English financial system, and decades before British credit was again considered fully trustworthy.

A basic factor behind the South Sea Bubble was the need to convert difficult-to-trade government war debt into exchange-traded low interest securities. The natural greed of man created the climate for the speculative mania to burst into the uncontrollable fire that then consumed the fragile finance that created it. The more substantial economy known as the Industrial Revolution grew from the ashes of the South Sea Bubble.

Bank of England notes were redeemable in coin on demand, but the bank maintained only a small reserve in gold for redemption purposes. Whenever the banks, including the Bank of England, increased the amount of paper, there was a run to the bank to redeem coin with notes, forcing the banks to buy expensive bullion. Serious runs led to a suspension of specie payments by the Bank of England twice in its early life, the most important one continuing for twenty-five years - 1797 to 1822 - but the business of England, and the Bank, continued without pause.

There is academic backing to my theory that booms and busts had their origins in excess credit which provided the fertile ground for money mania to flourish out of control. The Harvard economist Joseph Schumpeter stimulated my ideas when in his 1939 book "Business Cycles" he differentiated between inflationary financing of government expenditure and *"reckless banking"* which he classed with *"speculative madness, swindle and the like"*. Subsequent American financial crashes have enhanced this theory.

The beginning of the 18th century also appears to have sparked the start of paper speculation. The Bank of England was not the only bank to issue notes, and even when the Bank's monopoly was extended in 1742, London private bankers and country bankers continued to issue notes. I suspect that, as the use of paper money reduced the amount of bullion movements at sea, opportunities for piracy were reduced. Maybe it is only coincidence, noted by someone with misgivings about modern banking, that a founder of the Bank of England, William Patterson, had been a buccaneer in his youth.

Following the 1720 stock-market collapse of the South Sea Bubble, English resources were committed to privateering and colonisation in the West Indies and North America. There was little financial interest in Far East Company commerce. The great English resource was the export of people which resulted in around 60,000 emigrants to America 1720-40. The English colonists included middle-class families who looked forward to the acquisition of land for food cultivation.

Popularity of tea increased because of the attraction to a hot drink that could revive the spirits and reputedly cure colds, and which was easy to prepare. The imports of tea through the British East India Company quadrupled between 1720 and 1750. By 1766 exports of China *Tcha* from Canton sold at a profit four times the price paid.

The government was able to finance the war of 1739-48 with little difficulty. The national debt of 1750 was £78 million or debt/GNP ratio 107.5%. In 1751 a number of funds and annuities were grouped together at 3% to become known as *Consols*. The eventual cost of the Seven Years War was £160million of which £60million was raised in the money markets.

After the Seven Years War (1756-1763) the first modern style banking crisis arose. Intense demand from the Continent for funds for commercial and colonial development led to a shortage of cash which in turn led to increased sales of British securities. The British money market became tight. As export orders declined, those exports already shipped could not be paid for. Production was curtailed and commodities prices fell. For the first time the Bank of England operated like a central bank by operating as a lender of last resort. £2million was made available to commercial firms in London, Amsterdam and Hamburg. The slowing economy apparently allowed a decline in the Royal Navy during the years of peace.

The crisis of 1772 was possibly the first modern market and industrial crisis. Speculation and embezzlement caused at least 525 corporate failures. The East India Company bore heavy losses and its stock price fell significantly. As Dutch banking houses had invested extensively in the stock of the East India Company, they suffered the loss along with the other shareholders. In this manner, the credit crisis spread from London to Amsterdam. Dutch merchants, Imperial Russia and the Bank of Stockholm provided credit. Only belatedly did the Bank of England provide credit.

At the end of the American Revolution, the boom in foreign trade caused a balance of payments crisis when imports of raw materials outpaced exports. The Bank exercised control over the money market by restricting note issue and then easing credit when the drain on precious metals was reversed. In 1783 the younger Pitt introduced the Sinking Fund in order to stabilise the National Debt provided by the Bank of England. This provided Britain with debt for arms at far less cost than France. Pitt's fiscal reforms had improved the state's finances and restored its credit.

When France declared war in 1793 intense demand for redemption of provincial notes caused refusal by London banks to assist their correspondent banks in the country. The Pitt government had to step in to provide Commodity Secured credits. The government drew blithely on a reluctant Bank of England to finance the Napoleonic wars. Large amounts of bullion were sent to its continental allies. A rumour of French invasion caused a run on provincial banks in 1797. The run spread rapidly and within a week the credit structure of the nation was paralysed. The crisis deepened when the Bank of England suspended specie payments in February 1797 under the Bank Restriction Act of 1797.

The 1797 suspension of the Bank of England's obligation to convert its notes into bullion shifted the British monetary system from a commodity standard towards a flexible exchange rate. The actual transition was not an abrupt one, however, being complicated by the fact that, initially, illegal melting and export of coin, which continued to trade at par with Bank of England notes, limited the extent to which their price in terms of gold bullion could fall.

The Bullionist position in 1801 was that rising prices and the falling exchanges had a common source in an over-issue of Bank of England notes; that this had been undertaken to buy government debt, and that it would have been impossible had the Bank not recently been relieved of its obligations to convert its liabilities into gold on demand. The Report of the Bullion-Committee 1810 supported this view.

The Anti-Bullionist position was first, that rising agricultural prices were the result of poor harvests, and the falling exchange rate was both a by-product of the extra food imports that these had generated, and a consequence of an outflow of funds needed to pay subsidies to Britain's allies in the war against France. Secondly, to the extent that an over-issue of notes had anything to do with rising prices, the fault lay with the country bank note issue, which could fluctuate significantly and independently of that of the Bank of England. Thirdly, and at the very heart of the Anti-Bullionist position, there lay a precept for the proper conduct of monetary policy which could be called the *Real Bills Doctrine*.

The *Real Bills Doctrine* was an operating principle suitable, not to an individual competitive commercial bank, but to the Bank of England, not least by several of its directors; and, second, in the monetary system over which that Bank presided as a central bank, the price level was not anchored by gold convertibility. In 1810, even though it found that the inflation of the previous two years had been set in motion by a real shock to the balance of payments, the Bullion Committee clearly regretted that the Bank's response had not been constrained by specie convertibility. Its *Report* therefore recommended that convertibility be re-instituted at the 1797 parity, within two years, even though this would quite clearly require significant deflation, and in the midst of an ongoing war.

The findings of the Bullion Committee were placed before the House of Commons in a series of resolutions that were extensively debated during 1810-11. All of them were rejected, with that recommending an early return to convertibility failing by a significantly larger majority than any of the others. The House of Commons did, however, at the same time affirm the desirability of its ultimate restoration. It was not until after Waterloo and the war's end in 1815 that serious discussion of the issue began again.

Liverpool's chief economic problem during his time as Prime Minister was that of the nation's finances. British debt reached 226% of GDP in 1815 and a peak of 260% in 1821. The interest on the national debt, massively swollen by the enormous expenditure of the final war years, together with the war pensions, absorbed the greater part of normal government revenue. The refusal of the House of Commons in 1816 to continue the wartime income tax left ministers with no immediate alternative but to go on with the ruinous system of borrowing to meet necessary annual expenditure.

The basic economic issue, in essence, was food prices; the price of grain was central to the price of the most important food staple, bread, and the working man spent much of his wages on bread. The powerful landowner agricultural lobby in Parliament demanded protection for agriculture in the peace aftermath which had reduced the price of domestically grown grain. Liverpool was in principle a free-trader, but had to accept the bill as a temporary measure to ease the transition to peacetime conditions. The Liverpool Tory government passed the 1815 Corn Law to keep bread prices high. This resulted in serious rioting in London. Income Tax was abolished in 1816.

The Act of Parliament in 1816 defined the pound sterling solely in terms of gold at its 1797 price, thus removing the last vestiges of ambiguity about the role of silver in the British monetary system. Liverpool eventually facilitated a return to the gold standard in 1819. Legislation mandating the restoration of convertibility was passed by Parliament, a measure that was finally implemented in 1821, albeit not quite in the manner envisaged two years earlier. The Act in question required the convertibility of Bank of England paper in gold ingots to begin in May 1821, while deferring the start of redemption in gold coin until May 1823. In fact Parliament would set the ingot plan aside before it could be implemented. The pound sterling officially moved from silver to the gold standard and could be related to other currencies on their respective gold standard. This meant that one British pound was worth 4.85 US dollars.

In 1815, George Stephenson invented the modern steam locomotive, launching a technological race for bigger, more powerful locomotives using higher and higher steam pressures. Stephenson's key innovation came when he integrated all the components of a railways *system* in 1825 by opening the Stockton and Darlington line. It demonstrated that it was commercially feasible to have a system of usable length. London poured money into railway building—a veritable bubble, but one with permanent value. Speculation had already grown in bonds and stocks of South America as investors assumed that the British government would support Latin American bonds. When bonds crashed without any interference by government, the speculative bubble burst.

Early in 1825 as gold was being drained out of the country from speculation and inflationary banking practices, the stock market collapsed and there was a general financial crisis. The Bank of England fulfilled its function as a central bank by becoming a lender of last resort and providing credit on easy terms, with some difficulty. An infusion of gold reserves from the *Banque de France* saved the Bank of England from complete collapse. Despite expanded credit, more than 10% of banks in England and Wales failed. Scottish joint-stock banks basically survived so British parliament passed an act in 1826 encouraging joint-stock banks. Bigger banks swallowed minnows to commence the growth of huge banking institutions.

Another crisis in 1839 saw a rapid drain on reserves which cause a sharp rise in the discount rate and borrowing from abroad. The subsequent deflationary cost caused commercial and banking failures until 1842.

The Industrial Revolution increased British productivity on a sustained basis that increased national wealth and purchasing power. Average real wages rose 15-25percent between 1815 and 1850. Demand rose for foodstuffs and essential goods in a burgeoning population.

After 1840 Britain abandoned mercantilism and committed its economy to free trade, with few barriers or tariffs. The great rail expansion of the 1840s caused stock market speculation that also involved the Bank of England. Sir Robert Peel's *Bank Charter Act* of 1844, and parallel legislation for Scotland passed in 1845, essentially conferred a monopoly of the British note issue on the Bank of England. By 1847 the Bank was again losing reserves at a rapid rate facilitated by the repeal of the Corn Laws. Britain's joint-stock banks aggressively expanded enveloping smaller rivals when deposits expanded more than 400% between 1847 and 1857. This concentrated banking during a speculative boom including the rapid expansion of the Royal Bank of Scotland. The crisis of 1857 was the first global banking crisis, largely caused by the effects of excessive speculation in the US railroads at a time following bad harvests and costs of the Crimean War. A new feature of banking, discount houses, had insufficient reserves because they relied on their ability to borrow from the Bank of England which was not in fact available from 1858. The Bank of England refused to rescue Overend and Gurney which exacerbated the crisis.

In 1847, 1857 and again in 1866, the Bank Charter Act had to be suspended to give the Banking Department access to specie reserves held in the Issue Department in order to restore stability to financial markets.

In 1873 the US financial crisis brought pressure on the Bank of England mainly as gold fled London for rural areas. Only high interest rates at a time of falling commodities prices solved the reserves crisis. The Bank of England kept interest rates as high as 9 percent in the 1870s. The United Kingdom is often considered to have been the hardest hit; during this period it lost some of its large industrial lead over the economies of Continental Europe. While it was occurring, the view was prominent that the economy of the United Kingdom had been in continuous depression from 1873 to as late as 1896. It was known as the Great Depression until the 1930s. Britain came to fear American economic cycles.

Foreign trade tripled in volume between 1870 and 1914; most of the activity occurred with other industrialised countries. Britain ranked as the world's largest trading nation in 1860, but by 1913 it had lost ground to both the United States and Germany. London strengthened its position as the world's financial capital;

the export of capital was a major base of the British economy 1880 to 1913, the "golden era" of international finance.

The gold standard was suspended at the outbreak of the war in 1914, with Bank of England and Treasury notes becoming legal tender. Prior to World War I, the United Kingdom had one of the world's strongest economies, holding 40% of the world's overseas investments. By the end of the war, Britain owed £850 million (£35.1 billion as of 2013), mostly to the United States with interest costing the country some 40% of all government spending. The pound sterling was worth US$4.98. Inflation more than doubled between 1914 and its peak in 1920, while the value of the Pound Sterling fell by 61.2 percent to $3.92. The Debt/GDP ratio grew from 25.83% in 1913 to 154% in 1921.

In an attempt to resume stability, a variation on the gold standard was reintroduced in 1925, under which the currency was fixed to gold at its pre-war peg, although people were only able to exchange their currency for gold bullion, rather than for coins. This conversion was at the cost of deflation and unemployment. The undervalued French franc caused attraction to France of British securities and bills. The Bank of France commenced to withdraw its funds in 1928 which contributed to the demise of the post-war gold standard system. It was abandoned on 21 September 1931, during the Great Depression, and sterling suffered an initial devaluation of some 25%.

In 1940, an agreement with the U.S.A. pegged the pound to the U.S. dollar at a rate of £1 = $4.03. (Only the year before, it had been $4.86.) This rate was maintained through the Second World War and became part of the Bretton Woods system which governed post-war exchange rates. Under continuing economic pressure, and despite months of denials that it would do so, on 19 September 1949 the government devalued the pound by 30.5% to $2.80. The move prompted several other currencies to be devalued against the dollar. The pound was again devalued by 14.3% to $2.40 on 18 November 1967.

Advances in Technology

A number of innovations in the 1700s appeared in England which solved economic and technical problems. Thomas Lombe introduced a water-powered silk-throwing machine in 1719. By mid-century a number of throwing mills were established. The paper industry improved its machinery to pulp linen rags which were its main raw material. Benjamin Huntsman invented the coke-fired crucible in steel making in the 1740s. Thomas Newcomen introduced a practical coal-fired atmospheric engine to drain water from mines around 1716.

In the 1760s James Watt worked on a steam engine for pumping water from mines and formed a partnership with Matthew Boulton in 1775. Watt patented the application of "Sun and Planet Gear" to steam, and a steam locomotive in 1784. Although not particularly important to government at the time, the invention which possibly commenced the Industrial Revolution was the steam engine. The steam engine grew to be used to raise minerals from mines, provide heat for smelting iron ore, and drive machines in textile mills. The Industrial Revolution began to rely on coal to produce the high temperatures needed to smelt iron. Eventually it also became a source of heat for the steam engine. There was a huge increase in the production of coal in Britain. Very little coal was found in the south, but vast amounts were found in the Midlands, the north, the north-east and parts of Scotland. Because coal was so difficult and expensive to move, towns and other industries grew up around the coal mining areas so that the workers came to the coal regions. This in itself was to create problems as these towns grew without any obvious planning or thought given to the facilities the miners and their families would need.

In England the 1760s and 1770s saw the introduction of wage saving machinery in the manufacture of cotton, iron, steel and pottery, as well as the first practical applications of James Watt's and Matthew Boulton's steam engines. In 1779 Samuel Compton had combined the spinning jenny and the water-frame into one machine called the mule. The mule could produce 300 times as much yarn as a person on a spinning wheel. These machines produced more yarn than weavers could handle until 1787, when Edmund Cartwright invented the power loom. The Industrial Revolution had flowered.

The introduction of machines in the late eighteenth century had led to the development of the factory system. The large factory was more cost effective because it allowed the concentration of machines and workers in one place. It also reduced transportation costs and allowed for greater quality control. The factory owner had greater control of the work force and enforced much stricter discipline.

Inevitably taxes rose to compensate for borrowing and to pay off the government debt, which led to widespread disturbance between 1812 and 1822. Around this time, the group known as Luddites began industrial action, by smashing industrial machines developed for use in the textile industries of the

West Riding of Yorkshire, Nottinghamshire, Leicestershire and Derbyshire. Throughout the period 1811–16, there were a series of incidents of machine-breaking and many of those convicted faced execution

In 1821, a parliamentary bill was passed to allow the building of the Stockton and Darlington Railway which connected collieries near Bishop Auckland to the River Tees at Stockton. The gauge Stephenson chose for the line was 4 feet 8 $\frac{1}{2}$ inches (1,435 mm) which subsequently was adopted as the standard gauge for railways, not only in Britain, but throughout the world.

The first working electrostatic telegraph was built by the English inventor Francis Ronalds. He laid down eight miles of wire in insulated glass tubing in his garden and connected both ends to two clocks marked with the letters of the alphabet. Electrical impulses sent along the wire were used to transmit messages. He offered his invention to the Admiralty, describing it as "*a mode of conveying telegraphic intelligence with great rapidity, accuracy, and certainty, in all states of the atmosphere, either at night or in the day, and at small expense.*" There was little official enthusiasm for his device. The first commercial electrical telegraph, the Cooke and Wheatstone telegraph, was co-developed by William Fothergill Cooke and Charles Wheatstone. In May 1837 they patented a telegraph system which used a number of needles on a board that could be moved to point to letters of the alphabet.

Isambard Brunel's designs revolutionised public transport and modern engineering. He assisted in the building of the first tunnel under a navigable river and development of SS *Great Britain*, the first propeller-driven ocean-going iron ship, which was at the time (1843) also the largest ship ever built. *Great Britain* is considered the first modern ship, being built of metal rather than wood, powered by an engine rather than wind or oars, and driven by propeller rather than paddle wheel. She was the first iron-hulled, propeller-driven ship to cross the Atlantic Ocean.

A redesign of the Lee-Metford rifle which had been adopted by the British Army in 1888, the Lee-Enfield superseded the earlier Martini-Henry, Martini-Enfield, and Lee-Metford rifles. The military superiority of British weapons over native forces in colonial wars was epitomised by the battle of Omdurman, Sudan in 1898. Maxim machineguns and Lee-Enfield rifles destroyed 11,000 Dervishes for the loss of only forty-eight British troops.

Rule of Law

Law has always been central to British self-perception of civilisation. The heritage of a balanced constitution, the rule of law, and the 'rights of free-born Englishmen' has been as important to the historical formation of British identity as language and Protestant religion. The Constitution of the United Kingdom is the set of laws and principles under which the United Kingdom is governed. Much of the British constitution is embodied in written documents, within statutes, court judgments and treaties. The constitution has other unwritten sources, including parliamentary constitutional conventions and royal prerogatives. The bedrock of the British constitution has traditionally been the doctrine of parliamentary sovereignty, according to which the statutes passed by Parliament are the UK's supreme and final source of law.

There are three separate judicial systems in the United Kingdom: that of England and Wales, that of Scotland, and that of Northern Ireland. The essence of English common law is that it is made by judges sitting in courts, applying legal precedent (*stare decisis*) to the facts before them. Common law can be amended or repealed by Parliament. As the Parliament of England became ever more established and influential, legislation gradually overtook judicial law-making such that today, judges are only able to innovate in certain very narrowly defined areas. English criminal law derives its main principles from the common law. The main elements of a crime are the *actus reus* (doing something which is criminally prohibited) and a *mens rea* (having the requisite criminal state of mind). England exported English Common law and English Statute law to most parts of the British Empire, and many aspects of that system have survived after Independence or otherwise cessation of British rule.

A person who believes that a crime has been committed, contacts the police, who conduct an investigation. If, after arresting and interviewing a person, the police believe that he or she committed the crime, that individual is charged. A report of the case is then sent to the Crown Prosecution Service (CPS). If the CPS believes that the case has a reasonable prospect of success, and that it would be in the public interest to do so, it will start criminal proceedings against the suspect, who becomes the defendant in the case. In court, the CPS bears the burden of proving, beyond reasonable doubt, that the defendant committed the crime.

Minor offences, such as speeding, are heard by Magistrates' Courts. Many towns in England and Wales have their own Magistrates' Court, where cases are heard by three magistrates. Magistrates do not need any legal qualifications, and they are advised by a Clerk, who is a qualified lawyer. Magistrates do not state reasons for their decisions. Very serious offences, such as murder and rape, are heard in the Crown Court. The Crown Court is based in about 90 centres throughout England and Wales. A jury consisting of 12 people chosen at random from the local population will decide, without giving reasons, whether the defendant is guilty of the offence. Usually a jury's decision will be unanimous, but the judge may decide that an 11:1 or 10:2 majority is sufficient. The jury is advised about the law by the judge, whose role also includes imposing a sentence if the defendant is found guilty.

Appellate courts are those that only hear appeals from other courts. The two most senior appellate courts are the Court of Appeal and the Supreme Court. The Supreme Court's predecessor was the House of Lords Appellate Committee. Appeals were technically not to the House of Lords, but rather to the Queen-in-Parliament. By constitutional convention, only those lords who were legally qualified (Lords of Appeal in Ordinary, or Law Lords) heard the appeals, since World War II usually in what was known as the Appellate Committee of the House of Lords rather than in the chamber of the House.

The Court of Appeal, which encompasses only England and Wales, consists of a Civil Division and a Criminal Division. The Civil Division hears appeals against decisions of the High Court, while the Criminal Division hears appeals about alleged errors of law in the Magistrates' and Crown Courts. Cases are heard by three Lords Justices of Appeal, each of whom reaches an individual decision that may consist of a lengthy speech. The Court's decision may be reached either by unanimity or by a 2:1 majority.

The Constitutional Reform Act 2005, which came into force on 1 October 2009, abolished the judicial functions of the House of Lords (except on impeachment), and transferred them to a new body, the Supreme Court of the United Kingdom. Vacancies in the Supreme Court of twelve judges are filled by the Monarch based on the recommendation of a special selection commission consisting of that Court's President, Deputy President, and members of the judicial appointment commissions for the three judicial systems of the UK. Members of the Supreme Court may be removed from office by Parliament, but only for misconduct.

Initially, all Commonwealth realms and their territories maintained a right of appeal to the Judicial Committee of the Privy Council. Established by the Judicial Committee Act 1833 (or with the Privy Council Appeals Act 1832) to hear appeals formerly heard by the King in Council, it was the highest court of appeal (or court of last resort). Many of those Commonwealth countries that became republics, or which had indigenous monarchies, preserved the Judicial Committee's jurisdiction by agreement with the United Kingdom.

> *"How can you be the world's leading power when you're the world's leading borrower? It's the lenders who have the leverage."*
>
> Peter G. Peterson
> Blackstone Group c.1988

Government Management – Advance or Decline

Constitutional monarchy proved to be a resilient form of government for the capitalist era. England (then the United Kingdom) was governed by parliament that in return was dominated by nobility influenced by land wealth (Tories) and city crony capitalism (Whigs). The Orange/Georgian monarchs basically acquiesced to senior parliamentary figures such as Walpole, and the Pitts. Although England was nominally democratic, the middle and lower classes had little say in government until the nineteenth century, but they benefited indirectly from increase in trade in consumer goods promoted by government. The institution of the Bank of England which gradually became a central bank allowed some fiscal discipline. Parliament supported the Royal Navy as a dominant force. Great Britain had become an economic leader.

The rebellion of the American colonies was a shock to the aristocracy and not well handled by parliamentary leaders of George III. The nascent democracy in America was a shock to politicians and no doubt produced new trains of thought in the middle class. This was exacerbated by the French revolution, which although it produced a miserable government, wakened ideas of democracy throughout Europe. The British government became aware of its military inadequacies but the nascent industrial revolution produced widespread gains. After the loss of America, international trade became more important especially with India. France and Spain were continual enemies but were unable to cope with British economic strength. Britain was able to handle high levels of war debt.

Social legislation such as the Corn Laws and Catholic emancipation surfaced early in the nineteenth century and trade unions became more active. Politicians commenced to embrace democracy as aristocratic control in parliament declined. The Whigs in particular became involved in social reform and political parties changed to Conservatives and Liberals. Increased democracy coincided with disappointing military action in the Crimea and the growth of newspapers in informing civil opinion. I have assumed that 1850 was the peak of British dominance when Palmerston's aggressive foreign affairs interventions were still active, although another time is possible such as 1867 when the Reform Act was passed. The crisis of 1857 was the first global banking crisis, largely caused by the effects of excessive speculation in the US railroads at a time following bad harvests and costs of the Crimean War. After the 1850s governments were often short-lived or coalitions. More laws were passed to regulate the lower classes. The United Kingdom is often considered to have been the hardest hit by the Depression of 1873; during this period it lost some of its large industrial lead over the economies of Continental Europe. Between 1880 and 1910 Britain's portion of the world's trade fell from 23% to 17%. Britain's balance of payments remained reasonably strong on the back of banking, shipping, insurance and investments.

The 1897 Diamond Jubilee of Queen Victoria coincided with public admiration for the Anglo-Saxon empire assisted by the popular press, so that the Boer War was simply considered the natural extension of Empire in competition with the imperial reach of France, Italy, Russia and Germany. By 1900 a number of colonies sought independence even though they remained in the Empire. By 1906 the Unionists and Labour became factors in parliament so the Liberal government competed to expand the welfare state. The epitome of inefficient government was the secret treaty of 1906 to support the French in the event of war with Germany, which was unknown to the military until 1912. This meant the Britain was not prepared for war in 1914. Britain ranked as the world's largest trading nation in 1860, but by 1913 it had lost ground to both the United States and Germany. Management of the War was ineffective until 1916 when Lloyd George took over. Even then Lloyd George had little influence with the generals as the Treasury struggled with debt.

The Great War was a major economic catastrophe as Britain went from being the world's largest overseas investor to being its biggest debtor, with interest payments consuming around 40 percent of the national budget. Inflation more than doubled between 1914 and its peak in 1920, while the value of the Pound Sterling fell by 61.2 percent. The Debt/GDP ratio grew from 25.83% in 1913 to 154% in 1921.

CHAPTER 6

The Republic of the United States of America 1800 - 2010+

Chronology

1792	USA	Banking crisis
1800	**USA**	**President Thomas Jefferson**
1803	USA	Louisiana Purchase
1805		100 year warm-wet climatic peak
1803-05		**Sunspot Solar Cycle 5 peak**
1808	USA	President James Madison
1812	USA	War of 1812 against Britain
1814-22		drought Great Lakes
1815-17		Sunspot Solar Cycle 6 peak
1816	USA	President James Monroe
1816-35		Kondratieff Wave Autumn
1819	**USA**	**Panic of 1819; Recession**
1824	USA	President John Quincy Adams; mixed Congress
1825		**100 year hot-dry climatic peak**
1828	**USA**	**President Andrew Jackson; Jacksonian Democrat Congress**
1829-31		Sunspot Solar Cycle 7 peak
1830		100 year cold-wet climatic peak
1836	USA	Democrat President Martin Van Buren; Democrat Congress
1837	**USA**	**Panic of 1837; Depression**
1836-39		**Sunspot Solar Cycle 8 peak**
1840	USA	Whig President William Harrison
1841	USA	Whig President John Tyler; Whig Congress
1844	USA	Jacksonian Democrat President Polk; Democrat Congress
1847-49		**Sunspot Solar Cycle 9 peak**
1848	USA	Whig President Zachary Taylor; Democrat Congress

1850	USA	Whig President Millard Fillmore; Democrat Congress
1852	USA	Jacksonian Democrat President Pierce; Democrat Congress
1856	USA	Democrat President Buchanan; hostile Democrat Congress
1857	**USA**	**Panic of 1857; Recession**
1859-61		Sunspot Solar Cycle 10 peak
1860	USA	Republican President Abraham Lincoln; Republican Congress
1861	**USA**	**American Civil War**
1862		drought USA
1864-74		Kondratieff Wave Autumn
1865	USA	end Civil War; Lincoln assassinated; President Andrew Johnson
1865		**100 year cold-dry climatic peak**
1868	USA	Republican President Ulysses S. Grant; Republican Congress
1869-71		Sunspot Solar Cycle 11 peak
1873	**World**	**Panic of 1873; Great Depression**
1876	USA	Republican President Rutherford Hayes; split Congress
1882-84		Sunspot Solar Cycle 12 peak
1884	**USA**	**Panic of 1884**
1880	USA	Republican President James Garfield; split Congress
1881	USA	Republican President Chester Arthur
1884	USA	Democrat President Grover Cleveland; split Congress
1888	USA	Republican President Benjamin Harrison; Republican Congress
1890	**USA**	**Panic of 1890**
1892	USA	Democrat President Grover Cleveland; Democrat Congress
1892-94		Sunspot Solar Cycle 13 peak
1893	**USA**	**Panic of 1893; Depression**
1896	**USA**	**Panic of 1896; Depression**
1896	USA	Republican President James McKinley; Republican Congress
1898	**Cuba**	**Spanish/American War**
1901	USA	Republican President Theodore Roosevelt
1901	**USA**	**Panic of 1901**
1905-07		Sunspot Solar Cycle 14 peak
1907	**USA**	**Panic of 1907; Recession**
1908	USA	Republican President William Taft; Republican Congress

1911		**drought USA; Panic of 1910-11**
1912	USA	Democrat President Woodrow Wilson; Democrat Congress
1914	**Europe**	**World War I**
1916-18		Sunspot Solar Cycle 15 peak
1917	**USA**	**War declared against Germany/Prohibition**
1920	USA	Republican President Warren Harding; Republican Congress
1921-29		Kondratieff Wave Autumn
1923	USA	Republican President Calvin Coolidge; Republican Congress
1925		100 year warm-wet climatic peak
1927-29		Sunspot Solar Cycle 16 peak
1928	USA	Republican President Herbert Hoover; Republican Congress
1929	**USA**	**Wall Street crash; Great Depression**
1932	**USA**	**Democrat President Franklin D. Roosevelt; Democrat Congress**
1933	USA	end Prohibition
1934		drought USA
1935		**100 year hot-dry climatic peak**
1936-38		**Sunspot Solar Cycle 17 peak**
1940	USA	Democrat President Franklin D. Roosevelt; Democrat Congress
1941	**USA**	**War declared against Japan, Germany**
1944	USA	Bretton Woods Conference
1945	USA	End World War II
1945		100 year cold-wet climatic peak
1945	USA	Democrat President Harry Truman; Democrat Congress
1947-49		**Sunspot Solar Cycle 18 peak**
1948	USA	Democrat President Harry Truman; hostile Democrat Congress
1950	Korea	USA leads UN forces in Korean War
1952	USA	Republican President Dwight Eisenhower; Republican Congress
1956-58		**Sunspot Solar Cycle 19 peak**
1956	USA	drought USA
1956	Egypt	Suez Canal Crisis
1957	Russia	Sputnik I
1960	USA	Democrat President John Kennedy; Democrat Congress
1961	Vietnam	US commits troops to Vietnam

1962	USA	Cuban missile crisis
1963	USA	Democrat President Lyndon Johnson
1964	USA	Vietnam War
1967-69		**Sunspot Solar Cycle 20 peak**
1968	USA	Republican President Richard Nixon; Democrat Congress
1969		100 year warm-wet climatic forecast
1971	**USA**	**President Nixon closes gold window**
1973	**USA**	**US dollar gold link abandoned**
1973	USA	1973 oil crisis; 1973-74 stockmarket crash
1975		**500 year cold-dry; 100 year cold-dry climatic forecast;**
1974	USA	Republican President Gerald Ford
1975	Vietnam	USA withdraws troops from Vietnam
1976	USA	Democrat President James Carter; Democrat Congress
1978-80		**Sunspot Solar Cycle 21 peak**
1980	USA	Republican President Ronald Reagan; split Congress
1982-83		strong El Nino
1882-2000		Kondratieff Wave Autumn
1986	Libya	USA bombs Libya; Iran-Contra Affair
1987	World	Stockmarket crash
1988-90		**Sunspot Solar Cycle 22 peak**
1988	USA	Republican President George H. Bush; Democrat Congress
1989-91	USA	Savings and Loan Crisis
1990	USA	Iraq Kuwait Gulf War
1990	Japan	Japanese asset bubble burst
1991	Russia	Breakdown of Soviet Union
1992	USA	Democrat President William Clinton; Democrat Congress
1996	USA	Democrat President William Clinton; Republican Congress
1997-98	Asia	Asian Financial Crisis
1998	Russia	Russian Financial Crisis
1999-2001		**Sunspot Solar Cycle 23 peak**
2000	USA	"Dot-Com" Bubble burst; Recession
2000	USA	Republican President George W. Bush; Republican Congress
2001	USA	September 11 air attack on New York, Washington by terrorists
2003	Iraq	Invasion of Iraq by Coalition of Willing
2007	USA	Recession
2008	**World**	**Global Financial Crisis – Recession/Depression**
2008	USA	Democrat President Barack Obama; Democrat Congress

2012	USA	Democrat President Barack Obama; split Congress
2014?		**Forecast Sunspot Solar Cycle 24 peak extended**
2025		Forecast Sunspot Solar Cycle 25 peak
2023		100 year warm-wet peak forecast
2036		**100 year hot-dry peak** forecast
2032-34		Forecast Sunspot Solar Cycle 26 peak
2045		100 year cold-wet peak forecast
2091		100 year cold dry peak forecast

"It is incumbent on every generation to pay its own debts as it goes. A principle which if acted on would save one-half the wars of the world."

Thomas Jefferson

America Follows the Cyclical Pattern

The American Republic culture has been the dominant culture of the twentieth century, and there is no doubt that it can be considered just, prosperous and enduring by the criteria on which I examined ancient cultures. It is worthwhile examining the American culture in more detail because it brings the past into the present, and thus is the most important cycle to my readers. If the cyclical pattern holds true, not only will it justify my earlier cyclic conclusions, but it should allow me to forecast the future progress of the next dominant culture into the twenty-first century.

"America" was first printed on a map in 1507 when mapmaker Waldseemuller used the name to honour Amerigo Vespucci who had accepted that his discovery, South America, was a new continent. The American Republic culture was cultivated in North America from seeds planted with the English colony of the Virginia Company 1607, and the "Mayflower" Massachusetts settlement in 1620. Subsequently the relatively free colonies of religious New England, the trading Dutch New York, planned Puritan Pennsylvania and the slave-embracing southern tobacco states of Virginia, Carolinas and Georgia outpaced the state-governed colonies of France to the north, and Spain to the south.

The Seven-Year War (1756-1763) against France, triggered by a young Virginian, Lt. Colonel Washington, resulted in the British conquest of French Canada, and removal of any direct threat to America from France. Already chafing under the ineffective governorship of the British crown and trade restrictions designed to assist the motherland, the colonies became emboldened to revolt against a pro-Native Indian policy imposed by the distant British hegemony.

The War of Independence (1776-1783), so important to America, was not pressed strongly by the British who were ruled by constitutional monarch George III and his inefficient nobility at a time of hostility to Britain from France, Spain and Holland. The War brought America to the attention of the world, and allies from those countries hostile to Britain. The War of Independence might have coincided with the peak of British royal culture. Although the peak of British power was decades away, the royal power structure had already devolved to a basic democratic parliamentary culture.

Climate and Geographic Access to Resources

European culture was introduced to the continent of North America by the colonies of England, France and Spain in the seventeenth century. The thirteen English colonies stretched from French Canada to Spanish Florida, bounded to the west by the Appalachian and Allegheny Mountains. The climate was by no means mild but these hardy settlers could handle the harsh winters. The fertile soil could grow almost any food crop. There was a thirst for land which pushed the white man's expansion against the indigenous Indians. The expansion was not due to population pressure because in 1705 the colonials numbered less than 1.5million in an area inland from a coastline of thousands of miles. Carolina was the first slave state, corrupted by planters from West Indian Barbados who imported slaves to tend crops of rice, tobacco and indigo. American slavery was then on a small scale, with the exception of Carolina, and in 1714 there were fewer than 60,000 slaves in the colonies.

The French had intended to join their colonies in Canada and Louisiana through the Ohio and Mississippi valleys, but this pressure was relieved in 1763 when the British conquered Canada. The British themselves were forced to quit America after the War of Independence which from 1783 granted American colonies all territory west to the Mississippi. Immigrants from Scotland, Ireland, England and northern Europe were attracted by tales of land available and the freedom from oppressive governments. By 1800 the population had grown to 4 million.

The number of slaves had increased exponentially to 697,000 at the first census in 1790, following the cultivation of cotton for export in 1780. By 1810 the invention of the Whitney cotton gin had made the USA the main supplier of cotton to Britain where the consumption had been greatly stimulated by the Industrial Revolution. The expansion of cotton production would not have been possible in such quick time without slaves who cleared land, cultivated and harvested the crop. Regardless of climatic differences in the North, where men were busy farming their own fertile land, the high cost of labour, due to the shortage of free men, would not have allowed Northern cultivation of cotton.

In 1801, Napoleon forced Spain to cede its American territory to France. Thomas Jefferson (President, 1801-1809) took the opportunity of Napoleon's need for money, to successfully bid $15million for the huge Louisiana tract of land from Canada to Texas, Mississippi River to the Rocky Mountains.

Florida was bought from Spain in 1819. The United States and Britain jointly occupied the Oregon Country. In addition to the acquisition of Florida, the landmark Treaty of 1819 secured the border of the United States along the 42nd Parallel to the Pacific Ocean and represented America's first determined attempt at creating an "American global empire".

The Louisiana Purchase removed any barrier to further western expansion. It was found that Louisiana and the Mississippi delta were ideal for sugar-cane, with Kentucky and Tennessee suitable for tobacco. All needed cheap labour. In 1808, when importation of slaves ceased, there were approximately 1.75 million Negroes in the USA. After 1808 the plantations in the Old South of the Carolinas, Virginia and Georgia, were unsuitable for cotton, but could, and did, breed slaves to fulfil demand in the states of the Deep South.

A further flood of European immigrants pushed settlement westwards so that by 1820, 25% of America's 10 million population lived beyond the mountains in frontier states and territories. The huge distances between farm production areas and industrial centres were an economic burden to developing America. The invention of the steamboat in 1810 allowed the Ohio, Mississippi, Missouri Rivers, and the Great Lakes to become great waterways which allowed agricultural produce from the fertile farmlands to be moved efficiently to hungry European markets. The Santa-Fe covered-wagon trail ran southwest from St. Louis to the Rio Grande. The Oregon Trail ran past the Mormon settlement of Salt Lake City to the mouth of the Columbia River, claimed for the United States by explorers Lewis and Clark.

Texas, formerly part of Mexico, declared its independence in 1835, but in 1844 voted itself into the American Union. The Spanish Jesuit settlement of California, virtually independent since 1822, sparked the US war with Mexico in 1846. Following the 1848 Treaty of Guadalupe Hidalgo, the USA obtained California, New Mexico, Nevada, Utah and Colorado. In 1849 gold was discovered in California.

The Oregon Treaty of 1846 divided the Oregon Country along the 49th parallel, the original American proposal. Although there were many who still clamored for the entire territory, the treaty was approved by the Senate. The portion of Oregon territory acquired by the United States later formed the states of Washington, Oregon, and Idaho, and parts of the states of Montana and Wyoming.

The protestant Calvinist ethic of the New England states and Puritan Pennsylvania had differentiated culturally from the Southern states, Carolina, Maryland and Virginia, as early as the seventeenth century, even before the latter became slave based. The American Constitution barred slavery north of the Ohio River. In 1820 the Mason-Dixon Line was fixed as the northern limit of slavery. However in 1854, the Southern dominated Congress allowed the new territories of Kansas and Nebraska to have slaves. By 1861 irreconcilable differences between the North and the South, mainly over the right to secession, had led to civil war.

Railroads, introduced in 1829, proved vital for Northern military success and increased demand for iron and steel. The West was not directly affected by the war, and was able to expend its energies in mining of gold, silver and copper. Seven states, California, Nevada, Arizona, New Mexico, Colorado, Idaho, and Montana founded their mining bases, often ignoring Indian treaties, while the East was blasting ahead. The clear winners of the bloody Civil War were the Northern industrialists, the "robber baron" corporations which were the military/industrial complex of the era. Never-the-less by displaying the same resilience that extended the war, the South recovered amazingly fast. Instead of shipping cotton North, Southerners began to develop their own textile industry. Coal and iron deposits were developed in Alabama and Tennessee lumber from the hill country, and tobacco in North Carolina.

In 1859 the world's first commercial oil well came into production in Pennsylvania, with later wells in Oklahoma, Texas and California. John D. Rockefeller founded Standard Oil 1870 which achieved control of 90%of US refineries by 1882. The American continent offered more natural resources than any country except Russia, and presented huge rewards for the concentrated band of monopolist entrepreneurial capitalists and their banker friends.

In 1898, the United States gained all of Spain's colonies outside of Africa in the Treaty of Paris, including the Philippines, Guam and Puerto Rico. The treaty came into force in Cuba 1899, with Cubans participating only as observers. Cuba formed its own civil government. However, the US imposed various restrictions on the new government, including prohibiting alliances with other countries, and reserved the right to intervene. The US also established a perpetual lease of land in Guantánamo Bay.

William H. Seward, the United States Secretary of State, negotiated the Alaska Purchase with the Russians in 1867 for $7.2 million. Alaska was loosely governed by the military initially, and was administered as a district starting in 1884, with a governor appointed by the President of the United States. Alaska was officially incorporated as an organised territory in 1912 and officially proclaimed a state in 1959.

The Newlands Resolution was used to annex the Hawaiian Republic to the United States and it became the Territory of Hawaii in 1898. In 1959, Congress passed the Hawaii Admission Act and US President Dwight D. Eisenhower signed it into law.

Leaders and Commanders - The Paradigm of Political Control

Eighteenth Century

The American War of Independence (1775-1783) erupted when British troops seeking rebel arms were attacked by militia at Concord and Lexington. In June 1775 the Second Continental Congress passed Articles of Confederation and Perpetual Union, which allowed formation of the American Continental Army under the command of the delegate from Virginia, General George Washington. The Unanimous Declaration of the Thirteen United States of America (Declaration of Independence) was made on July 4, 1776.

The states then democratically revised their constitutions and made themselves sovereign. The Continental Army was poorly resourced against the might of far away Britain, but the patriotism of the Americans against the indifference of the

English people was an important factor in the eventual victory. Another factor was the first American leader, George Washington who waged a war essentially designed to test the endurance of the British and their long supply lines. In 1778 France, with the support of its ally Spain, entered the war on the American side to provide support by land and sea, but more importantly with supplies.

John Paul Jones took the war to England itself with a French sponsored squadron. He captured an enemy warship in 1779, and only an unfavourable wind stopped a Franco-Hispanic invasion. Benjamin Franklin negotiated recognition of America's independence from Britain in 1782, at the expense of the alliance with France and Spain, which became the big losers after the Peace of Paris 1783. The peace brought little toleration within the United States of British sympathisers. The largely aristocratic Tories, or Loyalists, had lands and possessions confiscated before being forced to flee to remaining British possessions. This removed a fair proportion of the upper class strata which further enhanced middle class democracy. Only adult white male property owners could vote. Enslaved Africans, most free black people and most women were not extended the voting franchise.

In peace, the American states were anything but united. They failed to honour monetary promises to Congress which was a root cause of post-war inflation and loss of credit. Their squabbling delayed the constitution of a Republic that could unite America. Many compromises were necessary, particularly about slavery, before a Constitution was eventually agreed in 1787, and ratified in 1790. The American Revolution had succeeded where the French Revolution of the same era did not.

The agreed Federal government would be led by a president, elected for four years by electoral bodies from the states on a population basis, with the right to choose ministers or secretaries who must not be members of Congress. The Congress would consist of two houses. The House of Representatives would be elected every two years in proportion to the population of the states. The Senate, or upper house, consisted of two elected members from each state, sitting for six years, one third retiring every two years. A Supreme Court would be appointed for life by the President, with the Senate's approval. In 1791 a Bill of Rights, largely drafted by James Madison, became part of the Constitution. The American Republic had been born.

In 1789 the Virginian, George Washington, was elected as the first President of the United States of America. His Vice President was John Adams, an acerbic New Englander from Quincy, Massachusetts. Washington appointed his wartime aide from New York, Alexander Hamilton, as Secretary of the Treasury, whose financial efforts managed to bring the fledgling nation back from the verge of bankruptcy. He created many new federal institutions, including the Bank of the United States. Balancing the federalist Hamilton in the six-man Cabinet was the States-rights liberal Virginian, Thomas Jefferson, who was Secretary of State. It was Jefferson who formed the anti-Federalist party, then known as the Republican Party which confusingly later evolved into the Democratic Party.

Washington was a ceremonial president, but his mediation talents between opposing factions made his presidency a success, so that he was re-elected in 1792, close to the outbreak of the French Revolution. *Francophile* Jefferson, sympathetic towards a French Republic, tendered his resignation over acts by a French envoy, and hastened the American Republic's political move towards party politics. Two treaties with Britain and Spain, negotiated in Washington's second term, removed the remaining obstacles to large westward expansion into the Ohio and Mississippi valleys. Washington declined a third term, thus creating a precedent that was followed until 1940. In his 1796 farewell address Washington maintained that the USA should avoid European quarrels and entangling alliances.

Nineteenth Century

The Vice President and Federalist Party candidate, John Adams, succeeded Washington as President in 1797 and followed the same neutralist policy towards the war in Europe. Jefferson, who had stood in 1796 for president as the Democratic-Republican Party's candidate, was instead made Vice President and advocated support for France. Adam's most important appointment was that of John Marshall as Chief Justice of the Supreme Court in 1801. Marshall dominated the American judicial system for over thirty years, and provided the legal backing for paper-money as equal in security to property that was important in the development of capitalism. The Supreme Court under Marshall ruled that it was in the power of the Court to review both state and federal legislation, and if necessary declare it unconstitutional.

The liberal Virginian, Thomas Jefferson, who had so much to do with the Declaration of Independence, won the 1800 presidential election against the New York political machinist Aaron Burr, through a secret deal with federalists. Jefferson's idealism was never reconciled in practice. He was against slavery but kept his own slaves. He was an intellectual puritan who enjoyed life's luxuries.

His political philosophy was *"agrarian democracy"* which based the Republic on independent yeoman farmers, but he encouraged Congress to pass the Embargo Act (1807) which effectively cut off farm exports. Jefferson had Aaron Burr as Vice President. Jefferson used his influence to bring Ohio into the Union in 1802, the first state under the Northwest Ordinance prohibiting slavery. In Congress, Jefferson had authored the Ordinance of 1787 in Congressional committee under the Articles of Confederation. He was therefore instrumental in prohibiting slavery not only to new territories, but in the new states to come, beginning with Ohio.

In 1801 Jefferson's cabinet voted unanimously to send three frigates and a schooner with marines to the Mediterranean with orders to make a show of force against Barbary pirates but to opt for peace. If a state of war existed they could use their own discretion. Tripoli had already declared war upon the United States. Jefferson and the young American navy forced Tunis and Algiers into breaking their alliance with Tripoli which ultimately moved it out of the war. Jefferson also ordered five separate naval bombardments of Tripoli, which restored peace in the Mediterranean for a while. Jefferson continued to pay the remaining Barbary States until the end of his presidency.

Jefferson made one of history's greatest bargains when, seeking to buy New Orleans from the French, was offered the whole of Louisiana, the Mississippi Valley and New Orleans for $15 million. The Louisiana Purchase in 1803, if nothing else, assured Jefferson's re-election in 1804. The young United States of America had been able to expand, albeit at the expense of the native American Indians. He followed up the Southern expansion by commanding Lewis and Clark to explore west of the Mississippi and Missouri Rivers, which was finally mapped in 1806. Burr was dropped from the Vice Presidency before the 1804 election, in favour of George Clinton, and was later to kill the financial wizard Alexander Hamilton in a duel. The Jefferson ticket won an overwhelming victory in 1804.

Relations with Great Britain had always been bad, due partly to the violent personal antipathy between Jefferson and the British Ambassador, Anthony Merry. After Napoleon's decisive victory at the Battle of Austerlitz in 1805, Napoleon became much more aggressive in his negotiations over trading rights, and American efforts failed. Jefferson responded with the Embargo Act of 1807, directed at both France and Great Britain. This triggered economic chaos in the US and was strongly criticised at the time, resulting in Jefferson abandoning the policy within a year. Also in 1807, Jefferson ordered his former vice president Aaron Burr tried for treason. Burr was charged with conspiring to levy war against the United States in an attempt to establish a separate confederacy composed of the Western states and territories, but he was acquitted. 1806 Jefferson denounced the "violations of human rights" attending the international slave trade, calling on the newly elected Congress to criminalise it on the first day possible. In 1807, Congress passed the Act Prohibiting Importation of Slaves, which Jefferson signed into effect in 1808. In contrast with modern Presidents, Jefferson was personally heavily in debt when he left office, but had managed to reduce the national debt by 30%.

Another Virginian founding father of the US Republic, Jefferson's Secretary of State (1801–1809), James Madison was the Republican Party choice for president in 1808. Madison easily defeated Federalist Charles Pinckney. He also won in 1812 by carrying the South and the West. Madison sought to continue Jefferson's agenda, in particular the dismantling of the system left behind by the federalists under Washington and Adams. One of the most pressing issues Madison confronted was the first Bank of the United States. Its twenty-year charter was scheduled to expire in 1811, and while Madison's Treasury Secretary said the bank was a necessity, Congress failed to re-authorise it. As Secretary of State, Madison had been involved in unfulfilled 1807 negotiations with Britain over commerce during the Napoleonic Wars. He continued to vacillate as President, subject to political pressure from New England merchants who were British maritime sympathisers, and the South and West who wanted confrontation with Britain as a path to further expansion. The declaration of the War of 1812 actually occurred after Britain had suspended the Act responsible for America's displeasure, but this had not been communicated to Madison.

The War of 1812, in which the brash independent nation of America declared war on Great Britain over embargoes on commerce, showed the world the potential of the Republic. The illusion of potential support from French-speaking Canadians, on which expansionist hopes were based, was shattered when ill-disciplined militias endeavoured to invade Canada. The US Navy was more successful on both the Great Lakes and the high seas. American ships were better designed and armed, with volunteer crews that were, ship-for-ship, superior to their pressed British counterparts. The actions with Europe did not allow full disposition of Royal Navy forces. However, the invincibility of British naval power was broken, shattering the basis of the theory that it was too big to be attacked.

Never-the-less, the fact that the British were able to land on the Chesapeake and burn the new city of Washington DC, indicated that Madison's administration provided poor leadership. The epitome of a strong leader rose to prominence in the last skirmish of the war, the Battle of New Orleans in January 1815 (after the peace Treaty of Ghent had already been signed in 1814). General Andrew Jackson organised the defence of the city by conscripting free blacks and local pirates into his small force of regular soldiers. Good planning and motivated US defenders defeated a poorly executed attack from overwhelming British numbers, making Andrew Jackson a popular hero.

The absence of a national bank had made war with Britain very difficult to finance. In 1814 Congress passed a bill chartering a second national bank but Madison vetoed it. In 1816, Congress passed another bill to charter a second national bank; Madison signed the act, having eventually learned from the war with Britain that the bank was needed. The Federalist Party, which had called for secession over the war at the Hartford Convention, dissolved and disappeared from politics. In 1816, two-thirds of the incumbents in Congress were defeated for re-election after having voted to increase their salary.

Madison's successor in 1817 was his Secretary of State, James Monroe, another founding father Virginian slave-owner against slavery. He had within his Cabinet two men of opposing moral philosophies - Secretary of State, John Quincy Adams of Massachusetts, and Secretary of War, John Calhoun of South Carolina. As a possible solution to the problem of the fate of slaves if freed, Monroe supported a Congressional scheme to repatriate freed slaves to an American sponsored colony in West Africa called Liberia, where the capital was named Monrovia. The scheme was greatly unsuccessful, so that American blacks preferred slavery rather than the fearful despatch to freedom in Liberia.

Monroe bought Florida from Spain in 1819 and sought to ease partisan tensions, embarking on a tour of the country that was generally well received. With the ratification of the Treaty of 1818, under the successful diplomacy of John Quincy Adams, the United States extended from the Atlantic to the Pacific, giving America harbor and fishing rights in the Pacific Northwest. The collapse of the Federalists in 1816 left Monroe with no organised opposition at the end of his first term, and he ran for reelection in 1820 unopposed, the only president other than Washington to do so.

In the period 1790-1820 immigration had been slowed by the Napoleonic Wars but American fertility rose to the challenge. It has been estimated that the large families of 6-8 children increased the American population by 250%. Such an estimate also includes the Negro population which was encouraged to grow by slave owners who also owned the progeny.

A conservative well-mannered man, Monroe enjoyed the nationalism that grew in America following success in the War of 1812, promoted initially to obscure the actual poor military record. The foreign policy of President Monroe basically declared that the continent of America was for Americans alone. The Monroe Doctrine of 1823 was to be the basis of American foreign affairs well into the twentieth century. The Doctrine rested on two principles - that European nations should not be allowed to colonise in the western hemisphere, and that Europe should not be allowed to interfere with nations in that hemisphere that had independent government. This openly warned Spain and France not to intervene in the hemisphere and, with the expansion of the American economy westwards, the power to actually enforce the doctrine grew. It allowed expansion of America into Mexican territory, as well as denying Russian claims to territory south of Alaska.

The presidential election of 1824 was fiercely contested by candidates from the traditional North and South, as well as two men from the West. The New Englander, John Quincy Adams, son of former President John Adams, had been groomed like a *princeps* for the presidency. William Crawford, Southern aristocrat from Georgia and Monroe's Secretary of the Treasury, suffered from accusations of corruption, but would have the Southern vote following a deal to have Secretary of War, John Calhoun of South Carolina, as Vice President. The charismatic Henry Clay of Kentucky had developed the role of Speaker of the House of Representatives into a powerful political position. Andrew Jackson of Tennessee was the Indian fighter and hero of New Orleans whose strong character many believed was preferable to the career politicians that the already political city of Washington had nurtured. In the election, Jackson actually received the largest number of electoral votes, but not enough overall to secure a majority. The 1824 election result went to the Democratic-Republican House of Representatives where Adams, with Clay's support won. Clay, the great compromiser, became Secretary of State. The Senate was Jacksonian but the House Anti-Jacksonian.

The aristocratic austere President Adams was an advocate of strong federal government which he tried to implement in a wise and prudent manner. Adams enacted a part of his agenda and paid off much of the national debt. During his term, Adams worked on transforming America into a world power through "internal improvements," as a part of the "American System". It consisted of a high tariff to support internal improvements such as road-building, and a national bank to encourage productive enterprise and form a national currency. During Adams' lifetime, technological innovations and new means of communication spread messages of religious revival, social reform, and party politics. Goods, money, and people traveled more rapidly and efficiently than ever before. In essence Adams' presidential term suffered from Jackson's long 1828 election campaign which commenced in 1825, and which started the American tradition of endless electioneering. Adams was thwarted by political opposition particularly by the Congressional supporters of Jackson.

The Jackson political backers (Jackson Men), including the New York Tammany Hall political machine, transformed Jefferson's Southern-based Democratic Republic Party into the powerful national Democratic Party. Adam's National Republican Party responded to Jackson's criticism of government, by raising malicious personal, often scurrilous, attacks on Jackson. The accusations of adulterer and murderer were thought to have caused the early death of his wife, and embittered Jackson against his political opponents. The accusations, if anything, made Jackson more popular with voters in lower economic brackets and the rough, rowdy, back-country people who provided vocal support. In 1828 Jackson, with the New York political machinist Martin Van Buren as proposed Secretary of State, enjoyed a clear mandate and Jacksonian majority Congress.

As the first popularly elected president, Jackson ("Old Hickory") was to a large degree beholden to his party's politicians - another first that endured in American politics. Jacksonian democracy changed the form of government in America, even though many of the actions in its name were not initiated by Jackson. The Jackson administration moved quickly to clear out allegedly inefficient and corrupt bureaucrats from the departments that had grown under previous oligarchic Republican governments. By moving his own partisans into power, Jackson was credited with bringing the Tammany Hall "spoils" system to the federal government.

Never-the-less, terming himself *"the tribune of the people"*, Jackson was a strong president who fully exercised the rights of America's chief executive, and who advocated the removal of the native Indian population west of the Mississippi. In 1833, after a landslide 1832 re-election, Jackson, the strong Unionist, was prepared to go to war with South Carolina over secession, until Clay negotiated a tariff reduction in return for the state withdrawing its Nullification Bill. When

Chief Justice John Marshall died in 1835, also extinguished was the capitalist legal influence, because Jackson appointed as Supreme Court Justice, his friend Roger Taney, who ruled the Court for thirty years along the principles of Jacksonian Democracy.

In 1831 Jackson vetoed the bill renewing the federal charter of the Second Bank of the United States, decrying it as a monopoly controlled by rich men and against the public interest. In 1834 the Whig Party Senate censured President Andrew Jackson for defunding the Second Bank of the United States. The late Jacksonian economic boom was based on an expanded number of banks issuing paper-money, fuelled by the cash surplus once the national debt had been repaid in 1835. Federal money went to private banks rather than to the previous Federal banker, the Second Bank of the United States. The paper-money financed a land boom which predictably ended when Jackson insisted in 1836 that paper money would no longer be accepted for federal land. Exacerbated by 1835 crop failures, and a failure of financial houses in London, the American financial system froze.

As Jackson's nominated successor, Martin Van Buren barely won the presidency for the Democratic Party in 1836, and immediately had to deal with the bank crisis caused by *Jacksonomics*, and which by 1837 had deepened into a depression. State elections of 1837 and 1838 were disastrous for the Democrats, and the partial economic recovery in 1838 was offset by a second commercial crisis in that year. Van Buren was scapegoated for the depression and called "*Martin Van Ruin*" by his Republican political opponents. He succeeded in setting up a system of bonds for the national debt. Van Buren put his political talents to work to develop a central bank that he called an independent treasury system, but it took until 1840 to get it passed by Congress. By this time the continued depression ensured his defeat at the subsequent election.

Another Indian fighter came briefly to the fore in the campaign of 1840. The Whigs chose as its candidate William Harrison, retired General and hero of Tippecanoe (1811 battle which broke Indian power in the North-west). The Whig Party had been established in opposition to "King" Jackson, and had assumed many of the conservative policies of the National Republic Party. Harrison died after only a month in office, to be succeeded by his Vice President John Tyler, a cultured Virginian politician. As President, Tyler opposed the Whig platform and vetoed several Whig party proposals. As a result, most of his cabinet resigned. Tyler dedicated his last two years in office to the annexation of Texas. Congress passed the resolution authorising the Texas annexation, which was carried out by

Tyler's successor. Tyler sought election to a full term, but he had alienated both Whigs and Democrats and his efforts to form a new party came to nothing. Tyler was followed as president by Democrat, Jackson protégé, James Polk of Tennessee.

Jacksonian Democrat James Polk was the surprise candidate for president in 1844, defeating Henry Clay of the rival Whig Party by promising to invade and annex Texas. President Polk fulfilled the hopes of his mentor, Jackson, and his Manifest Destiny policy, by successfully reaching an agreement with Britain over the border with Canada, before successfully fighting a war with Mexico in 1846-47. By obtaining California, and New Mexico, as well as Oregon, Polk's supporters claimed he had added more territory to the USA than any other president with the exception of Jefferson. In 1846, Polk approved a law restoring the Independent Treasury System, under which government funds were held in the Treasury and not in banks or other financial institutions. This established independent treasury deposit offices, separate from private or state banks, to receive all government funds.

In an 1848 confusing election, the Whig candidate, the hero of Buena Vista *"against Santa Ana's Mexican army"*, General Zachary Taylor of Tennessee, was successful. Once again an old war horse died in office, allowing anti-slavery moderate Vice President Millard Fillmore to succeed to the top job in 1850. Fillmore's term was basically spent overseeing debates in Congress over slave conditions and whether new states/territories should be allowed to adopt slavery. When the Whig Party broke up in 1854-1856, Fillmore and other conservative Whigs joined the American Party, the political arm of the anti-immigrant, anti-Catholic, "Know-Nothing" movement, though he himself was not anti-Catholic. He was the American Party candidate for President in 1856, but finished third. The Northern states, united by 1850 through the Industrial Revolution which had introduced labour-saving machinery, formed the Republican Party to oppose the Southern based Democratic Party.

Franklin Pierce was another Jacksonian Democrat even though he came from New Hampshire, before serving as brigadier-general in the Mexican War. At the 1852 Democratic Convention, Pierce was nominated on the forty-ninth ballot, and at the election easily beat the Whig candidate, his commander in the war, General Scott. President Pierce's administration was composed of men like Jefferson Davis, largely chosen to balance the political factions of slavery and anti-slavery, and who often proved inept in that role. Practically no policy at home or abroad was achieved, although some, like purchase of Alaska, were successfully executed by future presidents. Harriet Beecher Stowe's 1852 novel *"Uncle Tom's Cabin"* had spread anti-slavery sentiments from the North to the West, even to some degree in the South, but in 1856 the Republicans were still disorganised.

The Kansas-Nebraska Act 1854 provoked outrage among northerners, who already viewed Pierce as bowing to slave-holding interests. The passage of the Act resulted in so much violence between groups that the territory became known as *Bleeding* Kansas. Pro-slavery Border Ruffians, mostly from Missouri, illegally voted in the elections to set up the government, but Pierce recognised it anyway. The debate over slavery turned bloody in 1856 when the territory of Kansas applied for admission as a state. A mob attacked an abolitionist town which encouraged a fanatic, named John Brown, to attack a pro-slavery settlement. This contributed to the Republican Party cause, as well as to critical assessments of Pierce as untrustworthy and easily manipulated. Having lost public confidence, Pierce was not nominated by his party for a second term. The Civil War had in fact already started in Kansas.

The Democrat's James Buchanan was elected president in 1856, but had a hostile House and a Senate which would not pass bills seen to be pro-slavery. Buchanan's efforts to maintain peace between the North and the South alienated both sides. An ejected and re-elected Congressman, Preston Brooks, advised the South to *"tear the Constitution of the United States, trample it underfoot, and form a Southern Confederacy"*. The Southern states declared their secession in the prologue to the American Civil War. The division between northern and southern Democrats allowed the Republicans to win a plurality in the House election of 1858. Their control of the chamber allowed the Republicans to block most of Buchanan's agenda.

Railroads opened up remote areas, drastically cut the cost of moving freight as well as passenger travel, and stimulated new industries such as steel and telegraphy, as well as the profession of civil engineering. Due to radical innovations, the railroad became the first large-scale business enterprise and the model for most large corporations. Industrialists such as Cornelius Vanderbilt and Jay Gould became wealthy through railroad ownerships, as large railroad companies such as the New York Central, Grand Trunk Railway and the Southern Pacific, spanned several states.

One of the founders of the new Republican Party, Ohio lawyer, Abraham Lincoln, was chosen as the presidential candidate in 1860 following a series of debates against the more experienced Northern Democratic politician, Stephen

Douglas. Lincoln won the presidency mainly because of the Democratic rift which caused South put up another candidate, Buchanan's Vice President John Breckinridge, who split the Democratic vote. Unfortunately Congress was also split.

The secessionists commenced action immediately after the election, so that by January 1861, six states had seceded from the Union in protest against Lincoln's anti-slavery rhetoric. Before Lincoln's inauguration, Buchanan allowed the seceded states to take over Federal property within their borders including arsenals and forts, except Fort Pickens in Florida and Fort Sumter in Charleston Harbour. In February, the six seceded states adopted a provisional constitution of the Confederate States of America, and chose Jefferson Davis of Mississippi as President. The new Southern government voted itself a bond issue of $15 million which would support creation of an army of 100,000 men.

On inauguration, Lincoln basically issued the Confederacy with the ultimatum - to remain in the Union or make war to stay out. Lincoln then moved to re-provision Forts Pickens and Sumter. Before Sumter could be relieved, it was called upon to surrender, and fired upon. Lincoln called for 75,000 volunteers. The Civil War, so long promised, was fully under way.

Eleven states finally joined the Confederacy - South Carolina, Georgia, Florida, Alabama, Louisiana, Texas, Mississippi, Virginia, North Carolina, Arkansas, and (allied) Tennessee. The Confederacy was at such a disadvantage in terms of leadership, men and resources that it is a wonder that the war lasted as long as it did. By seceding from the Union, the South had already lost the question of slavery, because complete victory over the North was impossible. Lincoln was implacable that all states had to be re-united but hoped that the South would see reason to negotiate re-entry.

The two geographical areas on either side of the Mason-Dixon Line had developed radically diverse cultures which would have inevitably clashed along moral lines. The South, rich in cotton and slaves, was no match for the North which had a diverse economy as a result of the Industrial Revolution. The West would play little part. The two cultures, which had been growing further divided since the seventeenth century, made it impossible for the South to negotiate the complete subjugation of its culture. A bloody defeat was inevitable, at a bloody cost to the victors in an uncivilised war. It was only the extraordinary determination of the people of the South to defend their slave-based economy, and the unending courage of its soldiers, that allowed the war to last. The North's victory and resultant corrupt vicious occupying governments ("*Carpetbaggers*") imposed on the South meant that the two cultures would remain diverse, even though racism rather than slavery was to become the ostensible divisor.

Politics continued to provide friction despite, or because of, the war. Lincoln asserted that the fight was to preserve the Union, but many of his actions were criticised by the Radical faction of the Republican Party which insisted that the purpose of the conflict was the emancipation of slaves. In September 1862 Lincoln capitulated to the fractious rump by issuing the Emancipation Proclamation. The Northern Democratic Party was also split over the war, with the Peace Democrats (often called "*copperheads*") critical of, even subversive towards, the war effort. The stage was set for Lincoln's address at the Gettysburg battlefield cemetery in 1863 which became the most quoted speech in American history. Lincoln's use of martial law to deal with "*copperhead*" leaders lost him six states in the otherwise successful 1864 re-election.

In 1865, General Robert E. Lee's surrender to General Ulysses S. Grant effectively ended the Civil War. The huge losses on both sides during the four years of conflict in the misnamed Civil War, around 620,000, were more than American later losses in World War I, World War II and the Korean War put together.

Before the final Confederate forces had surrendered, Lincoln was assassinated. His Vice President, Andrew Johnson, who had been the only Southern Democratic Senator in Congress after secession, became President for the difficult task of reconstruction. The South was probably fortunate that President Johnson was foreman of reconstruction in the first years after defeat, because with Lincoln, he embodied the human face of Republicanism. Johnson favoured a middle-class agrarian South, controlled by the small farmer, merchant and artisan. He had no objection to Negro suffrage, but as a states-rights man, believed that only the states could give the freed slave the vote.

The Radical Republicans, representing Northern Industrialism, wanted to ensure that any Southern state in the Union was under Republican control, to continue their wartime domination of tariff, subsidy, taxes as well as disposal of land and resources. The Republicans wanted Negroes to be enfranchised by Federal decree so that they could obtain their vote. The harsh face of Republicanism was successful in passing the Fourteenth Amendment to the Constitution through Congress, ensuring Radical control of reconstruction and Southern state governments. Johnson had a showdown with the Radical Republicans and was nearly impeached in 1867.

The *"carpet-bag"* legislatures of the reconstructed Southern states were among the most corrupt that democracy has seen. Given Radical Republican control, and the painting of the Democrats as "the party of secession", it is surprising that General Ulysses S. Grant did not receive a greater majority in his successful bid for the presidency in 1868, and re-election in 1872. He had used the army to build the Republican Party in the South, based on black voters, Northern newcomers (*"Carpetbaggers"*) and native white supporters (*"Scalawags"*). As a result, African-Americans were represented in the Congress for the first time in American history in 1870. As a career military man Grant was used to following political dictates. It was not surprising that he allowed his administrations to be controlled by Radical Republican politicians, often to their own benefit and that of their big business backers.

Rapidly expanding home markets, including the West whose mineral exploitation had been relatively unaffected by the War, and an excellent transport system, had encouraged the growth of industrialism. Political control had allowed high tariffs, and the creation of monopolies which allowed the most resourced and rapacious companies to swallow competitors.

By the campaign of 1876, news of Republican corruption had filtered into the press, and the Democrats had gained support of Southern farmers, disillusioned by the *"carpet-bag"* reconstruction. A mirror image of the harsh face of the Radicals rose more violently in the South to terrify Negroes - the Klu Klux Klan. In a messy election, moderate Republican President Rutherford Hayes was narrowly elected, but, in a spirit of compromise, presided over removal of the remaining *carpet-bag* governments and Radical financial control. Big business in the North was then in such a dominant position that it possibly no longer needed to exploit the South. Companies had formed transcontinental corporations, and industrial complexes which operated their uncontrolled policies of ruthless domination. There were no laws to stop the *"robber-barons"* from feudal exploitation of people and resources. Hayes believed in meritocratic government, equal treatment without regard to race, and improvement through education. Hayes kept his pledge not to run for re-election, retired to his home in Ohio.

In 1880 Republican James Garfield was elected, but assassinated in July 1881. His position was taken by the Vice President Chester Arthur who had to face a Democratic House. To the surprise of reformers, Arthur took up the cause of reform, though it had once led to his expulsion from office in New York. He signed the Pendleton Act into law and strongly enforced its provisions to reform the civil service. Of the Cabinet members Arthur had inherited from Garfield, only Secretary of War Robert Todd Lincoln remained for the Arthur's entire term. Suffering from poor health, Arthur made only a limited effort to secure re-nomination in 1884; he retired at the close of his term.

In 1884 the Democrats were successful in having President Grover Cleveland elected with a Democratic House but Republican Senate. His crusade for political reform and fiscal conservatism made him an icon for American conservatives of the era. Cleveland won praise for his honesty, self-reliance, integrity, and commitment to the principles of classical liberalism. He relentlessly fought political corruption, patronage and *bossism*. In 1886, a bill to reduce the tariff was narrowly defeated in the House. The tariff issue was emphasised in the Congressional elections that year, and the forces of protectionism increased their numbers in the Congress, but Cleveland continued to advocate tariff reform. In response to monopolistic practices (such as price fixing) and other excesses of some railroads and their owners, Congress created the Interstate Commerce Commission (ICC) in 1887. The ICC indirectly controlled the business activities of the railroads through issuance of extensive regulations. Congress also enacted antitrust legislation to prevent railroad monopolies, beginning with the Sherman Antitrust Act in 1890.

In 1888 Grover Cleveland lost the election to Republican Benjamin Harrison who carried with him a Republican Congress. His administration is remembered most for economic legislation, including the McKinley Tariff and the Sherman Antitrust Act, and for annual federal spending that reached one billion dollars for the first time. One of the most volatile questions of the 1880s was whether the currency should be backed by gold and silver, or by gold alone. The issue cut across party lines, with western Republicans and southern Democrats joining together in the call for the free coinage of silver, and both parties' representatives in the northeast holding firm for the gold standard. Harrison attempted to steer a middle course between the two positions, advocating a free coinage of silver, but at its own value, not at a fixed ratio to gold. He also substantially strengthened and modernised the Navy, and conducted an aggressive foreign policy.

In 1890 an economist calculated that about 125,000 men controlled at least half of the national wealth. The ascendancy of individuals, such as Andrew Carnegie (United Steel) and John Rockefeller (Standard Oil), was in the American tradition of resourcefulness and self-reliance, so the *"robber-barons"* were in general admired for their enterprise. The ideology, that wealth was a just reward for industry, was promoted by the Republican Party as the party of industrial capitalism, assisted by financial support from big business. The influence of wealth on politics had the predictable outcome of placing powerful businessmen in an impregnable position.

The overbearing Republican attitude was resented by the population who in 1890 returned a Democratic Congress, and in 1892 returned Grover Cleveland to the presidency. Unfortunately the Panic of 1893 started a run on gold, and depression struck almost as soon as Cleveland returned to power. Railroads went into bankruptcy, banks collapsed, factories closed, unemployment soared and farm prices plummeted. Labour organised strikes against big business which responded with picket-busting private armies that precipitated bloody clashes. The American Federation of Labour had been formed in 1887, only to be countered by the National Association of Manufacturers in 1895. Cleveland's use of troops against strikers labelled him a tool of monopolies. It ruined his Democratic Party, opening the way for a Republican win in 1894 and for the agrarian and silverite seizure of the Democratic Party in 1896. The result was a political realignment that ended the Third Party System and launched the Fourth Party System as well as the Progressive Era.

After several unsuccessful attempts to create new political parties, the National People's Party was formed in 1891 from farm based organisations. The Populist Party expressed the rural dweller suspicion of largely urban politics which appeared to support the banks, trusts and monopolies that made farm life difficult. Populists were opposed to both major parties which appeared to exist simply to oppose each other. In the 1894 Congressional elections many Populists and independent representatives were sent to Congress at the expense of both major parties. Never-the-less the Republican Party retained the majority.

Criticism of monopolist Wall Street bankers who were thought to control the gold standard currency, led to a move to produce government notes backed by silver. Free silver became a rallying point for a number of politicians in all political parties. The Democrat, William Jennings Bryan, took both the Democratic and Populist 1896 nomination after his famous "*cross of gold*" speech, and raised hopes that a president could serve the common man. Popularity was no match for the Republican Party machine, amply financed by business under Senator Mark Hanna. Republican President James McKinley was elected on a gold standard platform, with control of Congress. McKinley presided over a new high tariff, the short Spanish-American War 1898, and the gold-standard Currency Act of 1900. The Gold Standard Act confirmed the United States' commitment to the gold standard by assigning gold a specific dollar value (just over $20.67 per Troy ounce).

Revolts against Spanish rule had occurred for some years in Cuba. After the mysterious sinking of the American battleship *Maine* in Havana harbor, political pressures from the Democratic Party and certain industrialists pushed the administration of Republican President McKinley into a war that he had wished to avoid. Compromise was sought by Spain, but rejected by the United States which sent an ultimatum to Spain demanding it surrender control of Cuba. First Madrid, then Washington, formally declared war in 1898.

The ten-week war was fought in both the Caribbean and the Pacific. American naval power proved decisive, allowing US expeditionary forces to disembark in Cuba against a Spanish garrison already brought to its knees by nationwide Cuban insurgent attacks and further wasted by yellow fever. The result was the 1898 Treaty of Paris, negotiated on terms favorable to the US, which allowed temporary American control of Cuba, ceded indefinite colonial authority over Puerto Rico, Guam and the Philippine islands from Spain. The defeat and collapse of the Spanish Empire was a profound shock to Spain's national psyche. The war marked American entry into world affairs. Since then, the US has had a significant hand in various conflicts around the world, and entered many treaties and agreements. I have considered that 1898 was the commencement of the United States rise to a dominant culture.

Twentieth Century

McKinley was re-elected in 1900 but assassinated in September 1901, to be succeeded by his Vice President, Roosevelt, as the youngest ever president. The Republican reform President, Theodore Roosevelt (1901-1909), attempted to move the Republican Party (GOP) toward Progressivism, including trust busting and increased regulation of businesses and would not have been the electoral choice of conservative Republican leaders except for his inheritance of the party machine on the death of Hanna. Roosevelt helped establish the Panama Republic in 1903, from which the US gained control of the Panama Canal. The Canal, which opened officially in 1914, provided the gateway to Europe for exports from the US west coast.

In 1904, Roosevelt was elected to a term in his own right, winning the largest percentage of the popular vote since the uncontested election of 1820. Roosevelt coined the phrase "*Square Deal*" to describe his domestic agenda, emphasising that the average citizen would get a fair share under his policies. Roosevelt successfully broke a number of trusts including tobacco, beef and fertilisers, but a conservative Republican-controlled Congress saved many other monopolies. Foreign policy was to demonstrate supremacy over South America. Roosevelt's policies were characterised by his slogan, "*Speak softly and carry a big stick*". He sent the Great White Fleet on a world tour to demonstrate American power; and negotiated an end to the Russo-Japanese War, for which he won the Nobel Peace Prize.

Uninhibited, government-sponsored railroad building had already peaked when the age of the automobile dawned. In 1907 Henry Ford commenced mass production of the automobile, followed by the famous Model T in 1909. Competition which sprang from General Motors increased demand for oil to make the USA the world's leading oil producer until the 1960s. Communication by the telegraph and telephone directly affected manufacturing and marketing.

Roosevelt's handpicked presidential successor in 1908, President William Taft, followed his mentor's domestic agenda which emphasised trust-busting, civil service reform, strengthening the Interstate Commerce Commission, improving the performance of the postal service, and passage of the Sixteenth Amendment (income tax). Taft was oblivious to the political ramifications of his decisions, often alienated his own key constituencies, and certainly alienated Roosevelt who stood against Taft for the Republican nomination in 1912. Taft ultimately outmaneuvered Roosevelt and obtained the Republican nomination. Roosevelt and his group of disgruntled party delegates and members bolted from the party to create the Progressive Party ticket, splitting the Republican vote in the 1912 election. Woodrow Wilson, the Democrat, was elected with 41% of the popular vote; Roosevelt got 27%, and Taft garnered 25%. Taft won a mere eight electoral votes, in Utah and Vermont, making it the worst defeat in American history of an incumbent President seeking re-election.

Former professor of history, President Woodrow Wilson, introduced his New Freedom philosophy which was a restoration of individual competition, with the government acting as coordinator and protector of individual's rights. Wilson's policy was that governments must remove special privilege and concentration of power that hindered competition. He persuaded the Democratic Congress to pass a legislative agenda that few presidents have equaled, remaining unmatched up until the New Deal in 1933. He followed his predecessors' trust-busting with the Federal Trade Commission Act and the Clayton Antitrust Act, instituted control of banking with the Federal Reserve Act, and introduced the Federal Farm Loan Act. Wilson, at first unsympathetic, became a major advocate for women's suffrage after public pressure convinced him that to oppose women's suffrage was politically unwise. Although considered a modern liberal visionary giant as President, Wilson was "deeply racist in his thoughts and politics" and his administration racially segregated federal employees and the Navy. Wilson spent 1914 through to the beginning of 1917 trying to keep America out of the Great War in Europe. Wilson won the support of the peace element (especially women and churches) by arguing that an army buildup would provoke war.

Narrowly re-elected in 1916 around the slogan, *"He kept us out of war"*, Wilson became the first Democratic president since Andrew Jackson to be elected to two consecutive terms of office. Wilson's second term with a Democratic Congress was dominated by World War I. Following the revelation of Germany's attempt to enlist Mexico as an ally against the U.S, Wilson asked Congress to declare war in April 1917 in order to make *"the world safe for democracy."* The government under Wilson introduced bureaucratic control of industry, food, fuel, housing and the media. He borrowed billions of dollars in war funding through the newly established Federal Reserve Bank and Liberty Bonds. In the late stages of the war, Wilson took personal control of negotiations with Germany, including the armistice. His view of a post-war world was that another terrible conflict could be avoided. In 1919, he went to Paris to aid the formation of a League of Nations to the Treaty of Versailles, with special attention on creating new nations out of defunct empires.

In January 1919 the women's and temperance movement's long lobbying resulted in the Eighteenth Amendment to the United States Constitution, authorising Prohibition of alcohol. In 1918 the Republicans won Congress amid isolationist backlash against the League of Nations and a postwar depression. Congress proposed the Nineteenth Amendment that prohibits any United States citizen from being denied the right to vote on the basis of gender in June 1919. It was ratified in August 1920. President Woodrow Wilson suffered a massive stroke in October 1919, leaving him partially paralysed. Despite his poor health, he tried to gain a two-thirds majority that would enable Congress to ratify the Treaty of Versailles, and attempted to run for a third term. Compromise Republican candidate, Warren G Harding, won the 1920 election with a Republican Congress. The USA never joined the League.

President Harding rewarded his friends and contributors with powerful positions that led to charges of corruption and prison terms for some appointees. Harding spurned the League of Nations, and, after Congress had rejected the Treaty of Versailles, signed a World War I peace treaty with Germany and Austria separate from the other Allies. Wilson's prescient warning, *that if the League were defeated, the United States would have to fight World War I all over again*, was ignored. Harding promised the nation a return to "normalcy", in the form of a strong economy, independent of foreign influence. This program was designed to rid Americans of the tragic memories and hardships faced during World War I. Domestically, Harding signed the first federal child welfare program, dealt with striking mining and railroad workers, including supporting an 8-hour work day, and oversaw an unemployment rate drop by half. He also set up the Bureau of the Budget to prepare the United States federal budget. Harding promoted a successful world naval program. In August 1923, Harding suddenly collapsed and died to be succeeded by Vice President Calvin Coolidge.

Elected in his own right in 1924, Coolidge gained a reputation as a small-government conservative, and also as a man who said very little. His famous quote was in 1925 *"After all, the chief business of the American people is business. They are profoundly concerned with buying, selling, investing and prospering in the world."* Under the Republican regime business again grew large. The Great War had ruptured much of Europe's industry, which in the early stages of reconstruction caused demand for American goods. Domestically, new products like automobiles and radios were made available to the lower economic classes through instalment payments, promoted as hire-purchase rather than debt. During the latter half of the 1920s, steel production, building construction, retail turnover, automobiles registered, even railway receipts advanced from record to record. US gold reserves and the cost to European combatants of the Great War raised the USA to financial pre-eminence in the world until the 1929 Wall Street stock market crash. The United States was undoubtedly the dominant culture of the time.

The combined net profits of 536 manufacturing and trading companies showed such an increase that stock-exchange speculation became rampant. The new Europe which sought to rise from the ashes of war was impressed with the force of American industrialism so those foreign investors with money were more than ready to participate in financing further expansion through the stock-market. Despite an apparently strong economy *"Silent Cal"* Coolidge did not seek a second full term as President in 1928, instead he supported the bid by his Secretary of Commerce, Herbert Hoover.

Republican President Hoover won in a landslide in 1928 with a Republican Congress. In 1929 the USA produced 70% of the world's oil, 50% of its copper, 38% of its lead, 46% of its iron and 62% of its corn. In 1930, fifty percent of the nation's corporate wealth was controlled by two hundred companies; the tobacco, utilities, aluminium, chemicals, dye, communications, and steel trusts dominated more than in 1900. Agriculture had suffered from the 1921 recession and, because of increased production, needed assistance from President Hoover in 1929 to establish the Federal Farm Board and Agricultural Marketing Act.

The collapse of the stock-market burst the Big Prosperity Bubble and exposed the frailty of debt behind corporate wealth. When the Wall Street Crash of 1929 struck less than eight months after he took office, Hoover tried to combat the ensuing Great Depression with government enforced efforts, public works projects such as the Hoover Dam, tariffs such as the Smoot-Hawley Tariff, an increase in the top tax bracket from 25% to 63%, and increases in corporate taxes. These initiatives did not produce economic recovery during Hoover's term, but served as the groundwork for his successor. Hoover was nominated by the Republicans for a second term in 1932 but, blamed as responsible for the Great Depression, he suffered a large defeat at the hands of Franklin D. Roosevelt.

Democrat President Franklin Roosevelt (FDR) set up his New Deal in 1933 and forged a coalition of labor unions, liberals, religious, ethnic and racial minorities (Catholics, Jews and Blacks), Southern whites, poor people and those on relief. He had a Republican Senate and only a narrow majority in the House of Representatives. President Roosevelt's New Deal philosophy was to instigate a major economic and social shift in the nation which would revitalise industry, away from industrial dictatorship and privileged enterprise to more equitable opportunities for the people to share in the nation's wealth. During the famous "hundred days" of 1933, anti-depression measures passed Congress with incredible speed. He created credit and extended government support (and control) over much of the US economy. In December 1933 the 21st Amendment to the Constitution was ratified ending the disastrous experiment of Prohibition. The big business of crime, enriched by illegal drinking, had expanded its substantial base into other areas. With the apparent success of early schemes evident, Roosevelt became bolder in 1934 and 1935 with introduction of the Social Security Act dealing with a raft of public social benefits, the Resettlement Act allowing farm reconstruction, and the Wheeler-Rayburn Act which targeted taxes from corporations and undivided profits. The USA had developed a limited welfare state, twenty years after extending voting rights.

One failure of the Big Deal was its failure to stop the growth of monopoly, or maybe oligopoly, in American economic life. In 1937 three companies produced 80% of the nation's cars, three companies made nearly 100% of the steel, and one manufacturer controlled nearly 100% of the aluminium output.

In the 1936 presidential election, Roosevelt campaigned on his New Deal programs and carried every state except Maine and Vermont. The New Deal Democrats won even larger majorities in Congress. The Supreme Court became Roosevelt's primary focus during his second term, after the court overturned many of his programs. Roosevelt stunned Congress in early 1937 by proposing a law allowing him to appoint up to six new justices but this was successfully opposed even by his own Party because it would have upset the constitutional separation of powers. Nevertheless, by 1941 Roosevelt had appointed eight of the nine justices of the court which began to ratify his policies.

The economy improved rapidly from 1933 to 1937, but then relapsed into a deep recession. Roosevelt at first had massive support from the rapidly growing labor unions, but they split into bitterly feuding AFL and CIO factions. Disunity weakened the Democratic Party in the elections from 1938 through 1946. In the November 1938 election, Democrats lost six Senate seats and 71 House seats.

In November 1937 Germany and Japan signed an anti- Comintern pact shortly after Mussolini had announced a Rome-Berlin axis. Japan invaded China and bombed USS Panay. US Congress was determined not to allow the US to get involved.

When war broke out in Europe in 1939, sentiment in the USA was with the Allies, but Roosevelt's hands were tied by the Neutrality Act of 1935 which denied trade with, or loans to, belligerent nations. Only after the fall of France in 1940 did Congress act to re-arm, with conscription for the first time, and provide loans to the allies. Roosevelt openly defied the Neutrality Acts by passing the Destroyers for Bases Agreement, which, in exchange for military base rights in the British Caribbean Islands, gave fifty WWI American destroyers to Britain. The agreement with Britain was a precursor of the March 1941 Lend-Lease Agreement, which began to direct massive military and economic aid to Britain, the Republic of China, and later the Soviet Union. The military-industrial complex was stimulated.

Roosevelt introduced White House staff under the Reorganisation Act 1939 which created the Executive Office of the President (EOP) which increased White House Staff from 33 people. From 1939 new units of EOP were established. Estimates of White House staff in 2005 were 1850 persons.

The two-term presidential tradition had been an unwritten rule since George Washington declined to run for a third term in 1796. FDR systematically undercut prominent Democrats who were angling for the nomination in 1940. At the Democratic Convention, Roosevelt sent a message saying that he would not run unless he was drafted, and that the delegates were free to vote for anyone. Then the auditorium sound system (controlled by the pro-FDR city administration) broadcast appeals to vote for Roosevelt. He was nominated overwhelmingly on the first ballot, and won the 1940 election with 55% of the popular vote and a Democratic Congress. Roosevelt became the first US president to serve three terms.

Important political figures, mainly from the opposition, were still determined to stop Roosevelt from involving the USA in a European war. Roosevelt initiated FBI and Internal Revenue Service investigations of his loudest critics, though no legal actions resulted. The military buildup spurred economic growth. There was a growing labor shortage, accelerating the Great Migration of African-Americans, farmers and rural populations to manufacturing centers. Roosevelt initiated a *"shoot on sight"* policy that effectively declared naval war on Germany. In July 1941, Roosevelt had ordered Henry Stimson, Secretary of War to begin planning for total American military involvement. Roosevelt was firmly committed to the Allied cause well before the December 1941 attack on Pearl Harbour by Japan, which might not have been a surprise to some. The government expressed shock because of no formal declaration of war, but history suggests that after two wars in the nineteenth century without formal declarations, this was the Japanese pattern. There was also the sour Japanese memory of Commander Perry enforcing US will on Japan in 1854 through armed might.

War against Japan was declared immediately. Roosevelt immediately converted the Depression government controls over the American people into the commitment of the USA to undertake the defence of Europe and the Pacific. The impact of forces and resources on the War was immediately tremendous, although the turning point was not apparent until late 1942. In 1942, war production increased dramatically, but still fell short of the goals established by the President, due in part to manpower shortages. The effort was also hindered by numerous strikes by union workers, especially in the coal mining and railroad industries, which lasted well into 1944. Roosevelt formed a new body, the Joint Chiefs of Staff, which made the final decisions on American military strategy. Roosevelt avoided the State Department and conducted high level diplomacy through his aides, especially Harry Hopkins.

Those parts of the economy not already controlled by the government were under new bureaucratic offices. World War II demonstrated the tremendous resources of the USA and its unbridled energy. Without in any way disparaging the courage of the men who fought to make the world safe for democracy, it was US resources that largely decided the result of the war. The Americans dominated armies and logistics. American financial dominance was also recognised by the international Bretton Woods Conference in 1944, which created the International Monetary Fund and effectively subordinated the world's currencies to the US dollar.

The tide of war was well in the Allies favour when a tired, reluctant Roosevelt was re-elected for a fourth term in 1944. He died not long after his inauguration in 1945, leaving his Vice President Harry Truman to deal with war and peace.

Roosevelt dominated the American political scene not only during the twelve years plus of his presidency, but also for decades afterward. He had orchestrated the realignment of voters that created the Fifth Party System. FDR's New Deal Coalition united labor unions, big city machines, white ethnics, African-Americans, and rural white Southerners. He also influenced the later creation of the United Nations and Bretton Woods currency realignment. The relative prosperity of America brought another wave of European immigration. The immigrants from many countries, coupled with the return of armed servicemen who had served throughout the world, softened the insular American culture.

It was left to Harry Truman to authorise the use of atomic weapons against Japan. Germany surrendered in May 1945, followed by Japan, shattered by the atomic bomb, in September 1945. Unlike the earlier World War, America was inclined to international co-operation, so that the first meeting in San Francisco of the United Nations in April 1945 enjoyed full United States support. Problems with wartime ally Russia, politically alienated from America since the advent of Communism in 1919, began at the Potsdam peace talks, to lay the foundation for the Cold War. It was Truman's policy "to *help free people maintain their institutions and their integrity against aggressive movements that seek to impose upon them totalitarian regimes*". Peace also brought problems to Truman at home, where he lost a number of more left-leaning Roosevelt appointees from his administration, and encountered a recalcitrant Congressional opposition.

In 1946 Congress was returned with a Republican majority for the first time since 1928. Truman's Doctrine continued *"to support free people who are resisting attempted subjugation by armed minorities or by outside pressures."* Congress accepted the Truman Doctrine and European Recovery Program (Marshall Plan) of 1947, but little else. Truman recognised that American isolationist sentiment was alive even in peacetime, so that his policies committed to containment of Russian expansion; and alliance, including financial support, with democratic anti-communist nations. Russia countered with the creation of Cominform and Comecon, involving its satellite neighbours. The Cold War had begun. The Central Intelligence Agency (CIA) was formed in 1947.

Another split between Northern and Southern Democrats over civil rights looked like giving the 1948 election to the Republican Dewey. By taking to the road, campaigning against a "do nothing" Republican Congress, Truman was narrowly re-elected. He still had a recalcitrant Congress, in which Southern Democrats often supported the Republicans to block legislation. In 1949 the government had agreed to the production of the new super bomb (the H-Bomb) of huge destructive capacity. After Republican success in the 1950 Congressional elections, only elements of Truman's foreign policy were successful.

The occupying forces of Korea, USSR in the north and the USA south of the 38th parallel, had forced Korean partition in 1945. In June 1950 elements of the North Korean army crossed the 38th parallel into South Korea, which triggered the UN Security Council (in the absence of USSR) to raise troops (mainly US) to oppose them. General Douglas Macarthur was Commander in Chief of UN Forces. In October 1950, Communist China entered the conflict on a "volunteer" basis. Truman immediately sent in US troops and gained UN approval for the Korean War. In 1951 Truman dismissed Macarthur over difference in policy, particularly the use of nuclear weapons, and encountered renewed public dissension.

By the 1952 election, right-wing sentiment was such that the war hero General Dwight Eisenhower, drafted by the Republicans, was easily elected. The public was sure that *"Ike would end the war in Korea and kick Communist butt"*. Under Eisenhower, the Republicans also controlled Congress by a thin margin, but were far from united as some factions had moved further to the right than others. The mood was epitomised by the spread of anti-communist *"McCarthyism"*, from the actions of Republican Senator Joseph McCarthy and his permanent investigations body, the House Un-American Activities Committee. Not until 1954 was McCarthy censured. In such an atmosphere, Eisenhower's "middle-of-the road" policy continued to face problems with Congress, so that many major issues were passed over.

On the foreign policy front, which by then was particularly important to America, Eisenhower was under the influence of his Secretary of State, the strongly anti-Communist John Foster Dulles, and his equally right-wing brother, Central Intelligence Agency (CIA) Director Allen Dulles. Under Eisenhower, a special committee was established to undertake clandestine activities without the direct knowledge of the President. Under its auspices the CIA undertook covert actions in Iran in 1953 to unseat the Mossadeq regime. The Dulles brothers dominated this committee, but similar committees continued under future US administrations to undertake dubious activities of which the President could deny that he approved. The later 1986 Iran-Contra affair would have been handled by such a special committee without President Reagan's direct knowledge. It was the Dulles' doctrine to launch a massive retaliation of nuclear weapons in the event of war with Russia or China.

Early in 1953, the French asked Eisenhower for help in French Indochina against the Communists, supplied from China, who were fighting the First Indochina War. Chief of Staff Matthew Ridgway dissuaded the President from intervening by presenting a comprehensive estimate of the massive military deployment that would be necessary. In February 1955, Eisenhower dispatched the first American soldiers to Vietnam as military advisors to Diem's army. After Diem announced the formation of the Republic of Vietnam (RVN, commonly known as South Vietnam) in October, Eisenhower immediately recognised the new state and offered military, economic, and technical assistance.

In 1955, the Supreme Court asked that desegregation of schools proceed *"with all deliberate speed"*, but this was resisted, sometimes violently by some states. *"Ike's"* personal popularity was more than sufficient to allow his re-election in 1956, but the Republicans lost control of Congress. In November 1956, Eisenhower forced an end to the combined British, French and Israeli invasion of Egypt in response to the Suez Crisis. Eisenhower had ended the Korean conflict without completely alienating China, and had acted decisively in the Suez crisis, despite offending England. After the Suez Crisis, the United States became the protector of unstable friendly governments in the Middle East via the *"Eisenhower Doctrine"* to stop the spread of Communism. In 1958, he sent 15,000 US troops to

Lebanon to prevent the pro-Western government from falling to a Nasser-inspired revolution. Eisenhower misread the world and domestic opinion following the launch of the Russian satellites Sputniks I and II. The President claimed that the satellites simply represented scientific achievement. The world and the US public were frightened that Sputnik represented military superiority which would allow Soviet domination. The mood was not helped by delays to America's own satellite program caused by an inefficient Defence Department and inter-service rivalry. Nor was it helped in 1957 when Eisenhower suffered a stroke.

In 1957, in response to the calling out of the Arkansas National Guard to prevent racial integration in Little Rock, Eisenhower sent in Federal troops. The issue of African-American (Negro) rights had festered since the civil war, and the Civil Rights Act 1957 endeavoured to strengthen voting safeguards, but the issue would continue to inflame the South, well into the 1960s.

With an eye to the 1960 election, Senator Lyndon Johnson of Texas attacked the shortcomings of the Eisenhower administration's military policies. He was joined by other Democrats, stimulated by reports from the competing military services of the weapons gap against Russia. The Democrats produced a clean sweep of the 1958 Congressional elections with the biggest majority in both Houses since Roosevelt in 1936.

In 1960 Eisenhower, the oldest serving US president, backed his Vice President Richard Nixon, who was chosen as Republican candidate on the first ballot. The Democrat opponent, John Kennedy, was the son of roguish multi-millionaire Joseph Kennedy, who had cultivated sufficient political and media influence necessary to push his son to the top of national politics. The surprise Democrat vice-presidential candidate was the political machinist, Lyndon Johnson, from Texas, a state notorious for electoral fraud but essential for victory. Credible accusations have been since made that Johnson was the choice made known to Joseph Kennedy by the shadowy criminal organisation known as *"the Mafia"* whose support was to be a key to Democrat success in Illinois. The narrow but successful election of the Kennedy *princeps* was the first of many based on a well financed public relations machine, but maybe the only one influenced by organised crime.

In his 1961 parting address Eisenhower warned America about the dangers from the military-industrial complex. *"This conjunction of an immense military establishment and a large arms industry is new in the American experience. The total influence -- economic, political, even spiritual -- is felt in every city, every State house, every office of the Federal government. We recognise the imperative need for this development. Yet we must not fail to comprehend its grave implications. Our toil, resources and livelihood are all involved; so is the very structure of our society. In the councils of government, we must guard against the acquisition of unwarranted influence, whether sought or unsought, by the military-industrial complex. The potential for the disastrous rise of misplaced power exists and will persist. We must never let the weight of this combination endanger our liberties or democratic processes. We should take nothing for granted. Only an alert and knowledgeable citizenry can compel the proper meshing of the huge industrial and military machinery of defense with our peaceful methods and goals, so that security and liberty may prosper together."*

The warning was not heeded because the first American Catholic president, and the youngest, Kennedy was immediately confronted by Russia in a warming Cold War, against which, in true Boston-Irish fashion, he issued the challenge that America was willing to pay any price for the survival of liberty. This stance was particularly liked by the military-industrial complex, as was America's competition in the Space Race triggered by the Russian April 1961 successful launch of a man into orbit. The abortive Bay of Pigs, Central Intelligence Agency (CIA) sponsored invasion of Cuba, was planned before his inauguration but Kennedy let it proceed in April 1961. As one of his first presidential acts, Kennedy asked Congress to create the Peace Corps with his brother-in-law, Sargent Shriver, as the first director. Through this program, Americans volunteered to help underdeveloped nations in areas such as education, farming, health care, and construction.

In May 1961 Kennedy dispatched Lyndon Johnson to meet with South Vietnam's President Ngo Dinh Diem. Johnson assured Diem more aid in moulding a fighting force that could resist the Communists. Kennedy announced a change of policy from support to partnership with Diem in defeat of Communism in South Vietnam. Late in 1961, the rebel Viet Cong began assuming a predominant presence, initially seizing the provincial capital of Phuoc Vinh. Kennedy increased the number of helicopters, military advisors, and undeclared US Special Forces in the area, but he was reluctant to order a full-scale deployment of troops. In early 1962, Kennedy formally authorised escalated involvement when he signed the *"National Security Action Memorandum – Subversive Insurgency War of Liberation"*. Secretary of State Dean Rusk voiced strong support for US involvement. "Operation Ranch Hand", a large-scale aerial defoliation effort, began on the roadsides of South Vietnam.

When Kennedy discovered in 1962 that the Soviet Union had installed missiles in Cuba that had the potential to deliver nuclear weapons to the USA, he ordered a blockade in the Caribbean. Armed with CIA intelligence that it was not possible for the Soviets to launch an *all-out* attack on the USA, Kennedy faced down the Soviet's Khrushchev. The fallible CIA intelligence did not reveal that Khrushchev was in fact ready to launch a nuclear missile. Following an exchange of letters Khrushchev found a way to back down an hour before the planned launch. The confrontation had brought the world to the brink of nuclear war.

In 1963, South Vietnamese generals, led by *"Big Minh"*, overthrew the Diem government, arresting and then killing Diem and Nhu. Kennedy was shocked by the deaths. He found out afterwards that Minh had asked the CIA field office to secure safe-passage out of the country for Diem and Nhu, but was told that 24 hours were needed to procure a plane. Minh responded that he could not hold them that long. Kennedy's domestic program was more Democrat oriented, calling for Federal aid to education, medical care for the aged, and enlargement of civil rights. A domestic confrontation occurred following civil rights riots in Alabama resulting in the arrest of campaigner Martin Luther King and the calling out of 3000 Federal troops. Kennedy's program for African-American (Negro) civil rights was not enacted before he was assassinated in 1963.

In addition to civil rights problems, Democratic President Lyndon Johnson (1963-1969) inherited the deteriorating situation of the undeclared war in Vietnam to which Kennedy had committed the first American troops in November 1961. In August 1964, Johnson was empowered by the Senate to *"repel armed attack"* following an alleged attack on a US destroyer in the Gulf of Tonkin. The captain of the USS Maddox is recorded as saying that his vessel was *".definitely attacked … I think"*. Johnson did not use this power to declare war until he had beaten the Republican hawk, Barry Goldwater, at the 1964 election. Former Defence Secretary McNamara later admitted that the Tonkin attack never happened, but that the Administration acted in good faith. The subsequent bombing of North Vietnam heightened the conflict but Johnson was not prepared to pay the cost, in men and money, of fully pursuing military armed victory.

US military planning was faulted in Vietnam because there appears to have been no realisation that jungle warfare, particularly in the monsoon season, was altogether different from past engagements. There was apparently no use of historical Chinese imperial failures in Vietnam and old intelligence from fighting of WWII in tropical regions such as Burma and New Guinea. No intelligence had been gleaned by the French account of Dien Bien Phu or the book written by their future nemesis General Nguyen Giap. Apparently no studies were followed about difficulties of a fixed army fighting a guerrilla war in hostile jungle terrain.

John F. Kennedy originally had proposed a civil rights bill in June 1963. In late October 1963, Kennedy officially had called the House leaders to the White House to line up the necessary votes for passage. Johnson overcame southern resistance and convinced the Democratic-controlled Congress to pass the Civil Rights Act of 1964, which outlawed most forms of racial segregation. In 1965, Johnson achieved passage of a second civil rights bill, the Voting Rights Act, which outlawed discrimination in voting, thus allowing millions of southern blacks to vote for the first time. In accordance with the Act, several states, *"seven of the eleven southern states of the former confederacy"* – Alabama, South Carolina, North Carolina, Georgia, Louisiana, Mississippi, Virginia — were subjected to the procedure of pre-clearance in 1965, while Texas, home to the majority of the African-American population at the time, followed in 1975.

Johnson's problems began to mount in 1966. The press had sensed a "credibility gap" between what Johnson was saying in press conferences and what was happening on the ground in Vietnam, which led to much less favourable coverage of Johnson. In the congressional elections of 1966, the Republicans gained three seats in the Senate and 47 in the House, reinvigorating the conservative coalition and making it more difficult for Johnson to pass any additional Great Society legislation. Johnson had escalated the war effort continuously from 1964 to 1968, and the number of American deaths rose. As casualties mounted and success seemed further away than ever, Johnson's popularity plummeted.

In domestic politics, Johnson had fared better than Vietnam policy with legislation that achieved objectives of improving civil rights, health care, housing and transport. Civil rights heated up after the assassination of Martin Luther King in April 1968. Unfortunately the financial cost of supporting bread and battles (Vietnam, Space, and the Cold War) was enormous and unsustainable. The "war tax" belatedly introduced by Congress in 1968 was far too little, too late. Between 1965 and 1975, the United States spent $111 billion on the war ($686 billion in FY2008 dollars). This resulted in a large federal budget deficit. In 1968, ahead of the Presidential election, Johnson decided to pursue negotiated peace in Vietnam and not stand for re-election. By this time Johnson had lost control of the Democratic Party, which was splitting into four factions, each of which despised the other three.

Republican Richard Nixon was narrowly successful in 1968 largely because the Democrats were in confusion in a climate of media criticism over the war. President Kennedy's brother Bobby was assassinated in June 1968 during the primaries before he could officially stand as a presidential candidate. Vice President Hubert Humphrey ran without Johnson's support. Democrats did not fully unite behind Humphrey. A third candidate, George Wallace, the segregationist from Alabama also split the Democrat vote. The Democrats however still controlled Congress. Nixon and his National Security Advisor, Henry Kissinger, were relatively successful in foreign policy, seeking rapprochement with China. Nixon's visit to the People's Republic of China in 1972 opened diplomatic relations between the two nations, and he initiated *détente* and the Anti-Ballistic Missile Treaty with the Soviet Union the same year. Although Nixon initially escalated America's involvement in the Vietnam War, he subsequently ended US involvement by 1973.

At home Nixon was not so successful, because of civil unrest from the civil rights movement which had become allied to the anti-Vietnam protest movement. Sentiments were aroused by the portrayal of the war on television. When in 1970 Nixon extended the military draft, students rebelled, at times violently. The general working public, many of whom knew men fighting, were somewhat appalled at the actions of what were portrayed as privileged students. These people reacted against the left-wing sentiment of the sixties in cyclical support of a relatively right-wing president.

The imposition of wage and price controls to combat inflation was of more concern to middle class America, than Nixon's forced break in August 1971 from the 1946 Breton Woods agreement, which finally recognised that the US dollar was unsound. By election time in 1972, inflation did appear under control and the economy sound. It was a sign of a divided nation that Republican Nixon won in a landslide, but the Democrats retained control of Congress.

Nixon's second term started badly. In June 1972 a number of men, directly connected to the President, were caught burgling the Democrat headquarters in the capital's Watergate building. This commenced the *"Watergate Scandal"*, investigated by a Democratic Congress and publicised by the Eastern liberal press which had harboured an editorial dislike for Nixon since the 1950s. In July 1973 it was discovered that the President's conversations in the White House were automatically taped. In October Vice President Spiro Agnew resigned under a Maryland corruption cloud. At the same time the Egypt-Syria/Israel war broke out, starting oil price rises that would greatly affect the oil-hungry US economy.

In March 1973 the gold link with the US dollar was permanently abandoned. The US dollar was then tumbling out of control.

Following moves to impeach, Nixon resigned as President in August 1974 in favour of the new Vice President Gerald Ford, who pardoned him the following month. The power of Congress over the Chief Executive, growing over decades, had been fully exercised. The US presidency would never again enjoy its primary role of leading the American people, at least for the remainder of the century.

Congress was also not in the mood to honour Ford's request to provide more assistance in Vietnam in March 1975. In April 1975 Saigon was evacuated of American officials just ahead of North Vietnamese troops. With the conquest of South Vietnam by North Vietnam, nine months into Ford's presidency, US involvement in Vietnam essentially ended. The world would watch on colour television, the might of democratic America humiliated in its first war defeat. In many respects the United States of America had also peaked in terms of global dominance, although economically the rise in the debt/GNP ratio was not confirmed until 1980.

As an example of America's impotence, President Ford and his adviser Henry Kissinger were non-committal when in 1975, Indonesian President Soeharto informed them of the Indonesian intention to occupy the Portuguese colony of Timor. The day after Ford and Kissinger left Jakarta, Indonesia invaded. The annexation of East Timor then became a UN problem at least until 1999.

In 1976 the Democrat Party thought that they could overcome popular rejection of Washington politicians by putting forward an outsider, peanut farmer James Carter of Georgia, whom the power-brokers thought that they could control. He nearly lost to Ford despite the bad press that the incumbent received. President "*Jimmy*" Carter proved to be the "*nice guy*" of his image, but impractical as a Chief Executive of a nation that was under economic strain at a time of international political upheaval. He took office during a period of international economic stagnation and inflation, which persisted throughout his term. The end of his presidential tenure was marked by the 1979–1981 Iran hostage crisis, the 1979 energy crisis, the Three Mile Island nuclear accident, the Soviet invasion of Afghanistan, the United States boycott of the 1980 Summer Olympics in Moscow (the only US boycott in Olympic history), and the volcanic eruption of Mount St. Helens in Washington state.

The Cold War with the Communist Bloc spread, at the same time that revolutions broke out in the Middle East and Central America. The inept Carter administration had no answer to Soviet intrigue and naval expansion, although it did manage to broker a peace accord between Egypt and Israel in 1979. Domestically the US economy suffered from the aftermath of the broken dollar/gold nexus, during which the relative decline of US industrial production was obscured by rising inflation. It appears to me that the bureaucratic domination of facets of American life, post World War II, coincided with an erosion of American leadership quality. I shall leave it to the reader to decide whether the decline of leadership after the 1970s became more marked.

The scene was set for the rise of a conservative politician who could dominate Washington and restore to prominence America's image of itself. The ex-Hollywood movie actor, Ronald Reagan had trouble obtaining the Republican nomination for the 1980 election, but once a runner, produced the "*father-figure*" image that the people were seeking in their time of hero-need. The first president from the Western USA, 70 year-old Reagan won handsomely over "*Jimmy*" Carter who is reputed to have conceded even before the polls closed in California.

In the style of "*Teddy*" Roosevelt, President Reagan was a right-wing figure who "*talked softly but carried a big stick*". His supporting-cast administration produced supply-side economic policies, dubbed "*Reaganomics*" designed to produce a budget surplus, but, through tax cuts and pandering to the military/industrial complex, the spending in fact greatly increased the deficit and government debt. In some respects the money was well spent. The military rearmament plan gave America back its confidence, and is credited with winning the arms race against an even more debt-ridden Russia. Reagan took a hard line against labor unions, announced a new War on Drugs, and ordered an invasion of Grenada. In 1984 President Reagan was overwhelmingly re-elected.

It was under President Reagan that the Wall Street/Washington power complex grew into a strong political power. The combination of powerful Wall Street banks, notably Goldman Sachs, JP Morgan Chase and Morgan Stanley, and the US Treasury allowed financial deregulation which would allow the excesses of the nineteen nineties to expand through to the twenty-first century.

By the mid 1980s, Health Management Organisations (HMOs) began to dominate both the organisation of health care and reimbursement to physicians. This led to the healthcare industry alliance with government that allowed extremely high costs of pharmaceuticals and hospitals/doctor services with little systematic oversight and control. There was no political will to reform the healthcare sector despite the damage to low and middle ranks of the populace.

In 1985 the USA had 520,000 members of its armed forces abroad (including 65,000 afloat). That number was substantially more than British Empire deployments in peacetime at the height of its power. Never-the-less the Joint Chiefs of Staff opined that the numbers were insufficient despite a trebling of the defence budget since the late 1970s. The deficit had ballooned to $202.8 million and debt to $1823.1 million.

In 1986 a scandal overtook the Reagan administration (Iran-Contra Affair) under which the proceeds from covert arms sales to Iran were used to fund the Contra rebels in Nicaragua, specifically outlawed by Congress. President Reagan professed ignorance of the plot's existence (plausible deniability). A report by Congress concluded that *"If the president did not know what his national security advisers were doing, he should have"*.

Reagan's Vice President George H. Bush won the Republican nomination for 1988 largely because he was associated with the Reagan popularity. Bush and his running mate Dan Qayle were successful after another relatively dirty campaign against Democrat Michael Dukakis, governor of Massachusetts. However Bush's Republican presidency was restrained by a Democratic Congress. Foreign policy drove the Bush presidency: military operations were conducted in Panama and the Persian Gulf.

The undeclared Cold War between the capitalist West and the communist East, first manifested in the Soviet blockade of Berlin in 1948, and occasionally heated with conflicts such as Korea, Cuba and Vietnam, lasted well into the 1990s. The Soviet Union, at times allied with China in the Cold War, was the only major power to threaten American world cultural dominance, at a huge cost to its domestic economy and that of Eastern Europe. Reagan's Strategic Defence Initiative (SDI) against the Soviet Union, assisted by the cost of the Russian involvement in Afghanistan, was finally successful when the Soviet economy commenced to disintegrate in 1989. The Berlin Wall, separating East and West Germany was breached and torn down in November 1989. The Russian regime and economy collapse in 1991 caused the break-up of the USSR, and largely freed Eastern Europe from Communist dominance.

The 1980s also saw a wave of Hispanic immigration into the US from Mexico, the Caribbean and South America. Mexican immigration in particular, legal and illegal, had a great effect on the culture of the southern border areas that America had conquered in the 1830s and 1840s. Florida saw a great influx of refugees from Cuba, with the *Mariel* boatlifts. Most of the *"Marielitos"* were people wanting to escape from communism, and have succeeded in establishing their roots in the US. Fidel Castro sent some 20 thousand criminals directly from Cuban prisons, as well as mentally ill persons from Cuban mental institutions, with the alleged double purpose of cleaning up Cuban society and poisoning the USA.

Saddam Hussein, the dictator of oil-rich Iraq effectively challenged the hegemony of the world's remaining superpower, when he invaded Kuwait in 1990. Under the influence of major oil corporate/military transport complex, Bush crafted an international alliance to respond to Iraq, which was remarkably successful in the five days Gulf War. The fighting alliance, which included Arab states, would not support the invasion of Iraq's capital Baghdad, or the destruction of Saddam Hussein. The Iraqi dictator's continued defiance took the bloom off victory.

At $220 billion in 1990, the deficit had grown to three times its size since 1980. Bush was dedicated to curbing the deficit, believing that America could not continue to be a leader in the world without doing so. He began an effort to persuade the Democratic controlled Congress to act on the budget; with Republicans believing that the best way was to cut government spending, and Democrats convinced that the only way would be to raise taxes. Bush faced problems when it came to consensus building. Bush reneged on a 1988 campaign promise not to increase taxes and after a struggle with Congress, signed an increase in taxes that Congress had passed.

The apparent triumph in US foreign policy failed to create the image of Bush as a strong leader but he might still have been re-elected in 1992 had the campaign not turned into a three-way race. Bush's Democrat opponent was William *"Bill"* Clinton, the smooth governor of Arkansas, whose youthful image was compared to that of the assassinated John Kennedy. Splitting the vote was Texan millionaire independent Ross Perot who had a strong Reform Party economic platform but showed political ineptness.

Several factors were significant in Bush's defeat. The ailing economy which arose from recession may have been the main factor in Bush's loss. Conservative Republicans pointed to Bush's 1990 agreement to raise taxes in contradiction of his famous *"Read my lips: no new taxes"* pledge. Clinton won, but immediately ran into trouble with a recalcitrant Congress. The Republicans pushed an investigation of Clinton's links with a financial scandal in Arkansas where his wife Hillary Clinton had been involved with the Whitewater Development Corporation. In the 1994 mid-term elections the Republicans won control of both houses of Congress, as well as the biggest states' legislative victory in a generation. This led to the appointment of a partisan Special Prosecutor who expanded the investigation to include Bill Clinton's sexual peccadilloes.

It is possible that the expensive relentless pursuit of evidence against the President, especially of sexual misconduct, produced a sympathy vote or a rebound against a divided Republican leadership in 1996. As well, Clinton had presided over the longest period of peacetime economic expansion in American history, and signed into law the North American Free Trade Agreement. Whatever the cause, Clinton was narrowly re-elected. The Congress stayed Republican. Clinton's second term was dominated by consistent Republican pursuit of presidential sexual misconduct and later lying to the American people. He rapidly became a *"lame duck"* when the Special Prosecutor discovered his sexual relationship with a White House intern. An impeachment movement failed.

In response to the 1998 Al-Qaeda bombings of US embassies in East Africa, that killed a dozen Americans and hundreds of Africans, Clinton ordered cruise missile strikes on terrorist targets in Afghanistan and Sudan. First was a Sudanese Pharmaceutical company suspected of assisting Osama Bin Laden in making chemical weapons. The second was Osama Bin Laden's terrorist training camps in Afghanistan.

To stop the ethnic cleansing and genocide of Albanians by anti-guerilla military units in the former Federal Republic of Yugoslavia's province of Kosovo, Clinton authorised the use of US Armed Forces in a NATO bombing campaign against Yugoslavia in 1999, named Operation Allied Force. The U.N. Court ruled genocide did not take place, but recognised, *"a systematic campaign of terror, including murders, rapes, arsons and severe maltreatments"*. The term *"ethnic cleansing"* was used as an alternative to *"genocide"* to denote not just ethnically motivated murder but also displacement, though critics charge there is no difference. Slobodan Milošević, the President of Yugoslavia at the time, was eventually charged with the *"murders of about 600 individually identified ethnic Albanians"* and *"crimes against humanity."*

Twenty-First Century

Clinton oversaw an apparent boom of the US economy. Under Clinton, the United States had a projected federal budget surplus for the first time since 1969. The *dot-com* bubble burst, numerically, in March 2000, when the technology heavy NASDAQ Composite Index, peaked on the stock exchange at 5,048.62. By 2001 the bubble was deflating at full speed. A majority of the *dot-coms* ceased trading after burning through their venture capital, many having never made a profit. Investors often referred to these failed *dot-coms* as "*dot-bombs*".

The 2000 election was between Clinton's Vice President Albert Gore, and the son of past President Bush, George W. Bush. Although Gore won the popular vote, the Electoral College vote was so close that it hinged on Florida, governed by Bush's brother. After several legal contests, the election was moved to the Supreme Court which decided on a recount to Bush in a split decision. Bush thus became the first President since Benjamin Harrison in 1888 to win the presidency while losing the popular vote. The influence of the small states is exaggerated in the Electoral College and in the Senate, and tends to favour the Republicans. The Senate was narrowly Republican but in June 2001 Senator Reynolds declared himself an independent available to the Democratic caucus, giving Democratic control.

Less than a year into the George "*Dubyah*" Bush presidency, Islamic terrorists flew passenger planes into the twin tower World Trade Centre in New York, and the Pentagon in Washington. The Bush response to the loss of over 2000 people was to declare *War on Terror* and, in particular, on the suspected terrorist mastermind Osama bin Laden, Saudi-born leader of the Al Qaeda war band in Afghanistan. Afghanistan was then governed by the Islamic Taliban regime which apparently supported Al Qaeda. The US and allies invaded Afghanistan in October 2001 to engineer a change of government and search for Al Qaeda leaders.

The Bush regime came to be dominated by right-wing *neo-conservatives* led by Defence Secretary Donald Rumsfeld who advocated war against Iraq. It had long been a *neo-conservative* plan to take over Iraq as part of Middle East realignment to protect Israel. The potential to control Iraqi oil appealed to Bush political supporters. The Bush Administration attempted to persuade the United Nations to sanction the invasion of Iraq, but failed to convince the Security Council of the presence of Iraqi weapons of mass destruction. The UN had become a huge unwieldy partisan bureaucracy. The increase in membership of the large number of ex-colonial nations had caused an excess of democracy, not unlike that experienced by the Roman Senate in Empire, and, then also being enjoyed in US domestic politics. On doubtful intelligence, Bush convinced the Republican Congress to allow him to wage a pre-emptive war, and Iraq was invaded by a

"Coalition of the Willing" (USA, UK and Australia) in 2003. The US declaration of war in Iraq was the first since 1941 because the wars involving the USA in the interim (including Vietnam) were undeclared wars.

It has been stated that the abrogation by Congress to President George W.Bush of the right to determine United States ability to conduct war, was non-democratic and an example of a dictatorial Presidency. However the Bush Presidency was extended in 2004 when the *religious right* energised a popular vote. Bush won the South and Mid-America which outvoted the Democrats from the cities. The subsequent revised Cabinet was slightly more right-wing in reflection of the apparent Bush right-wing mandate.

With a Republican Congress, Bush also promoted policies on the economy, health care, education, social security reform, and amending the Constitution to disallow same-sex marriage. He signed into law broad tax cuts, the Patriot Act (criticised for ignoring civil liberties concerns), and Medicare prescription drug benefits for seniors. Bush announced the US would not implement the Kyoto Protocol on global warming that had been negotiated by the Clinton Administration in 1997, and agreed to by 178 other countries, but never ratified by the US Senate.

Bush successfully ran for re-election against Democratic Senator John Kerry in 2004, in another relatively close election. After his re-election, Bush received increasingly heated criticism from across the political spectrum for his handling of the Iraq War, Hurricane Katrina, and numerous other controversies. As a result, the Democratic Party won control of Congress in the 2006 elections. In December 2007, the United States entered its longest post–World War II recession, which included a housing market correction, a subprime mortgage crisis, soaring oil prices, and a declining dollar value. The *"Great Recession"* was re-branded the *"Global Financial Crisis"* prompting the Bush Administration to enact multiple economic programs intended to preserve the country's financial system. In September 2008, the crisis became much more serious, beginning with the government takeover of *Fannie Mae* and *Freddie Mac,* followed by the collapse of Lehman Brothers and a federal bailout of American International Group for $85 billion. Bush proposed a financial rescue plan to buy back a large portion of the US mortgage market. A key part of the proposal was the federal government's plan to buy up to $700 billion of illiquid mortgage backed securities (MBS) with the intent to increase the liquidity of the secondary mortgage markets and reduce potential losses encountered by financial institutions owning the securities.

Barack Obama began his presidential campaign in 2007, and in 2008, after a close primary campaign against Hillary Clinton (former President Clinton's wife), he won sufficient delegates in the Democratic Party primaries to receive the presidential nomination. He then defeated Republican nominee, Vietnam veteran John McCain, in the general election, and was inaugurated as the first African-American president on January 20, 2009. Nine months after his election, Obama was named the 2009 Nobel Peace Prize *laureate*.

During his first two years in office with a Democratic Congress, Obama signed into law economic stimulus legislation in response to the *Great Recession* in the form of the American Recovery and Reinvestment Act of 2009 and the Tax Relief, Unemployment Insurance Reauthorisation, and Job Creation Act of 2010. Other major domestic initiatives in his first term include the Patient Protection and Affordable Care Act, often referred to as *"Obamacare"*; the Dodd–Frank Wall Street Reform and Consumer Protection Act; and the *Don't Ask, Don't Tell* Repeal Act of 2010. He later became the first sitting US president to publicly support same-sex marriage. In foreign policy, Obama ended US military involvement in the Iraq War, increased US troop levels in Afghanistan, signed the New Start arms control treaty with Russia, ordered US military involvement in Libya, and ordered the military operation that resulted in the death of Osama bin Laden by US Navy SEALs.

The Tea Party movement was an American political movement that was primarily known for advocating a reduction in the US national debt and federal budget deficit by reducing US government spending. The Tea Party made public protests in 2009 and was apparently aligned with the Republican Party. 38 candidates for Congress were identified with significant Tea Party support in the 2010 mid-term elections and all were running as Republicans. Tea Party candidates were less successful in the 2012 election, winning four of 16 Senate races contested, but losing approximately 20% of the seats in the House that had been gained in 2010.

In November 2010, the Republicans regained control of the House of Representatives, as the Democratic Party lost a total of 63 seats, and after a lengthy debate over federal spending and whether or not to raise the nation's debt limit, Obama signed the Budget Control Act of 2011 and the American Taxpayer Relief Act of 2012.

A controversy arose in July 2011 over the raising of the federal debt limit, which was needed to prevent a default by the United States government. Republicans in

Congress, led by Tea Party followers, demanded spending cuts in the budgets for 2012 and subsequent years in return for raising the debt limit. On August 1, the Budget Control Act of 2011 passed the House 269–161, with 66 Republicans and 95 Democrats voting against the bill. On August 2, it passed in the Senate 74–26, and was signed into law by President Obama the same day. August 2 was also the date estimated by the department of the Treasury that the borrowing authority of the US would be exhausted.

Obama was re-elected president in November 2012, defeating Republican nominee Mitt Romney, and was sworn in for a second term on January 20, 2013. The Republican Party retained its majority in the House of Representatives, but the Democrats picked up slight majority control of the Senate, winning two net seats.

During his second term Obama promoted policies related to gun control in response to the Sandy Hook Elementary School shooting, called for full equality for Lesbian Gay Bisexual Transgender (LGBT) Americans, and his administration filed briefs which urged the Supreme Court to strike down the Defense of Marriage Act of 1996 and California's Proposition 8 as unconstitutional. In foreign policy, Obama continued the process of ending US combat operations in Afghanistan.

A similar controversy to 2011 began in January 2013 and ended in October 2013 with the passing of the Continuing Appropriations Act, 2014, though the debate continues. In August 2013, Treasury informed Congress that if the debt ceiling was not raised in time, the United States would be forced to default on its debt sometime in mid-October. In September, Treasury announced that extraordinary measures would be exhausted no later than October 17, leaving Treasury with about $30 billion in cash, plus incoming revenue, but no ability to borrow money. The US Government went into a partial shutdown on October 1, 2013, with about 800,000 Federal employees being put on temporary leave. On October 16, the Senate passed the Continuing Appropriations Act, 2014, a continuing resolution, to fund the government until January 15, 2014, and suspending the debt ceiling until February 7, 2014, thus ending both the United States federal government shutdown of 2013 and the United States debt-ceiling crisis of 2013. In February, 2014 the Congress agreed to raise the debt ceiling to its legal limit until March 2015 so that the matter would not be fought over in the Mid-term Election.

As well as injecting government funds into the economy, the Federal Reserve has been printing money by buying large amounts of government debt.

In early 2014 Obama's approval ratings had fallen to below 40% as left-wing liberals blame the Tea Party ideologues of interfering with big-spending policies. Conservatives blame Obama's populist lurch to the left in a centre-right nation that is discouraging the work ethic in an over-regulated society. At time of writing many Americans reflect a fear that the nation is losing its position as the world super-power and heading in the wrong direction. The harsh split of political parties is making the USA ungovernable at a time when monetary discipline will be required to control the effects of money-printing.

> *"I used to say that politics was the second lowest profession and I have come to know that it bears a great similarity to the first."*
>
> Ronald Reagan 1979

US Monetary History

America has been printing money in times of crisis since the Continental Congress printed money at a rapid rate to fund the Continental army's expenses and pay off loans from foreign nations. As a result, the colonies experienced severe inflation and depreciation of the Continental dollar. Debts incurred during the American Revolutionary War and under the Articles of Confederation amounted to $75,463,476.52 on January 1, 1791. The United States has continuously held public debt ever since, except for about a year during 1835–1836.

In 1792, Congress passed the Mint and Coinage Act. It authorised the Federal Government's use of the Bank of the United States to hold its reserves, as well as establish a fixed ratio of gold to the US dollar. As America's largest lender, the Bank of the United States affected other banks when credit was tightened. In 1792 a busted cartel of William Duer sparked the bust of the speculative boom in the markets of Philadelphia and New York. Alexander Hamilton used the Bank of the United States to funnel cash to troubled lenders, and stopped the crisis. Hamilton thus set the precedent for public finance as a remedy for over-extended lending by private banks.

Gold and silver coins were legal tender, as was the Spanish *Real*. In 1792 the market price of gold was about 15 times that of silver. Silver coins left circulation, exported to pay for the debts taken on to finance the American Revolutionary War. At the time gold was priced at $17.92 per ounce which lasted until 1834.

When President Madison assumed office in 1809, the federal government had a surplus of $9,500,000 and by 1810 the national debt continued to be reduced, and taxes had been cut. There was a sharp increase in the debt as a result of the War of 1812.

The first Bank of the United States' twenty-year charter was scheduled to expire in 1811. While Madison's Treasury Secretary said the bank was a necessity, Congress failed to re-authorise it. As the absence of a national bank made war with Britain very difficult to finance, in 1814 Congress passed a bill chartering a second national bank. Madison vetoed it. In 1816, Congress passed another bill to charter a second national bank; Madison signed the act, having learned from the war with Britain that the bank was needed.

With the Coinage Act of 1834, Congress passed an act that changed the mint silver/gold ratio to approximately 16 to 1. Gold discoveries in California in 1848, and later in Australia, lowered the gold price relative to silver; this drove silver money from circulation because it was worth more in the market as bullion than as money. The gold price rose to $20.67 per ounce which lasted until 1934.

In January 1835, President Jackson paid off the entire national debt, the only time in US history that has been accomplished. However, this accomplishment was short lived. A severe depression from 1837 to 1844 caused the national debt to increase to over $3.3 million by January 1, 1838 and it has not been paid in full since. Strongly against the national bank, Jackson vetoed the renewal of the charter of the Second Bank of the United States and ensured its collapse. Some modern economists have argued that the *Panic of 1837* was caused by the bank policies of the Jackson administration, with the power to create money being distributed into decentralised banks, most of which would then continue to cause a massive inflationary bubble.

The *Panic of 1837* was followed by a five-year depression, with the failure of banks and then-record-high unemployment levels. Van Buren's *"Independent Treasury"* system did not pass Congress until 1840. It gave the Treasury control of all federal funds and had a legal tender clause that required (by 1843) all payments to be made in specie. Passage of the Independent Treasury Act of 1848 placed the US on a strict hard-money standard. Doing business with the American government required gold or silver coins.

The *Panic of 1857* began in summer of that year, brought on mostly by the people's over-consumption of goods from Europe to such an extent that the Union's specie was drained off; overbuilding by competing railroads, and rampant land speculation in the West. Britain financed America's current account by buying American assets which included railroad stocks. Most of the state banks had overextended credit, to more than $7.00 for each dollar of gold or silver. The crisis was precipitated by the collapse of an insurance company, Ohio Life, which had been highly leveraged in railroad stocks. Banks dumped stocks which exacerbated falls. British banks associated with America began to fail. A new class of banking, discount houses, was most vulnerable because of lending without even reasonable reserves.

The Republicans considered the Congress to be the culprit for having recently reduced tariffs. In 1857 the final crisis of the free banking era began as American banks suspended payment in silver, with ripples through the developing international financial system.

President Buchanan's response, outlined in his first Annual Message to Congress, was "*reform not relief*". While the government was "*without the power to extend relief*", it would continue to pay its debts in specie, and while it would not curtail public works, none would be added. He urged the states to restrict the banks to a credit level of $3 to $1 of specie, and discouraged the use of federal or state bonds as security for bank note issues. The economy did eventually recover, though many Americans suffered as a result of the *panic*.

Another sharp increase in the debt occurred as a result of the Civil War. The debt was just $65 million in 1860, but passed $1 billion in 1863 and reached $2.7 billion by the end of the war. Due to the inflationary finance measures undertaken to help pay for the most uncivil US Civil War, the government found it difficult to pay its obligations in gold or silver, and suspended payments of obligations not legally specified in specie (gold bonds). This led banks to suspend the conversion of bank liabilities (bank notes and deposits) into specie. In 1862 paper money was made legal tender. It was a *fiat* money (not convertible on demand at a fixed rate into specie). These notes came to be called "*greenbacks*". During the following forty-seven years, 55% of the national debt was paid off by inflated "*greenbacks*" but the debt would never get below $900 million again.

At the end of his first term in early 1873, President Grant signed the Coinage Act making gold the only money standard (dollars would be exchanged on demand only for gold) in furtherance of hard money policy. The collapse of a New York brokerage house in 1873 sent ripples through Wall Street and other banks and brokerages that owned railroad stocks and bonds found themselves ruined as well in the *Panic of 1873*. Grant believed that, as with the collapse of the Gold Ring in 1869, the *panic* was merely an economic fluctuation that affected bankers and brokers. He responded cautiously, instructing Treasury Secretary William Adams Richardson to purchase $10 million in government bonds, thus injecting cash into the system. These purchases curbed the panic on Wall Street, but a five-year industrial depression, later called the Long Depression, nonetheless swept the nation. Eighty-nine of the nation's 364 railroads went bankrupt.

In 1867 Alaska, rich in gold had been purchased from Russia. In 1874, a year after the 1873 crash, the United States Congress passed legislation called the Inflation Bill of 1874 designed to confront the issue of falling prices by injecting fresh greenbacks into the money supply. Under pressure from business interests, President Grant vetoed the measure. Grant later pressured Congress for a bill to further strengthen the dollar by gradually reducing the number of greenbacks in circulation. After losing the House to the Democrats in the 1874 elections, the lame-duck Republican Congress did so. In January 1875, Grant signed the Specie Payment Resumption Act into law.

President Hayes vetoed the Bland-Allison Act that would have put silver money into circulation and raised prices, insisting that maintenance of the gold standard was essential to economic recovery. In 1878, Congress overrode Hayes's veto to pass the Silver Purchase Act, in a similar but more successful attempt to promote "easy money." With the resumption of convertibility in June 1879, the government again paid its debts in gold, accepted greenbacks for customs and redeemed *greenbacks* on demand in gold. *Greenbacks* were therefore perfect substitutes for gold coins.

One of the most volatile issues of the 1880s was whether the currency should be backed by gold and silver, or by gold alone. The issue cut across party lines, with western Republicans and southern Democrats joining together in the call for the free coinage of silver, and both parties' representatives in the northeast holding firm for the gold standard. Because silver was worth less than its legal equivalent in gold, taxpayers paid their government bills in silver, while international creditors demanded payment in gold, resulting in a depletion of the nation's gold supply.

Shortly after Grover Cleveland's second term began, the *Panic of 1893* struck the stock market, and he soon faced an acute economic depression. The *panic* was worsened by the acute shortage of gold that resulted from the increased coinage of silver, and Cleveland called Congress into special session to deal with the problem. The debate over the coinage was as heated as ever, but the effects of the *panic* had driven more moderates to support repealing the coinage provisions of the

Sherman Silver Purchase Act. Depletion of the Treasury's gold reserves continued nonetheless, but at a lesser rate, and subsequent bond issues replenished supplies of gold. At the time, the repeal seemed a minor setback to *silverites*, but it marked the beginning of the end of silver as a basis for American currency.

Rapid economic growth marked McKinley's presidency. He promoted the 1897 Dingley Tariff to protect manufacturers and factory workers from foreign competition, and in 1900, he secured the passage of the Gold Standard Act.

By 1907 there were 22,000 banks in America without any central bank. As well, the growth of trusts expanded the money supply when these "trustees" undertook acceptance of deposits, and riskier activities of underwriting and distribution of shares, in competition with banks. Whereas banks were required to hold 25% assets as cash, trusts faced only a 5% minimum. Large sums of money were attracted to trusts by higher rates than banks could pay.

The prestigious Knickerbocker Trust suffered from a run on banks caused by a failed corner of United Copper shares by two embezzling bankers who triggered the *panic of 1907*. Then flowed runs on the Trust Company of America and Lincoln Trust. Although John Pierpont Morgan tried to organise pools of cash, interest rates reached 125% and the run on banks spread. Surviving banks commenced innovative but illegal cheques to make up for lack of cash, which eventually calmed the panic. The obvious need for a reserve bank of last resort resulted in a National Monetary Commission that led to the 1913 Reserve Bank Act.

Debt increased again during the Great War (1914–1918), reaching $25.5 billion at its conclusion (19.1%GNP). This was followed by eleven consecutive surpluses that saw the debt reduced by 36% at the end of the 1920s. Under President Harding, federal spending declined from $6.3 billion in 1920 to $5 billion in 1921 and $3.3 billion in 1922. The financing of the Great War through loans ($10,000million+) meant that with peace, gold had to flow from Europe across the Atlantic in quantities in excess of the sixteenth century precious metals flow to Europe from the New World. Arguments over war debts embittered relations on both sides. The policy of Capitalism meant that debts had to be repaid, rather than be forgiven as a gesture of international co-operation. The WWI debts were never all repaid, and eventual defaults in the 1930s encouraged America's further national isolationism.

The fledgling Reserve Bank was in a quandary because prices in shops were falling while the stockmarket boomed. Should interest rates be raised to slow speculation or should rates be lowered to stimulate the economy. In 1928 the Fed raised rates. The increase from 3.5% to 5% was insufficient to slow speculation but did hurt America's flagging industries.

The *1929 crash* followed the speculative stockmarket boom that had taken hold in the late 1920s. During the latter half of the 1920s, steel production, building construction, retail turnover, automobiles registered, even railway receipts advanced from record to record. A crescendo of stock-exchange speculation had led hundreds of thousands of Americans and Europeans to invest heavily in the stockmarket. A significant number of them were borrowing money to buy more stocks. By August 1929, brokers were routinely lending small investors more than two-thirds of the face value of the stocks they were buying.

Stockmarkets are always sensitive to the future state of commodity markets and the slump in Wall-street predicted for May by Sir George Paish, arrived on time. In June 1929 the commodity position was endangered by a severe drought in the Dakotas and the Canadian West, plus unfavorable seed times in Argentina and Eastern Australia. When it was seen that, at this figure, the American farmers would get rather more for their smaller crop than for that of 1928, stocks went up again, and from far and wide orders came to buy shares at bargain prices for the profits to come. Then in August the wheat price fell when France and Italy were bragging of a magnificent harvest and the situation in Australia improved. This sent a shiver through Wall Street and stock prices quickly dropped. On October 24, 1929, with the Dow just past its September 3 peak of 381.17, the market finally turned down, and panic selling started. Bank failures followed. Nearly 11,000 banks failed between 1929 and 1933 and the money supply dropped by over 30%.

Together, the 1929 stock market crash and the Great Depression formed the largest financial crisis of the 20th century. The *Panic of 1929* has come to serve as a symbol of the economic contraction that gripped the world during the next decade. Reflecting the advance of modern communications, the falls in share prices on October 24 and 29, 1929 were practically instantaneous in all financial markets, except Japan. In 1933 the Federal Reserve refused to lend and shut its doors. A week long bank holiday was called across the nation. The Federal Deposit Insurance Commission was established in 1934 to insure bank deposits up to $2500. Customers saw that deposits in banks were risk-free so recommenced depositing.

The 1929 crash brought the *Roaring Twenties* to a shuddering halt. As tentatively expressed by economic historian Charles Kindleberger, in 1929 there was no lender of last resort effectively present, which, if it had existed and was properly exercised, would have been key in shortening the business slowdown[s] that normally follows financial crises. The crash marked the beginning of widespread and long-lasting consequences for the United States. The Glass-Steagall Act separated banking deposits from bank stockmarket activities which provided some comfort until the twenty-first century. The Glass-Steagall Act was effectively repealed in 1999.

The decline in stock prices caused bankruptcies and severe macroeconomic difficulties including contraction of credit, business closures, firing of workers, bank failures, decline of the money supply, and other economic depressing events. The resultant rise of mass unemployment was seen as a result of the crash, although the crash was by no means the sole event that contributed to the depression.

President Franklin Roosevelt instituted the New Deal—a variety of programs designed to produce relief (government jobs for the unemployed), recovery (economic growth), and reform (through regulation of Wall Street, banks and transportation). The economy improved rapidly from 1933 to 1937, but then relapsed into a deep recession. Debt held by the public was $15.05 billion or 16.5% of GDP in 1930. When Roosevelt took office in 1933, the public debt was almost $20 billion, 20% of GDP. Roosevelt increased the price of gold (devalued the dollar) to $35 per ounce in 1934. Decreased tax revenues and spending on social programs during the Great Depression increased the debt and by 1936, the public debt had increased to $33.7 billion, approximately 40% of GDP. Because of the much larger GNP of the United States, it is difficult to compare the debt/GNP ratio to that of the United Kingdom. As well, the debt figure of the US government does not include that of the individual States.

By 1939, the debt held by the public had increased to $39.65 billion or 43% of GDP. The buildup and involvement in World War II, during the presidencies of Democrats Franklin D. Roosevelt and Harry S. Truman, led to the largest increase in public debt. Public debt rose over 100% of GDP to pay for the mobilisation before and during World War II. Public debt was $251.43 billion or 112% of GDP at the conclusion of the War in 1945 and was $260 billion in 1950. State debt would have increased the overall figure by a further 5%GNP. Public debt for war effectively stimulated the US economy but no one has called it Quantitive Easing.

Delegates from all forty-four Allied nations gathered in Bretton Woods, New Hampshire, United States, for the United Nations Monetary and Financial Conference, also known as the Bretton Woods Conference. The delegates deliberated during July 1944, and signed the Agreement on its final day. The chief features of the Bretton Woods system were an obligation for each country to adopt a monetary policy that maintained the exchange rate by tying its currency to the US dollar, and the ability of the IMF to bridge temporary imbalances of payments. The US dollar was pegged to the price of gold at $35 per ounce. After the end of World War II, the US held $26 billion in gold reserves, of an estimated world total of $40 billion (approx 65%). The strength of the US economy, the fixed relationship of the dollar to gold ($35 an ounce), and the commitment of the US government to convert dollars into gold at that price, made the dollar as good as gold. In fact, the dollar was even better than gold: it earned interest and it was more flexible than gold.

The public debt fell rapidly after the end of World War II, as the US and the rest of the world experienced a post-war economic expansion. Unlike previous wars, the Korean War (1950-53) was largely financed by taxation and did not lead to an increase in the public debt.

In 1960 Robert Triffin, Belgian/American economist, noticed that holding dollars was more valuable than gold because constant US balance of payments deficits helped to keep the system liquid and fuel economic growth. What would later come to be known as Triffin's Dilemma, was predicted when Triffin noted that if the US failed to keep running deficits, the system would lose its liquidity, not be able to keep up with the world's economic growth, and, thus, bring the system to a halt. But incurring such payment deficits also meant that, over time, the deficits would erode confidence in the dollar as the reserve currency created instability.

The first effort to maintain the official gold price was the creation of the London Gold Pool in November 1961 between eight nations. The theory behind the pool was that spikes in the free market price of gold, set by the morning gold fix in London, could be controlled by having a pool of gold to sell on the open market, which would then be recovered when the price of gold dropped. In 1967, there was an attack on the pound sterling and a run on gold in the sterling area, and in November 1967, the British government was forced to devalue the pound. US President Lyndon B. Johnson was faced with a brutal choice, either institute protectionist measures, including travel taxes, export subsidies and slashing the budget—or accept the risk of a *"run on gold"* and the dollar.

In January 1968 Johnson imposed a series of measures designed to end gold outflow, and to increase US exports. This was unsuccessful; however, as in mid-March 1968 a run on gold ensued. The London Gold Pool was dissolved, and a series of meetings attempted to rescue or reform the existing system. All attempts to maintain the peg collapsed in November 1968, and a new policy program attempted to convert the Bretton Woods system into an enforcement mechanism of floating the gold peg, which would be set by either *fiat* policy or by a restriction to honour foreign accounts. In March, 1968 Congress repealed the 25% requirement of gold backing of the dollar, as well as the US pledge to suspend gold sales to governments that trade in the private markets. This led to the expansion of the private markets for international gold, in which the price of gold rose much higher than the official dollar price.

Another aspect of the internationalisation of banking was the emergence of international banking consortia. Since 1964 various banks had formed international syndicates, and by 1971 over three quarters of the world's largest banks had become shareholders in such syndicates. Multinational banks can and do make huge international transfers of capital not only for investment purposes but also for hedging and speculating against exchange rate fluctuations. By 1968, the attempt to defend the dollar at a fixed peg of $35/ounce had become increasingly untenable.

At the time President Nixon took office in 1969, inflation was at 4.7%pa— its highest rate since the Korean War. The *Great Society* had been enacted under Johnson, which, together with the Vietnam War costs, was causing large budget deficits. There was little unemployment, but interest rates were at their highest in a century. Nixon's major economic goal was to reduce inflation; the most obvious means of doing so was to end the war. This could not be accomplished overnight, and the US economy continued to struggle through 1970, contributing to a lackluster Republican performance in the midterm congressional elections (Democrats controlled both Houses of Congress throughout Nixon's presidency). Reinforcing the relative decline in US power, and the dissatisfaction of Europe and Japan with the system, was the continuing decline of the dollar—the foundation that had underpinned the post-1945 global trading system and expansion.

With inflation unresolved by August 1971, and an election year looming, Nixon convened a summit of his economic advisers at Camp David. He then announced temporary wage and price controls, allowed the dollar to float against other currencies, and ended the convertibility of the dollar into gold. Unusually, this decision was made without consulting members of the international monetary system or even his own State Department, and was soon dubbed the *Nixon Shock*. Meeting in December 1971 at the Smithsonian Institution in Washington D.C., the Group of Ten signed the Smithsonian Agreement. The US pledged to peg the dollar at $38/ounce with 2.25% trading bands.

After he won reelection, Nixon found inflation returning. He re-imposed price controls in June 1973. The price controls became unpopular with the public and businesspeople, who saw powerful labor unions as preferable to price board bureaucracy. The controls produced food shortages, as meat disappeared from grocery stores and farmers drowned chickens rather than sell them at a loss. The Smithsonian Agreement failed to encourage discipline by the Federal Reserve or the United States government. The dollar price in the gold free market continued to cause pressure on its official rate. Soon after, 10% devaluation was announced in February 1973 to $42.22 per ounce. Japan and the EEC countries decided to let their currencies float. A decade later, all industrialised nations had done so. I have included the prices of gold because the rise in gold price accompanies the devaluation of the US dollar. The average price for gold rose from $97.39 per ounce in 1973 to $615.00 in 1980. The US dollar had effectively devalued 94% from 0.0286oz. gold to 0.0016oz. At $35 per ounce, the dollar was worth 0.0286 ounces of gold. At the peak price of $1924 per ounce in 2011 the US dollar was only worth 0.0005 ounces or 98% devaluation since 1970.

In a 1951 paper, Dr Raymond Wheeler suggested that 1975 or 1980 would be the termination of the fifth 500 year climatic cycle since the sixth century BC. He suggested that the period might be the centre of a cold-dry climatic period corresponding to one in the first century AD, and one in the tenth century. Coincidentally the peak of a golden culture in a 200year cycle was due c.1978. The period 1798 -1975 is only 177 years, but is still within the time-frame indicated by past cycles. I have estimated that the US dominant culture peaked in 1975-80 when the world saw political weakness coupled with the collapse of the US dollar.

In 1974, the Congressional Budget Act reformed the budget process to allow Congress to challenge the president's budget more easily and, as a consequence, deficits became increasingly difficult to control. National debt held by the public increased from its post-World War II low of 24.6% of GDP in 1974 to 26.2% in 1980.

Paul Volcker, a Democrat, was appointed Chairman of the Board of Governors for the Federal Reserve System in August 1979 by President Jimmy Carter and reappointed in 1983 by President Ronald Reagan. Inflation was high and peaked in 1981 at 13.5%pa. In order to counter the high inflation, the Federal Reserve Board led by Volcker raised the federal funds rate, which had averaged 11.2% in

1979, to a peak of 20% in June 1981. The prime rate rose to 21.5% in 1981 as well. Thus, the unemployment rate climbed up over 10%. However, the economy was restored since the tight-money policy was over in 1982.

The actions of the Federal Reserve in raising interest rates so high were unpopular, particularly by consumers who had increasingly become dependent on credit card debt. American dependence on debt had allowed the Federal Reserve had become a fourth pillar of government and not under control of the president. Unfortunately individual banks were not under control of the Federal Reserve so imposed high interest rates were the only way to influence banking credit.

US debt as a percentage of GDP rose throughout the 1980s and early 1990's as federal spending grew; only stabilizing after 1993 as the growth of federal spending slowed relative to the growth of GDP. Federal debt was stable as a percentage of GDP between 1993 and 1997, and dropped nearly 10% as a percent of GDP after 1997. Public debt reached 49.5% of GDP at the beginning of President Clinton's first term in 1993. However, it fell to 34.5% of GDP by the end of Clinton's presidency. The budget controls instituted in the 1990s successfully restrained fiscal action by the Congress and the President and together with economic growth contributed to the budget surpluses at the end of the decade.

The *dot-com bubble* was a historic speculative bubble covering roughly 1997–2000 (with a climax in March 2000. The period was marked by the founding (and, in many cases, spectacular failure) of a group of new Internet-based companies commonly referred to as *dot-coms*. Companies could cause their stock prices to increase by simply adding an "e-" prefix to their name which one author called "*prefix investing*", or a "*.com*" to the end. A combination of rapidly increasing stock prices, market confidence that the companies would turn future profits, individual speculation in stocks, and widely available venture capital created an environment in which many investors were willing to overlook traditional metrics such as Price/Earnings ratio in favor of confidence in technological advancements. The collapse of the bubble took place during 1999–2001. During the presidency of George W. Bush, debt held by the public increased from $3.339 trillion in September 2001 to $6.369 trillion by the end of 2008.

It is not only government debt that was the problem. Modern capitalism has evolved so that debt is essential for the economy to operate. Corporations and small companies cannot continue to expand without borrowed money. Banks do not actually loan money. They create credit by allowing debt, and charge interest for the use of debt. Bankers tend to form an unholy alliance with governments and the Federal Reserve to expand debt. When interest rates are high, debt cannot be expanded at a fast enough pace to keep the economy moving. The economy prospers until the time when debt cannot be repaid. Of course government debt is not as fragile as private debt, but tends to become more vulnerable when debt levels reach gigantic proportions. At that stage all debt becomes a problem.

In the third Christian millennium it has become impossible to expel bankers, as Jews were so often deported by governments to write off debt in the distant past. As the Japanese government in the 1990s has found, bank debt has the potential to collapse a national economy. Eventually, as it has been throughout history, it is the people, and particularly the merchants who will pay the price to save governments and banks from their own folly.

The bursting of the US housing bubble, which peaked in 2006, caused the values of securities tied to US real estate pricing to plummet, damaging financial institutions globally. The *2008 financial crisis* is considered by many economists the worst financial crisis since the Great Depression of the 1930s. It resulted in the threat of total collapse of large financial institutions, the bailout of banks by national governments, and downturns in stockmarkets around the world. In many areas, the housing market also suffered, resulting in evictions, foreclosures and prolonged unemployment. The crisis played a significant role in the failure of key businesses, declines in consumer wealth estimated in trillions of US dollars, and a downturn in economic activity leading to the 2008–2012 global recession and contributing to the European sovereign-debt crisis.

In 2009, President Obama signed the American Recovery and Reinvestment Act of 2009, a $787 billion economic stimulus package aimed at helping the economy recover from the deepening worldwide recession. The Act included increased federal spending for health care, infrastructure, education, various tax breaks and incentives, and direct assistance to individuals, which is being distributed over the course of several years. In March, Obama's Treasury Secretary, Timothy Geithner, took further steps to manage the financial crisis, including introducing the Public-Private Investment Program for Legacy Assets, which contains provisions for buying up to two trillion dollars in depreciated real estate assets. Obama intervened in the troubled automotive industry in March 2009, renewing loans for General Motors (GM) and Chrysler to continue operations while reorganising. Over the following months the White House set terms for both firms' bankruptcies, including the sale of Chrysler to Italian automaker Fiat and a reorganisation of GM giving the US government a temporary 60% equity stake in the company, with the Canadian government taking a 12% stake.

In June 2009, dissatisfied with the pace of economic stimulus, Obama called on his cabinet to accelerate the investment. He signed into law the Car Allowance Rebate System, known colloquially as *"Cash for Clunkers"*, which temporarily boosted the economy. Although spending and loan guarantees from the Federal Reserve and the Treasury Department authorised by the Bush and Obama administrations totaled about $11.5 trillion, only $3 trillion had been spent by the end of November 2009.

Obama and the Congressional Budget Office stated that the budget of 2012 contained $2.469 trillion in receipts and $3.796 trillion in outlays, for a deficit of $1.327 trillion. In October 2013, debt held by the public was approximately $12.122 trillion or about 72.8% of Q2 2013 GDP. Of course the US national debt does not include the debt incurred by State and local governments, so the national debt/GNP ratio, which some already assume is above 100%, is actually higher than the above figures.

The Chairman of the Federal Reserve, Ben Bernanke, had been a student of the Great Depression and apparently reached the opinion that the worst of the depression could have been avoided if more money had been pumped into the economy. Bernanke served as a member of the Board of Governors of the Federal Reserve System from 2002 to 2005. In one of his first speeches as a Governor, entitled *"Deflation: Making Sure It Doesn't Happen Here"*, he outlined what has been referred to as the Bernanke Doctrine.

In late November 2008, the US Federal Reserve started buying $600 billion in mortgage-backed securities in a monetary expansion called Quantitive Easing (QE). Quantitative Easing increases the money supply by flooding financial institutions with capital in an effort to promote increased lending (debt) and liquidity. By March 2009, it held $1.75 trillion of bank debt, mortgage-backed securities, and Treasury notes, and reached a peak of $2.1 trillion in June 2010. Further purchases were halted as the economy had started to improve, but resumed in August 2010 when the Fed decided the economy was not growing robustly. After the halt in June, holdings started falling naturally as debt matured and were projected to fall to $1.7 trillion by 2012. The Fed's revised goal became to keep holdings at $2.054 trillion. To maintain that level, the Fed bought $30 billion in two- to ten-year Treasury notes every month.

In November 2010, the Fed announced a second round of Quantitative Easing, buying $600 billion of Treasury securities by the end of the second quarter of 2011. The expression "*QE2*" became a ubiquitous nickname in 2010, used to refer to this second round of quantitative easing by US central banks. A third round of quantitative easing, "*QE3*", was announced in September 2012. In an 11–1 vote, the Federal Reserve decided to launch a new $40 billion per month, open-ended bond purchasing program of agency mortgage-backed securities. Additionally, the Federal Open Market Committee (FOMC) announced that it would likely maintain the federal funds rate near zero "at least through 2015".

In December 2012, the FOMC of the Federal Reserve announced an increase in the amount of open-ended purchases from $40 billion to $85 billion per month. In June 2013, Ben Bernanke announced a "tapering" of some of the Fed's QE policies contingent upon continued positive economic data. Specifically, he said that the Fed could scale back its bond purchases from $85 billion to $65 billion a month during the upcoming September 2013 policy meeting. He also suggested that the bond buying program could wrap up by mid-2014. The stock market took a hit in June. In September 2013, the Fed decided to hold-off on scaling back its bond-buying program. In 2014, prior to stepping down from the post as Chairman, Bernanke reduced the bond buying program by a further $10 billion per month.

Quantitative Easing has been nicknamed "printing money" by some members of the media and financial analysts, as well as myself. However, central banks state that the use of the newly created money is different in QE. With QE, the newly created money is used to buy government bonds or other financial assets, whereas the term *printing money* usually implies that newly created money is used to directly finance government deficits or pay off government debt (also known as *monetising the government debt*). The Fed is actually reducing banks' bond assets and replacing them with cash, which could be a problem in a future bank crisis. In my opinion the central banks play with semantics.

Quantitative easing will no doubt prevent deflation of assets (including the stockmarket) but may cause higher inflation than desired if the amount of easing required is overestimated and too much money is created by the purchase of liquid assets. The Fed might have confidence that no inflation will occur, based on the Japanese experience 2001-2006 when the result of their QE was disappointing but at least with minimum inflation. Certainly the American velocity of money which should have been rising due to the increased money supply has in fact been falling, in a similar situation to the Japanese experience. In the recent example in the USA, much of the increased money supply appears to have entered the stock market which has slowly increased while other assets have been deflating. The other reason for lack of money velocity has been that banks have not been lending. Banks have increased their reserves with the Federal Reserve to a massive $2.6trillion. Inflation will be a danger when money flows out of the stockmarket and the velocity of money commences to rise. The Fed will probably prefer inflation to deflation.

Increasing the money supply tends to depreciate a country's exchange rates versus other currencies. This feature of QE directly benefits exporters living in the country performing QE, as well as debtors whose debts are denominated in that currency, since as the currency devalues, so does the debt. However, it directly harms creditors and bond holders of the currency, as the real value of their holdings decrease. Devaluation of a currency also directly harms importers, as the cost of imported goods is inflated by the devaluation of the currency.

An estimated increase of 3.5 trillion in the dollar money supply should have had an effect on the value of the US dollar but by April 2014 there was no sign of concerted selling. One reason for lack of dollar selling is that there is no alternative currency which is attractive to investors. There were early signs of the Chinese renmimbi appreciating against the dollar, which could eventually lead to attraction to the currency by international investors.

Throughout hundred years of history the printing of money has proved disastrous to various economies from that of the thirteenth century Chinese Sung Dynasty, fifteenth century Yuan Dynasty, nineteenth century France to the twentieth century Weimar Republic of Germany, and Stalinist Russia. If the US Federal Reserve has a plan to avert such disasters, it has not publically shared it. On the basis of history a devaluation of the US dollar has to be considered likely, but the timing is unknown at the time of writing.

Cohesive Religion

The European Protestant dissenters from Roman Catholicism during the sixteenth century religious revolution were far from united. The important new sects that emerged were Calvinism in Geneva and Holland, Anglicanism in England, and Lutherism in Germany. Soon those sects splintered further. Early in the reign of English Queen Elizabeth I, the sects of Puritanism arose in dissent against the political and Catholic influences of Anglicanism. Following a basically Calvinist doctrine were the Presbyterians, Congregationalists, Baptists and Puritans.

The American Republic was built on a religious foundation brought to the New World initially by Anglican adventurers and Puritan pilgrims. From the first landing, Americans devoted themselves to religion which was the centrepiece of their daily life, guided by clergy elected by the parishioners. In a similar manner to the developing politics, from which early religion was difficult to separate, hierarchical democracy guided the colonies.

As befitting a colony named after Elizabeth I, the *virgin* Queen of England, Virginia in 1607 enjoyed the first non-Catholic church services in America at the Anglican Church in Jamestown. After 1624 Virginia became a royal colony, which attracted further Anglican settlers during the Puritan Revolution. Although forced to adhere to the Puritan Commonwealth under Cromwell, Virginia was practically independent, and prospered under its own representative government. In 1693, an Anglican missionary, James Blair, founded the College of William and Mary. This was not the first university in America. A college for training orthodox Puritan ministers of religion had been founded in 1636, initially called Harvard after the founding beneficiary, but then renamed Cambridge.

John Winthrop became the elected political and religious leader of the Puritan Massachusetts Bay colony in 1637, and enforced orthodoxy through punishment, exclusion and banishment. Democracy still throws up dictators, even if they do come to power in a relatively democratic manner. Winthrop's intolerance and that of his supporters stimulated dissenting settlements in New England such as Providence, later Rhode Island, which became Baptist. The religious breakaways did not secede from their religion but separated their social life away from Puritan control. These colonies were more religiously tolerant than Massachusetts Bay, so attracted other Protestant sects such as Quakers and Baptists. Rhode Island implemented complete separation of church and state, with freedom of speech for all.

The Puritan intolerance was exemplified by the Salem witchcraft trials of 1692 during which self-righteous religious hysteria caused the death of a number of women who did not conform to expected behaviour. The Puritan faith peaked around the turn of the century, as increased Boston mercantilism watered down religious intensity.

Catholicism came to the English colonies through Lord Baltimore who founded the feudal settlement of Maryland in 1633. The feudal settlement rapidly became democratic, even if stratified from the class-based cultivation of tobacco. The initial Maryland religious tolerance was tested during a period of Puritan control in the English Civil War but was formally imposed in 1649 with an Act Concerning Religion. By the 1670's, despite attempts at restriction by the Jesuits, Maryland had become home for a number of refugees of all sects, particularly Quakers.

In 1682 the Quakers had their own settlement established in Pennsylvania, under William Penn. Philadelphia lived up to its name as the "city of brotherly love" when, by the eighteenth century, it became central to a number of religious sects - Quakers, Baptists, Presbyterians, Lutherans, Anglicans, as well as Catholics.

The Carolinas were settled by Barbadian planters to whom religion was not central to their way of life, even though they tended nominally to be Anglican. Coming from a slave-owning society, they imported workers to cultivate the rice-fields, after sugar and tobacco proved less than successful, to create a stratified society.

New York tended to be under both Catholic then Anglican influences, after the earliest Dutch Protestant farmer settlers were left alone when James, the Catholic Duke of York, gained control of the colony around 1674. When James II became King, his official, Sir Edmond Andros, expanded the commerce of New York through warehouses and better anchorages. New York's commercial bias was continued after William of Orange became the Protestant King of England.

The Protestant religion of the colonies was further boosted by the early eighteenth century immigration from Ulster, Scotland, Switzerland and Germany. Commencing in the Housatonic Valley of West Massachusetts, the settlers moved into Connecticut and what became Vermont. Then religiously tolerant New York and Pennsylvania attracted so many immigrants looking for land that they flowed along the inland valleys into the future states of North Carolina, Kentucky and Tennessee.

The sense of independent statehood that grew before the Revolutionary War included a development of a native religion, which through evangelism gave a distinctive American flavour to a number of denominations. The factors behind the American Revolution were mercantile and political, which overshadowed religious issues. The Constitution of the United States was crafted during a period of American history in which religion was not dominant in the life of leading citizens.

Thomas Jefferson and Benjamin Franklin were Deists. George Washington, most probably also a Deist, was not religious and was tolerant of the religions of others. Although many Founding Fathers were practising Christians, the view prevailed that federal laws should exclude religion. The states could concern themselves with religion as they saw fit. The formal separation of church and state was accomplished through the Bill of Rights, and later state legislation.

Anglicanism had been damaged by the Revolution against Britain, particularly in New York, where many Anglicans had remained loyal to the English crown. Those Anglicans, who did not flee to England and Canada, sought to establish a native church. The result was the Protestant Episcopal Church formally established in 1789.

Puritan and Calvinist values already had been weakened by more mercantile interests, and the religious Awakening after Independence overshadowed the orthodox churches in favour of the more American denominations of Deism, Methodism, Baptism and Unitarianism. These were the religions which were transported westward in the great geographic expansion of the nineteenth century, together with revivalist Congregationalism, Presbyterianism and the missionary Episcopal church. Mormonism was popular among great numbers of the lower and lower-middle classes.

The early nineteenth century also bought great numbers of European immigrants, most important of which, in terms of numbers, were Irish Catholics which depleted southern Ireland of a third of its population to have a great influence on Boston and New York. The large scale Catholic immigration caused such social pressure that an anti-Catholic movement took decades to dissolve in the cultural melting pot.

The South had never been particularly affected by Puritan values, and the development of a stratified social order dominated by the slave labour cotton plantation, encouraged a similar hierarchical religion for the upper classes. In the nineteenth century, the Episcopal Church in the South was as selective as the royalist Church of England.

Even the Southern churches of more liberal denominations sublimated their doctrine to defend slavery. The Roman Catholic Church, which had not perceived any moral dilemma with the earlier Spanish and Portuguese slave trade, had been able to expand in America with the acquisition of Florida and Louisiana from the

Spanish and French. The religion might have been attractive to some aristocratic Deep Southern planters of European ancestry, but the smaller immigrant planters tended to be Protestant. Socially conservative evangelical Protestantism grew gradually over the next century as a series of religious revival movements, many associated with the Baptist denomination, gained great popularity in the region. South-eastern and south-central United States became known as the *Bible Belt*. The Southern expansion of Catholicism was also limited because of Protestant propaganda about a Catholic political and military conspiracy, as well as the inability of the hierarchical Catholic Church to convert the majority of the population, the slaves.

In 1839, Joseph Smith, Jr., the founder of the Latter Day Saint movement, visited President Van Buren to plead for the US to help roughly 20,000 Mormon settlers of Independence, Missouri, who were forced from the state during the 1838 Mormon War. The Governor of Missouri, Lilburn Boggs, had issued an executive order on in 1838, known as the "Extermination Order". It authorised troops to use force against polygamous Mormons to "*exterminate or drive [them] from the state*". In 1839, after moving to Illinois, Smith and his party appealed to members of Congress and to President Van Buren to intercede for the Mormons.

In 1844, Joseph Smith and his brother Hyrum were killed by a mob in Carthage, Illinois. Brigham Young assumed leadership over the majority of the Church. To prevent war, Brigham Young led the Mormon pioneers (constituting most of the Latter Day Saints) to a temporary winter quarters in Nebraska and then eventually (beginning in 1847) to what became the Utah Territory. Colonising efforts were seen as religious duties, and the new villages were governed by the Mormon bishops (local lay religious leaders). In 1857 President James Buchanan sent an army to Utah, which Mormons interpreted as open aggression against them. In 1878 the Supreme Court ruled in Reynolds v. United States that religious duty was not a suitable defense for practicing polygamy, and many Mormons went into hiding; later, Congress began seizing church assets. Relations with the United States markedly improved after 1890, such that Utah was admitted as a US state.

The humanitarian evangelism of the mid nineteenth century, combined with the democracy of Northern churches, produced secular movements intended to cure social ills. The temperance movement viewed alcoholic beverages as a major obstacle to social progress, and a cause of poverty and crime. Encouraged by emerging women's suffrage, the Temperance Society managed to promote ineffective laws in thirteen states before 1860. It was only the Civil War that delayed abolition of alcohol until the twentieth century.

The church-inspired anti-slavery movement provided fuel for what became the Civil War. In the 1840s the previous mild verbal disapproval of slavery, particularly in the North, changed to an aggressive intemperate demand for abolition. The Protestant Churches took the view that it was impossible for an American church to remain Christian while condoning slavery. Such talk caused the Southern Methodists to split from the Methodist organisation to found the Methodist Episcopal Church, South. The Southern Baptist Convention and Southern Presbyterian congregations split away from the Northern bodies.

The slavery abolition movement was not based solely on religious grounds, but the Northern churches provided the moral backing for other economic and political ideas. Southern exponents of slavery argued on the basis that men were born neither free nor equal, and that natural rights to liberty do not exist. It was civil society which could grant rights and freedom to those who deserve them. Southern preachers could find justification for slavery in the Bible without too much trouble, since slavery was natural to the Middle East culture of the time when the Bible was written.

Despite the efforts of politicians, the smouldering slavery issue would not go away, for which the churches must take much of the praise, or blame. Abraham Lincoln did not belong to a church, so that his mild opposition to slavery was based on humanitarian grounds, but his political backing came from Northern religious groups. It was the political pressure from, and the economic domination of, the North that led the South to secede. Lincoln's determination to maintain the Union then resulted in the American Civil War. It was however, the support that politicians felt they had from their religious communities that enabled those actions to occur.

The violence of war, and the disastrous destruction of the South apparently shocked the Northern churches out of politics, and the main religious revival in the South was that of the racist Klu Klux Klan. Geographic expansion and economic advancement became much more important to the American people than activist religion, well into the twentieth century.

The apparent need of American Protestants to evangelise did not stay dormant for too long. It was taken by the American churches that the economic success of the United States was due to Protestantism which should be exported to the world as an alternative to the Catholicism that had been spread by *"old Europe"*.

By the 1890s American missionaries had increased their influence in the Pacific Ocean to the stage where they had an influence on local politics. The missionaries and sugar interests were behind political machinations that led Hawaii to become a US territory, which also happened to provide an attractive naval base. The Spanish-American War in 1898 had anti-Catholic overtones, particularly in the Philippines which had excluded Protestant missionaries. American missionaries were among the group proselytising the Chinese which triggered the Boxer Rebellion and US military involvement.

The dawn of the twentieth century saw another religious revival as the churches reached a compromise with Darwinism, and the population sought a social anchor against the storm tide of rapid change. Congregationalists, Methodists, Presbyterians, and Baptists, all multiplied their churches, often including an increasing number of Negroes. The Catholic Church became the numerically dominant single denomination around 1890. New sects such as the Church of Christ Scientist attracted converts from the orthodox churches. In the early years of the century, religious organisations spread their interests into social activities through such avenues as the YMCA and Salvation Army, imported earlier from Britain. The Social Gospel movement tried to influence social and industrial relations. It is indicative that the supporters of Theodore Roosevelt's Progressive party in 1912 should have chosen *"Onward Christian Soldiers"* as their campaign song.

The American expansion of home labour-saving devices and industrial need for labour led to change in the status of women. The women's movements and apparent success of church interference in society, led to a revival of the Temperance movement. The political use of religious and feminist muscle saw success in 1920 with the passing of the 18th and 19th amendments to the Constitution. Some would say that both were proven less than successful, but only the 19th amendment survived, granting the vote to women. The 18th amendment which forbade manufacture, sale and import or export of liquor, was repealed in 1933 by the 21st amendment, after a period of unprecedented lawlessness and illegal drinking.

The social reform movement of the churches was undermined by the ostentatious economic success of the *Roaring Twenties* and the factual failure of prohibition. It was kept alive only when the many poor required assistance in trying to avoid the worst effects of the Great Depression in the 1930s.

There was another burst of religious revivalism after World War II which led to a rise in church attendance by post war America. In 1954 *"In God We Trust"* was adopted as the country's credo. As the 1960s progressed, religion was victimised to some degree by racial turmoil and the Vietnam War, when the nation polarised over legal but unpopular actions by state and federal governments. The Southern churches were active in promoting civil rights, which was supported in principle by the Northern churches. When the civil disobedience over racial issues became blurred with the anti-Vietnam movement, the churches lost favour with both the nation's youth and ruling elite.

In the forty years since the 1960s the major churches have lost between a fifth and half of their membership, and the average age of church members in 1999 was well into middle age. However the new millennium saw a religious revival in rural areas and the South, mainly in the charismatic revivalist protestant faiths. It was held (by Professor Samuel Huntington) that the 2004 presidential election was the most influenced by religion in history. George W Bush owed his re-election to a formula that included conservative Catholics, mainline Protestants, Hispanics, Jews and Mormons. Catholics were the key group with 52% voting for Bush. Barack Obama was assisted to his second presidency by the Muslim vote.

Religion was an integral part of the American Republic since its inception, and was responsible for the development of many of the most commendable features of democracy. In a similar manner to ancient Rome, politicians in the national capital must be seen attending church by their constituents. Only future historians will be able to tell whether the sublimation of religion in the United States since the late 1960s coincided with the peaking of the American Republic culture in the mid 1970s. Certainly aggressive Islam is causing civil problems.

Advances in Technology

Possibly the first important American machinery invention was Eli Whitney's cotton gin, which in 1794 separated cotton lint from the seeds so efficiently that production increased fifty-fold from each gin. By 1810 the invention of the Whitney cotton gin had made the USA the main supplier of cotton to Britain where the consumption had been greatly stimulated by the Industrial Revolution. It was the cotton gin, often later a pirated copy, which increased the South's cotton production and British demand to the levels which changed the culture of the nation. Whitney went on to develop other labour saving machinery in the North which was to provide impetus for its industrialisation. At the behest of Thomas

Jefferson in 1798, Whitney is credited with producing muskets with standardised gun parts to a make America independent of overseas armourers. The idea of standard gun parts was that of a Frenchman, Honore Le Blanc, and there were two other American gun-makers producing guns, but Whitney is credited with the invention of the American System of Manufacture.

In 1814 the Boston Manufacturing Company built an automated version of a Manchester textile mill. Over the next fifty years the Automotive System was used in factories to produce products as diverse as locomotives and sewing machines. In the 1880s an engineer, Frederick Taylor, used a stop watch to further systemise production, and an engineer/psychologist couple, Frank and Lillian Gilbreth, used slow-motion film to improve manufacturing activity. Thus standardisation, automation and time/motion had already been operating before the famous Model-T automobile production line of Henry Ford was commenced in 1908.

America's access to fine cheap timber from its vast forests made shipbuilding a competitive industry from the late seventeenth century. Unheralded American craftsmen improved marine architecture to produce bigger and better ships for fishing and whaling. Commerce with Europe led to the evolution of the Baltimore clippers and Atlantic packet-ships, the designs of which influenced the naval vessels which proved superior to the British ships in the War of 1812. One heralded inventor was Robert Fulton (1765-1815) who, as early as 1798, had designs for a submarine. Fulton was a pioneer of steam, and who in 1811 built the first steamboat on the Ohio River from his shipyard in Pittsburgh.

Although it was the superior naval sailing vessels that earned wartime respect from the British, Fulton scared the enemy with the production in 1814 of the world's first large armoured steam ship. In 1815 Henry Sheve took a paddle-steamer up the Mississippi River from New Orleans to Louisville in twenty-five days, and pioneered the American river steam trade. The majority of domestic commerce was undertaken by water until the building of the railroads. After the 1812 War, steam ships were introduced into the trans-Atlantic trade, which stimulated the building of the clipper ships in Boston and Baltimore. The clippers, with a huge sail area and streamlined hull, initially out-competed steam-ships in the Atlantic because of their speed. The slower, often British, steam vessels became larger to eventually banish the clipper to long voyages around Cape Horn to China and Australia, which still stimulated American global trade.

American trade was initially based on the agricultural exploitation of vast areas of fertile land. The invention of barbed wire in the mid 1870s by two Illinois farmers, Glidden and Haish, to protect agriculture from cattle, opened up vast areas of the South and West to cattle grazing. By the 1840s farmers had the use of iron plows and mechanical reapers, produced by American technology. Combine harvesters appeared in the 1880s. Those parts of America unable to enjoy the river and canal trade were serviced by wagon trade and communicated by pony express.

The English steam powered railroad was introduced to America with the Baltimore & Ohio line in 1830. The railroads expanded at a phenomenal pace to reach 30,000 miles of track, mainly in the North and Northwest, until brought to a pause by the Civil War. The distance dictatorship over American domestic commerce was thus overcome by steam technology.

Commercial communication was still a problem until an American artist/ tinkerer, Samuel Morse, built a practical electrical telegraph in 1837, and obtained government assistance in 1844. In 1856 the Western Union Telegraph Company was formed to cut competition from wildcat line operators, and extended the telegraph line to California in 1861, killing the pony express in the process. The railroads then realised the value of the telegraph, so lines were extended along their tracks.

At the beginning of the Civil War, America imported all of its steel rails, before an ex-telegrapher, Andrew Carnegie, revolutionised the steel business by producing a cheaper superior product than the British. Carnegie used his network of railroad contacts to produce one third of America's steel output.

In 1875 a Scots immigrant who was teaching the deaf in Boston, combined the work of earlier inventors to make a sound reproducing machine. Alexander Graham Bell revolutionised telecommunication through the Bell Telephone Company in 1877.

The manufacture of electricity could not be said to be invented by any one person, because its evolution followed experimentation by many in a number of countries, including America's Benjamin Franklin. Englishman Michael Faraday developed a dynamo c.1825 but it was not until 1858 that the first steam driven electric generator went into operation.

One of the reasons for the slow development of electricity was lack of demand, which was corrected by American Thomas Edison. Edison, another ex-telegrapher, used his experimental skills to make ingenious improvements to the telegraph system, before successfully inventing many devices with wide commercial appeal. His development of the repeating telegraph sparked the idea for the Edison Phonograph, patented in 1877. He applied his ingenuity and perseverance to find a solution to the relatively short life of arc lights. In 1879, apparently independent from an English inventor, Joseph Swan, he produced a carbonised filament light bulb that stayed lit for 170 hours. He was quick to patent his invention and followed up by constructing, in 1881-2 New York City, the electrical power plant to power his light bulbs. Edison then experimented with an electric railroad. In 1887, an electric-powered safety elevator was developed which encouraged further development of "sky-scraper" buildings in New York and Chicago. A hydro-electric power station was constructed in 1893.

Edison's effect on America is so large as to be incalculable. By providing electric power and electric devices (over 1300 US and foreign patents) Edison provided great impetus to civilised living and the consumer society. He researched the production processes of a potential invention, and its market, before utilising the talents of staff in his industrial research laboratory, so that he can be said to be the father of the American process of Research and Development. He also introduced the idea of change for change sake, by improving consumer products which also then had a degree of obsolescence.

After 1912 when the Wright Brothers had successfully manufactured aircraft for commercial use, the Americans enjoyed better practical commercial air-travel connections than were possible in older and smaller countries.

Starting with scientific breakthroughs made during the 1930s, the United States, the United Kingdom and Canada collaborated during World War II in what was called the Manhattan Project to counter the suspected Nazi German atomic bomb project. In August 1945 two fission bombs were dropped on Japan ending the Pacific War. The Soviet Union started development shortly thereafter with their own atomic bomb project, and not long after that both countries developed even more powerful fusion weapons known as "*hydrogen bombs.*" In 1946 Congress established the civilian Atomic Energy Commission (AEC) to take over the development of nuclear weapons from the military, and to develop nuclear power. The AEC made use of many private companies in processing uranium and thorium and in other urgent tasks related to the development of bombs. Work in the United States, United Kingdom, Canada, and USSR proceeded over the course of the late 1940s and early 1950s. Electricity was generated for the first time by a nuclear reactor in 1951. The world's first nuclear submarine was launched in 1954.

Most of today's major pharmaceutical companies were founded in the late 19th and early 20th centuries. Key discoveries of the 1920s and 1930s, such as insulin and penicillin, became mass-manufactured and distributed. Switzerland, Germany and Italy had particularly strong industries, with the United Kingdom, the United States, Belgium and the Netherlands following suit. Legislation was enacted to test and approve drugs and to require appropriate labeling. Prescription and non-prescription drugs became legally distinguished from one another as the pharmaceutical industry matured. The US industry progressed in earnest from the 1950s, due to the development of systematic scientific approaches, understanding of human biology (including DNA) and sophisticated manufacturing techniques. Attempts were made to increase regulation and to limit financial links between companies and prescribing physicians, including by the relatively new US Food and Drug Administration (FDA). Legislation allowing for strong patents, to cover both the process of manufacture and the specific products, came into force in the 1970s. Pharmaceutical manufacturing became concentrated, with a few large companies holding a dominant position throughout the world and with a few companies producing medicines within each country.

Most historians would not classify monetary policy as technology, but I feel that America's climb to world dominance has been due as much to its innovative financial methods, as to its industrial and agricultural technology.

In 1711, the New York City Common Council made Wall Street the city's first official slave market for the sale and rental of enslaved Africans and Indians. In the late 18th century, there was a buttonwood tree at the foot of Wall Street under which traders and speculators would gather to trade securities. In 1792, traders formalised their association with the Buttonwood Agreement which was the origin of the New York Stock Exchange. In 1817, a constitution was drafted which renamed itself the "New York Stock & Exchange Board". It is now by far the world's largest stock exchange by market capitalisation of its listed companies at US$16.613 trillion as of May 2013.

In keeping with what was to become the epitome of capitalism, American colonial governments created paper credit as early as 1690 to overcome the shortage of English specie. The bills of credit were traded at a discount to silver, and the discount grew deeper as excess paper money was printed. Additionally, bankers issued doubtful paper credit on the security of real estate. The English government attempted to stop the practice of money creation, without trying to alleviate the shortage of silver. By 1764 an estimated $22million of unlawful paper was circulating in the colonies. The US Civil War was paid for in paper, after the suspension of specie payments, and only a quarter of the immense cost of war was financed by taxes.

The US dollar was placed in a position of dominance by the system of fixed exchange rates imposed by the Bretton Woods structure of 1945. This system was assisted by legislative restrictions on capital export, including John F. Kennedy's Exchange Equalisation Act. By the early 1970s the maintenance of the gold/dollar standard was restricting domestic monetary supply.

One hundred years after the Civil War, Lyndon Johnson's dilemma in financing the Vietnam conflict without increasing taxes, has been compared with Lincoln's necessity to finance preservation of the Union without lifting tax levels. The morality was entirely different in that Lincoln did not want to increase suffering in the Civil War, whereas Johnson was worried that taxes would turn the public against the Indochina war. Johnson was later blamed, although the actual cause was the American political culture in which raising taxes and cutting spending was politically impossible. However, both presidents printed money to cover the financial deficit.

Lincoln printed "*greenbacks*", not backed by gold reserves. Johnson hid the true cost of the war, and undertook deficit financing where Federal Reserve created money through the banking system, which the government then borrowed through the issue of bonds. The resultant increase in dollars, insufficiently backed by gold reserves, was the same as printing "*greenbacks*". The result was inflation. During the Civil War prices doubled in only a few years in wartime. The inflationary surge of the 1960s and 1970s was not as steep, but it persisted, tripling prices in less than twenty years.

After the Civil War, not the least in response to inflation, the money supply had to be lessened by retiring "*greenbacks*" so that dollars backed by gold could be accepted in international trade. After Vietnam, the inflated US dollar could not be backed by gold, so lost value and forced the world's currencies into a floating-rate regime. The Federal Reserve then had to push interest rates to very high levels to cure inflation and put some value back into the dollar in the 1980s.

America's financial prowess enabled it to lead the world in the production of many technologies that had originated elsewhere. Early experiments in cinema were made in Europe but the first moving pictures to be projected onto a screen were in New York in 1896. The movie house originated in 1902 Los Angeles, which after 1913 became the movie capital of the world (Hollywood).

Television was first demonstrated by Englishman J.L. Baird in 1926, but it was the Russian emigrant to the USA, V.K. Zworykin who patented electric scanning in 1928. Television as a product took years to perfect before it came to market after World War II in 1945. Television allowed the USA to export its culture to the world.

One of the most notable achievements of American technology was the space program and its success of placing man on the moon in 1969. The success of the civilian National Aeronautics and Space Administration (NASA) was based on the scientific ingenuity of former German Nazi aeronautical engineers who were smuggled to America immediately after World War II to work on the USA rocket program. The central figure, Werner von Braun (1912-1977), had his wartime SS records sanitised so that he could attain US citizenship in 1955. Von Braun and colleagues, Karl Debus and Arthur Rudolph, had developed the German military rockets (V1 and V2) during the War, which provided the basis for development of rockets for US satellites and Inter Continental Ballistic Missiles. The first US satellite (Explorer I) was launched by the military in 1958, and Neil Armstrong stood on the Moon's surface in 1969.

The first signs, in the 1970s, that the USA had stumbled as a world technological leader appeared with the transistor. Transistors were invented in the USA by scientists at the Bell Telephone Laboratories in 1948, but the country's electronics industry preferred to protect its investment in vacuum-tube products, so it was left to Japan to incorporate transistors into new consumer products.

Because the twentieth century was an age of technology, there are countless American inventions and innovations which I have not included in the above brief description. I have a deep admiration for the ingenuity of American individuals who thrived under the freedom of democracy, to produce improved devices that enhanced the way of life for most people in the world. However, without denigrating such genii as Edison, there was a pattern similar to that of earlier golden cultures, where innovation was often sourced elsewhere, to be improved vastly by American scientists and technicians.

The Rule of Law

A system of law was initiated in America by the governor of the Virginia Company, Lord de la Ware, and established as early as 1611. In 1629 the

Massachusetts Bay Company became self-governing with the power to pass laws, as well as correct, punish and rule all plantation inhabitants, as long as nothing was contrary to English law. American settlers had a strong desire to live independently under the rule of law, as enforced by elected magistrates from their own, often religious, society. It was the thought that England would take away this liberty, and subvert the laws that had allowed settlers to prosper, which encouraged the War of Independence perhaps more than commercial threats.

After Independence was declared, the states enacted constitutions which by and large adopted the laws that had been made under the old company charters. During the War, fought under the Articles of Confederation, courts under federal judiciary were created by the Continental Congress to hear Admiralty appeals from state courts. After the Revolutionary War, the United States Constitution was drawn up to be finally ratified in 1790. The Judiciary Act 1789 formally established the Supreme Court, in addition to the circuit courts, and federal district courts, which oversaw the Constitutional provision that state constitutions, as well as law, were subordinate to the federal Constitution and laws enacted by Congress. Washington's farewell address in 1796 was a strong statement that America was a country under the rule of law, to which the government would brook no defiance from any association or constituted authority. The number of Supreme Court Justices was originally six, and ranged between five and ten before the 1869 change to the present day nine. The early Justices were often partisan lawyer-politicians, but the culture of the Supreme Court as defender of the public interest evolved to bloom under a far-seeing lawyer-politician, Chief Justice John Marshall.

James Madison (1751-1836) had originally proposed in Constitutional discussions that the federal system exercise a power of veto over state laws, but this was rejected as mirroring the English royal veto. John Marshall, appointed Chief Justice in 1801 by John Adams, effectively implemented Madison's proposal by making the Supreme Court the supreme branch of government above the executive and legislative branches, and the undoubted arbiter of state law. Marshall was a federalist, who approved the philosophy of industrial capitalism, financed by banks, as a means of providing prosperity to an expanding nation within the law. He was opposed in his ideas by the land-owning republican aristocracy who saw the financial power of paper-money bankers as undermining the power of hard working farmers.

In Marbury -v- Madison (1803) Marshall established the Supreme Court's right to declare void and unconstitutional all or part of an Act of Congress or state legislature. In Fletcher -v- Peck (1810), the Court established the inviolability of contracts, placing them beyond reach of state courts and legislatures. Dartmouth College -v- Woodward (1819) established that corporation charters were also contracts and thus protected from legislative interference. McCulloch -v- Maryland (1819) and Osburn -v- Bank of the United States (1824) denied states the right to tax federal institutions, and affirmed the right of Congress to establish a federal bank. In his thirty-four years dominating the Supreme bench, John Marshall guided some 1100 rulings, which affirmed the superiority of federal power with the principle that the federal government may do things not specifically stated in the Constitution providing that the purpose of those acts agrees with the spirit of the Constitution and with the national interest.

The ideas of central power promoted by Marshall were important in nineteenth century America where the frontier spirit was exploding into a multitude of settlements busy creating their own laws, or at least local laws of convenience. The notion of the rule of law in all settlements created a multitude of lawyers who provided themselves with livelihood by dominating state legislatures and following circuit judges. Frontier justice was often abrupt and physically violent, particularly against thieves who disrupted the orderly life of farmer settlers. Whipping, branding and hanging were more effective, and economical, than imprisonment in emerging societies. Attorneys were however often able to minimise the use of the branding iron and the hangman's rope, so, of course were viewed as parasitical by the aggrieved tillers of the soil. A future president of the USA, Andrew Jackson, was an example of the nearly uneducated frontier lawyer, who engaged in land speculation, court pleading and office seeking. Duelling was also common form of justice on the frontier, and Jackson fought his first duel in Tennessee, over court-room abuse, at the age of twenty-one.

It was President Andrew Jackson, a natural opponent of "money power", who clashed constantly with John Marshall and the Supreme Court. Jackson, whose party slogan was *"Equal rights for all, special privileges for none"*, was in conflict with concentrated economic power that had been able to develop under Marshall's legal opinion. In particular President Jackson declared war on the Bank of the United States which was a corporate entity effectively operating as the country's central bank. In his "Veto of Re-charter" Jackson stated *"the authority of the Supreme Court must not be permitted to control the Congress or the Executive when acting in their legislative capacity, but to have only such influence as the force of their reasoning may deserve..."* At the same time Jackson was prepared to go to war with

Southern Carolina when that state attempted to nullify federal law by state law in contravention of the Constitution as earlier affirmed by the Supreme Court.

Jackson extended his philosophical influence when, on John Marshall's death in 1835, he selected as Chief Justice successor, his own crony, Roger B. Taney, who then conducted the Court for thirty years on convictions opposite to Marshall's principles. The Taney Court limited the results of the Marshall Court on Dartmouth College by ruling that a state charter of private business did not imply any privileges greater than those expressly granted. The later Court held the view that a state was entitled to make reasonable regulatory laws even if they appeared to override provisions of the Constitution. The Taney Court is best remembered for the dismissed appeal by a Missouri slave in 1857, known as the Dred Scott Case. The main rulings stated that a negro was not a citizen, and had no right to sue in a federal court; that one could not sue in one state against laws of another state; and that Congress could not forbid slavery in the territories of the United States because it was unconstitutional (Fifth Amendment) that persons be deprived of property ("slaves") without due process of law.

The Dred Scott Case appalled the North, and gave hope for the South that the constitutional law could be interpreted to allow slavery to be extended. The atmosphere created by the Supreme Court decisions provided a climate that enabled the South to be confident in Secession. In his unsuccessful bid for a Senate seat in 1858, an Illinois lawyer, Abraham Lincoln, spelled out his opposition to the threat to the constitution represented by the Dred Scott decision, and the necessity that the Union of the United States must be preserved in its principles as well as territory. Southern secession was already fact when Lincoln was inaugurated as President of the USA in March 1861, but it was Lincoln's insistence on the integrity of the Union that eventuated in Civil War from April 1861. Lincoln ignored Taney's ruling (Merryman *ex parte*) that Congress alone, and not the president, had the power to suspend a writ of habeas corpus in case of rebellion or invasion. Taney was considered a foe of Lincoln until his death in 1864, when Lincoln appointed another lawyer-politician as Chief Justice successor, wartime Treasury Secretary and failed presidential hopeful Salmon P. Chase.

It was Chase's burden to preside over the Supreme Court during Reconstruction, in which cases he took a moderate view, and was less dominating than his immediate predecessors. After the adoption (1868) of the Fourteenth Amendment, the character of litigation before the Court was altered, with many cases alleging that state legislation took liberty or property without due process of law or denied equal protection of the laws. Chase held a dissenting view on the Slaughterhouse case appeal in 1873, in which the Court held that Section 1 of the Fourteenth Amendment was to be considered in connection with the purpose of its framers to guarantee the freedom of former Negro slaves, and was not intended to deprive a state of its legal jurisdiction over the civil rights of its citizens. The Chase dissenting opinion to the conservative position on states' rights subsequently became the accepted position of the courts (Plessy -v- Ferguson 1896) as to the restrictive force of the Amendment.

The women's suffrage movement also tried to use the Fourteenth Amendment, to require states to let women vote, but the Court ruled (Minor -v- Happersett 1875) that *"the Constitution does not confer the right of suffrage on anyone"*. The Court also ruled (United States -v- Reece 1876) that although the Fifteenth Amendment forbade the states to disenfranchise blacks because of race, there was still the power to exclude certain people from the vote for reasons other than race. Women and many Southern blacks would have to wait until the twentieth century to gain access to the democratic process.

As often occurs in history, expansion of the population into new areas did not coincide with a similar expansion of the legal system. In the Western expansion 1850-1920 violence became endemic and communities were forced to establish their own vigilante justice. The popular Southern concept of duelling and honour led in a number of states to the legal right of a man to stand ground if threatened and to kill in self-defence. Gun fighting became the Code of the West, not only by individuals but by corporations such as railroad companies. Law enforcement tended to be localised around townships, and bands of vigilantes led by elected gunmen, town marshals, were not uncommon. It was only well into the twentieth century that courts were sufficiently respected, so that violent vigilante law faded. Even so the right of Americans to bear arms has been ingrained into the American Republic culture, and in the new millennium is causing great concern in densely populated cities where law enforcement is proving difficult against drug gun culture.

The early years of the twentieth century brought America prosperity from industrial expansion, assisted by conservative opinions from the Supreme Court which tended to concentrate on the principle of precedent (*stare decisis*). States were restricted from enforcing laws that restricted businesses in their employment practices and other activities. In a notable exception (Muller -v- Oregon, 1908) the Court, under Chief Justice Melville Fuller, upheld state law limiting the maximum working hours for women. The 1890 Sherman Act was intended to reinforce an anti-trust movement to restrict business monopolies, but was ineffective against business, although successful against labour unions. Trusts continued to concentrate business and capital in few hands through major trusts which numbered 318 in 1904. The Standard Oil Company of Ohio, founded by John D. Rockefeller was one of many ruthless monopolies which successfully avoided anti-trust investigations. In 1911 the Supreme Court, under conservative Taft appointee Edward D. White, dissolved the Standard Oil Trust, and laid the groundwork for the 1914 Federal Trade Commission Act. The Court included Oliver Wendell Holmes, who was known as the "great dissenter" because of his objections to his judicial colleagues' nullification of social legislation as unconstitutional. In 1916 Holmes was joined on the federal bench by another non-political reform-minded jurist in Louis D. Brandeis, and together they presided over a period of the Court's social jurisprudence. Women acquired the right to vote in 1920 with the Nineteenth Amendment to the Constitution. In 1921 another political lawyer was appointed Chief Justice, ex-President William H. Taft.

The prosperous 1920s came to an end with the 1929 stock-market crash, and the subsequent depression introduced the New Deal policies of Democrat President Franklin D. Roosevelt. The "bold experimentation" of Roosevelt's social legislation was not viewed with approval by the Supreme Court from 1935. Taft had been succeeded in 1930 as Chief Justice by another lawyer politician, Charles E. Hughes who had been Secretary of State in the Republican Harding and Coolidge administrations. Hughes was a moderate conservative but was not dominant on the Court, and, with Associate Justice Roberts formed split moderate opinions with the conservative Associate Justices, Butler, McReynolds, Sutherland and Devanter. The liberals were Justices Cardoza, Brandeis and Stone. The conservatives were successful more often than not, in their opinion that the delegation of powers to the President was unconstitutional in that it interfered with the exclusive powers of the states over interstate commerce. Some laws were ruled unconstitutional by the narrow margin of five to four.

In 1937 Roosevelt proposed to reform the Federal judiciary, and get rid of the "nine old men", but Congress was opposed to a measure that could be seen as "*stacking*" the Court. In the event, Hughes' and Roberts' opinions became more liberal so that New Deal measures then enjoyed a slim majority. After some aged Justices retired, Roosevelt was able to replace them with his own appointees. The Court then ruled that Congress was not limited to carrying out its express powers as listed in Article 1 of the Constitution, but might pursue any general welfare objective. It further empowered Congressional ability to tax various state-supported activities, while denying state taxation. The Supreme Court limited the scope of Federal law by an opinion that state law was to be used in Federal courts for diversity suits. By 1941 seven of the nine Justices were Roosevelt appointees, including the influential Felix Frankfurter. World War II in Europe brought with it increased conservative opinions, even from Roosevelt himself, so that the powers of government became even more dominant. At the same time the interpretation of Federal law provided an impetus to the growth in the number of lawyers skilled in compliance with, and contravention of, the increased wide-ranging laws and regulations. Corporation lawyers and Washington attorneys became a feature of the twentieth century.

In the 1950s, individual constitutional rights became a concern for the Court as freedom of speech, and other civil liberties, were brought before it in a climate of government Communist conspiracy investigations. In general the Court ruled that freedom of speech and due process was guaranteed above the alleged needs for internal security and suspected sedition. In this era, it was Congress, rather than the President, which expressed concern that the Supreme Court would not bend to its will. Again, attempts to curb the Court's jurisdiction failed.

By 1954, the Court, although liberal under Chief Justice Earl Warren, was again divided, this time between judicial pacifists and activists. The pacifists, led by Justice Frankfurter, suggested that the Court should avoid the role of policy making. The activists, led by Justices Black and Douglas, argued that it was the duty of the Court to shape the law to ensure that freedoms guaranteed by the Bill of Rights were absolute. The activists achieved success when the Court unanimously ruled (Brown -v- Board of Education of Topeka 1954) that segregated schools were unconstitutional in that they violated the Fourteenth Amendment guaranteeing equal protection under the law. In 1955 the Court issued guidelines for desegregating schools under Federal courts supervision, and urged that the process take place with deliberate speed. The politicians eventually came into line with the Court when the Civil Rights Act passed in 1964, and creation of the Equal Employment Opportunities Commission which had the power to act on complaints of discrimination.

The Court moved further into law enforcement when it ruled (Miranda -v- Arizona 1966) on the steps which need to be taken by law-enforcement officers in detaining alleged criminals, including the right to silence and to be represented by an attorney. Congress effectively overturned Miranda in 1968, but no presidential administration has enforced the political legal interference which was viewed as unconstitutional. Because the Congressional 1968 legislation has not been implemented, there has been no reason for the Court to rule on its legality.

The judicial liberalism of the Warren Court (1953-69) receded in the 1970s with the appointment of Chief Justice Warren Burger by President Nixon, and appointments by other Republican Presidents, Reagan and Bush. The Equal Employment Opportunities Commission had been taking direct action by imposing minority quotas in defiance of the Civil Rights Act, and to a degree this action was legitimised by the Court (Griggs -v- Duke Power Company 1971). The ruling gave protected minorities an automatic presumption of discrimination, with the right to sue without having to show that acts of discrimination had occurred. Race quotas were introduced in government and business, creating a fertile new field for civil rights lawyers. Race, always a problem in America, became a legal minefield as the previously downtrodden exercised real or imagined rights in the courts, universities and the workforce in the 1970s and 1980s. It would appear that in discriminating against majorities, such as white males, the Court did not fulfil the motto inscribed on the outside of the Supreme Court Building – *"Equal Justice Against Law"*. I note that racial problems, involving Hispanics as well as Afro-Americans, increased from around the time when I suggest that the American Republic dominant culture was peaking.

Another Burger Court ruling which possibly should have been in the political domain was that on abortion, which certainly enraged the religious right. In Roe -v- Wade 1973, the Court ruled that a woman has a right to an abortion in the first trimester of pregnancy, contending that it is part of her right to privacy guaranteed by the Fourteenth Amendment. The religious anti-abortionists did not accept the decision and took civil disobedient action ranging from blockades of abortion clinics to murdering pro-choice doctors and activists. The lawlessness of one sector of the community, that one would normally take to be law-abiding, coincided with a large increase in crime in the general population. The sentiment grew that the legal system was not functioning as a justice system.

In 1986 William Rehnquist succeeded Burger as Chief Justice. Under his leadership the Court, still conservative, had taken an active role in reversing or modifying some Supreme Court decisions. The Court restricted the number of cases that it would review by refusing writs of *certiorari* to all but around 4000 of the most important cases. The Rehnquist Court generally took a limited view of Congress's powers under the commerce clause, as exemplified by *United States v. Lopez* (1995). The Court made numerous controversial decisions, including *Texas v. Johnson* (1989), which declared that flag burning was a form of speech protected by the First Amendment; *Lee v. Weisman* (1992), which declared officially-sanctioned, student-led school prayers unconstitutional; *Stenberg v. Carhart* (2000), which voided laws prohibiting late-term abortions; and *Lawrence v. Texas* (2003), which struck down laws prohibiting sodomy. Perhaps the most controversial decision made by the Court came in *Bush v. Gore* (2000), which ended election recounts in Florida following the presidential election of 2000, allowing George W. Bush to become the forty-third US President.

The last quarter of the twentieth century saw law in America become involved in nearly every aspect of a citizen's life, through an expansion of civil rights, both in reality and aspiration, at a time when the regulations under which government exercised its powers increased far beyond those considered necessary, even in wartime. The resultant conflicts, and increased crime, caused a flood of litigation and criminal appeals to higher courts. The expansion of demand for legal services resulted in a huge increase in the number of attorneys and judges, whose importance in society was reflected in their sumptuous remuneration. As is natural when there is a rapid expansion in a profession, there have been a number of legal practitioners whose conduct can be criticised, and others who have become vocal politicians. The high cost of litigation had the effect of restricting legal redress to the more affluent, except in speculative contingent litigation in which lawyers took a large percentage of any successful settlement. The unfortunate effect of having more than three lawyers per thousand population has been the spread from distain of lawyers, to disrespect of law.

Chief Justice John G. Roberts was confirmed by the United States Senate in 2005. Under Roberts the Court has drifted primarily to the right in areas like the death penalty (*Kansas v. Marsh*), abortion (*Gonzales v. Carhart*), the right to privacy (*Hudson v. Michigan*), and campaign finance (*Citizens United v. Federal Election Commission*). In 2008 the Supreme Court heard arguments concerning the constitutionality of a District of Columbia ban on handguns. The Supreme Court ruled that "*The Second Amendment protects an individual right to possess a firearm unconnected with service in a militia, and to use that arm for traditionally lawful purposes, such as self-defense within the home.*"

In 2009, Sonia Sotomayor became the first Hispanic-American to serve on the Supreme Court after being nominated by Barack Obama and confirmed by the Senate to replace the retiring Justice David Souter. In 2010, President Obama nominated Elena Kagan to replace retiring Justice John Paul Stevens. This marked the first time in the history of the Court that three women served as justices, and that no Protestants served (instead, there were six Roman Catholics and three Jews).

A poll conducted in June 2012 by The New York Times and CBS News showed that just 44 percent of Americans approve of the job the Supreme Court is doing. Three-quarters said the justices' decisions are sometimes influenced by their political or personal views.

As a non-American citizen viewing the culture from a distance, I can suggest that the society in the twenty-first century is less imbued with the old values of justice. The retention/improvement of the wealth/power of the ruling class appears to be a dominant factor of practical legal activity in the USA, despite the apparent advancement of individual rights.

> *"Knowledge is of no value unless you put it into practice".*
>
> Anton Chekhov

Government Risk Management - Advance or Decline

The great early strength of the American Republic was its diverse society which became partly unified under religion and the rule of law, so that it was able to raise an army of soldier settlers to enforce its Declaration of Independence from England. The subsequent States were far from united in their cultures, but each State was willing to conform their military duties to the cause. The rank and file were farmers who returned to their small holdings to till the soil after military engagements, but who fought with commendable zeal. The upper classes sought honourable duty in the army, often utilising their own wealth, and once independence became fact, toiled to unite the states under law. The United States of America were lucky in their early leaders, who produced a philosophy which was acceptable to the vast majority of the population, whose main interest was in exploiting the natural riches that the great land had to offer.

Risk from outside the American continent was recognised after Independence in President George Washington's 1796 farewell speech warning that America should keep clear of foreign entanglements, but maintain a respectable defensive policy. The philosophy was formally stated in the message to Congress by President James Monroe in 1823. The Monroe Doctrine asserted that the American continents were no longer to be considered as a field for colonisation by European powers, and that, although the United States would not interfere in European affairs, it would view with displeasure an attempt by the European powers to subject the nations of the New World to their political systems. The doctrine became important in the 1840s and 1850s when Texas, Oregon, Yucatan and Mexico suffered disturbances. America asserted its will.

After a dispute with Britain over Venezuela in 1899, President Theodore Roosevelt raised the *ante* with the 1904 Roosevelt corollary to the Monroe Doctrine, which justified United States intervention in Latin America's affairs to forestall any European intervention. The war with Spain over Cuba was justified by the new view of America's hegemony in the region. The United States acted as an imperial power with economic strength that meant it could not be lightly challenged. This was the sign of the beginning of the climb to global dominance.

When World War I broke out, the Monroe Doctrine allowed the United States to remain neutral without offence to any of the warring parties. The sinking of the Lusitania in 1915 started to affect the American resolve, and after increased German submarine action, President Woodrow Wilson received Congress approval for a declaration of war in April 1917. Because of the isolationist neutrality stance, the United States was not prepared for war in 1916, but quickly mobilised its considerable forces. For the first time men were conscripted into military forces, despite the fact that many would willingly have served. The US Army grew from 200,000 in 1917 to over 4 million at the end of the war. The Navy was better prepared and by mid 1917 eighteen destroyers were operating in the north Atlantic. The Americans introduced new technology in anti-submarine and mine warfare, that seriously impaired the German Navy. It was the "big push" under General Pershing that broke the Hindenburg Line and German morale. It was the need to send armies overseas and the establishment of a competent navy, which justified government curtailment of civil liberties. Further, Wilson's efforts ensured a great degree of independence for the American Expeditionary Forces. The independence of America continued after the war, when it refused to join the League of Nations. Maybe Congress recognised that the USA had already eclipsed Great Britain as a dominant power.

The great Depression, which swept the world in the 1930s, exacerbated the yoke of World War I settlements in Europe, and provided the fertile ground for the rise of totalitarian governments. The National Socialist (*Nazi*) German government of Adolf Hitler and Fascist Italian government of Benito Mussolini re-armed and broke international treaties with apparent impunity. The League of Nations, without the United States, was powerless. The British and French governments operated policies of appeasement. In 1933 Japan left the League of Nations, and no country tried to check Japanese aggression in North East Asia. President Franklin Roosevelt, apparently with the comfort of the popular Monroe Doctrine, concentrated on American domestic policies without seeing the need to study the international lessons of World War I. The Neutrality Acts (1935-9) of Congress empowered the US government to place embargoes on participants from both sides in war, so that assistance could not be provided to previous allies, even after the formal outbreak of war in Europe in September 1939. Despite Japan's proclamation of the "New Order" in Asia, America was still neutral in 1940. Only after the fall of France in June 1940, did Roosevelt allow himself to be persuaded by Bernard Baruch to push for Congressional assistance to European allies. The Lend Lease Act (1941) provided much needed war material for Britain, Russia and China, but risk management measures were still constrained by neutrality.

America's neutrality dilemma changed in November 1941 when the US destroyer "Reuben James" was sunk by German torpedoes. Neutrality was finally dissolved in December 1941 when the Japanese surprise attack destroyed the US naval fleet at the Hawaiian port of Pearl Harbour. If the government had studied Japanese history, it would not have been surprised by the attack. The United States immediately mobilised and depression government controls were extended to convert industry to a war footing, co-ordinate armed forces, ration food and fix prices. Without the sentiment engendered by what was termed "*the infamous Japanese attack*", it is unlikely that the independent-minded American population would have accepted such burdens on their freedom.

Once in the war, the power of a fully focussed dynamic nation allowed the USA to invigorate international fighting forces, even though a turning point was not seen until late 1942. Following the successful invasion of Europe by allied forces in 1944, under US General Dwight Eisenhower, (and President Roosevelt's death in April 1945) Germany surrendered in May 1945. The war in the Pacific had already pushed Japanese forces into retreat when new president, Harry Truman, authorised the atomic bomb to be dropped on Japan in August 1945. US General Douglas MacArthur accepted Japan's unconditional surrender on September 2, 1945.

American past isolationist approach to government risk management was shown to be unreliable after World War I, but it was the surprise attack by Japan which shocked the United States to adopt a new approach to national defence through the establishment of the United Nations (UN) in October 1945 and the International Monetary Fund (IMF) from 1944. As the leading economy and undisputed military leader, the USA could have expected to dominate the international stage, but a recalcitrant Russia threatened American influence. The totalitarian regime of Soviet Russia used its territorial advantage from the close of the War to press for expansion of the Stalinist Communist movement. British Prime Minister Winston Churchill said (1946) *"an iron curtain has descended across the continent of Europe"*. America's response in March 1947 was the Truman Doctrine, basically *"to support free peoples who are resisting subjugation by armed minorities or by outside pressure"*. Thus, in a similar manner that ancient Rome recognised the need to influence internationally after Punic War II, the United States undertook to defend democracy with military and economic might.

In 1947 Truman made former WWII Army Chief of Staff, George Marshall, his Secretary of State who promptly promoted the European Recovery Plan, to provide financial pump-priming for the European democratic economies. Known as the Marshall Plan, ratified by Congress in 1948, the scheme provided over US$10billion to invigorate Europe, with the capitalist by-products of expanding US exports from the military/industrial complex, and establishing the dominance of the US dollar as the currency of international trade. Also in 1947, the Central Intelligence Agency (CIA) was created from a number of wartime intelligence agencies, including the Office of Strategic Services (OSS).

The response from Stalin was to blockade the allied enclave of West Berlin in Communist East Germany. The first victory, in what became known as the Cold War, was from air-power used in the 1948 Berlin Airlift, less publicly backed by movements of US troops and bombers at bases in Britain and Germany. Following the evidence of Soviet aggression, the North Atlantic Treaty was signed in 1949 by the United States, Great Britain, France, Italy, Canada, the Netherlands, Belgium, Denmark, Norway, Portugal, Luxembourg and Iceland. General Eisenhower served as first Supreme Allied Commander, NATO.

The United States did not confine its influence to Europe. In other areas of the world, a huge amount of foreign aid provided assistance to many poorer countries, accompanied with the construction of a network of American military bases, as a buttress against Communism. In 1948 Israel's declaration of independence was supported by the US. One area outside US persuasion was East Asia where the Communist forces of Mao Tse Tung had gained control of China, and Kim Il-Sung had become a Stalin influenced dictator of partitioned North Korea. Stalin's European setback and his courting of China led to his sanction, in 1950, of North Korea's invasion of South Korea.

The USA quickly used its dominance of the UN Security Council to arrange a United Nations defensive force under the command of Japan-based US General Douglas MacArthur. The defence then brilliant victory by MacArthur, maybe the Roman *"Pompey"* of his day, allowed UN forces to advance north of the 38th parallel into North Korea. China, which had swallowed Tibet while the world was focussed elsewhere, introduced *"volunteer"* forces into Korea. The Chinese offensive was contained but MacArthur then planned full scale attacks on China, which he believed were necessary for future peace. Truman was not prepared to countenance such attacks nor the use of atomic weapons. Truman sacked MacArthur, and signalled that the United States was not prepared to risk total war in defence of democracy. The Korean War lapsed into stalemate, then cease-fire in 1953 which remains unresolved by decades of peace-talks.

Truman's presidential successor in 1953, General Dwight Eisenhower, had experienced at first hand the battles against totalitarian power. He proved less belligerent than expected from a military man, while firmly containing Soviet Russia and China. Eisenhower made it known to the Communists that aggression would be resisted with ultimate force if necessary, but that provocation would not be attempted by the USA. The South East Asian Treaty Organisation was established in 1954, with signatories US, Britain, France, Australia, New Zealand, Philippines, Thailand and Pakistan, to resist the spread of Communism from China. Eisenhower did not believe in limited war such as the UN operations in Korea, so was opposed to war over Suez in 1956. He initially refused to involve the US in Indo-China. The Eisenhower Doctrine, which extended the Truman Doctrine to the Middle East, saw US troops in Lebanon in 1958 to avert a Middle East war. The peak of United States risk management was probably reached under Eisenhower.

Eisenhower's departure from the presidency in 1961, appeared to coincide with the emergence of more CIA-dominant US policy. Although the CIA-sponsored Bay of Pigs operation had been planned before his inauguration, President John Kennedy allowed the ill-fated invasion of Cuba to proceed in April 1961. This might have been a response to the Russians putting the first man into Space five days earlier. Soviet Russia, led by Nikita Khrushchev, had already increased Cold War pressure through national liberation struggles in Africa and South America sponsored by the KGB ("*Komitet Gosudarstvennoye Bezhopaznosti* - Committee of State Security). As part of the competition between secret-police influenced super-powers, Russia commenced to install missiles in America's *back-yard*, Cuba. When Kennedy discovered this provocation in October 1962, he confronted Khrushchev in a face-down that brought the world to the brink of nuclear war. Khrushchev blinked first. The missiles were removed.

America had been already giving military (CIA) aid to the South Vietnamese government before Kennedy committed the first 7000 troops in November 1961. Apparent difficulties with Prime Minister Diem led to a CIA-sponsored Vietnam military coup in November 1963 during which Diem was murdered. Kennedy himself was assassinated three weeks later, leaving an increased US involvement to his successor Lyndon Johnson. It is said that the Texan Johnson described Vietnam to members of the National Security Council as "*just like the Alamo*", which, in view of the subsequent disaster, proved to be remarkably prescient.

In August 1964, following a purported North Vietnam attack on the American electronic espionage destroyer "Maddox", Johnson was empowered by the Senate to "*repel armed attack*". He did not use this power until he had beaten the Republican hawk, Barry Goldwater, at the 1964 election. The subsequent bombing of North Vietnam heightened the conflict but Johnson was not prepared to pay the cost, in men and money, of fully pursuing armed victory. The failure to fully commit undoubted forces, and instead to use minimally trained conscripted troops in a war which the Soviet Union was supporting, simply extended an unwinnable campaign. The Vietnam War became increasingly unpopular within the USA where unsavoury fighting scenes involving conscripted working-class youth could be viewed on colour television. Johnson decided not to pursue the 1968 election but to try for peace negotiations. Committed North Vietnam was not interested in a negotiated settlement. President Richard Nixon withdrew military support from Vietnam while pursuing peace negotiations with North Vietnam, and courting China as a counter to the Soviet Union pressure. A cease-fire was negotiated in 1973, but was broken by North Vietnam which gained increasing military superiority. The United States lost its first war when Saigon was overrun and evacuated in April 1975. The military weakness of the USA as a dominant nation was revealed.

A market in US dollars, known as the *Eurodollar* market had developed outside the USA, and outside the control of the US Government. The US balance of payments crisis in 1971, fuelled by Vietnam War spending, had uncovered the fact that the once proud US currency lacked the disciplined foundation laid down by the 1944 Bretton Woods IMF agreement. President Nixon was forced to renounce convertibility of dollars for gold. By 1973, the world's currencies were forced to divorce themselves from the weak US dollar into a floating rate regime.

The October 1973 attack on Israel by Egypt and Syria in the Yom Kippur War was not foreseen by the CIA, and occurred at a time when President Nixon was under intense pressure of Congressional impeachment. Already upset by the inflation caused by a weak US dollar, the Organisation of the Petroleum Exporting Countries (OPEC) was emboldened by the Yom Kippur War into sharply raising the oil price. The USA economy had become dependent on imported oil so that an oligopoly like OPEC could damage the entire fabric of American society. The respect of the United States people for the office of the presidency was already waning when Nixon experienced the Watergate crisis. Following media sensations that organised huge public demonstrations and dollar chaos, Congress increasingly took power away from the presidency. Only distrust between China and the Soviet Union might have maintained the freeze on the Cold War when the USA was particularly vulnerable.

The United States had lost its monetary power and the president had lost his power over Congress c.1975. The monetary and leadership weakness of the US as a dominant nation was revealed. It is my opinion that the United States of America reached its peak as a dominant culture in 1975 simultaneously with a forecast peak of a 500year climate cycle.

With Congress in control, the activities of Nixon's immediate successors would most likely have been constrained, even if they had been stronger personalities. The apparent policy was to try to persuade potential antagonists to make peace not war. Gerald Ford's attempts in 1976 to reach agreement with Strategic Arms Limitation Talks (SALT) with the Soviet Union's Brezhnev had no apparent effect on the expansion of Soviet influence in South America. Jimmy Carter's Secretary of Defence Rumsfeld admitted in 1977 that America would be hard pressed to defend its allies or reinforce NATO but no apparent presidential action was taken to remedy weakness. Carter hosted the 1978 Camp David peace accord between Israel and Egypt, but was powerless to act in 1979 when the fundamentalist Muslim Iran government allowed students to imprison hostages at the US embassy in Tehran. Congress noted, but did not act, on the Carter Doctrine which asserted that the USA would be justified in intervening to protect Persian Gulf oil reserves.

Whether or not the American psyche was reminiscent of the strength of the previous oldest president, Eisenhower, the electorate gave power in 1980 to septuagenarian Republican President Ronald Reagan with a Republican Congress. By the time of Reagan, the White House staff had become huge compared with the relatively few aides of Eisenhower, so it is difficult to discern whether Reagan was the strong leader that his public relations machine promoted. He fostered self confidence in the domestic economy, particularly after the release of the hostages from Iran.

The negotiations with Iran were later found to have been possibly tainted by the illegal provision of arms organised by White House advisers. Reagan attempted to reverse the decline of US military power by channelling money into defence spending. The apparent strategy of the Strategic Defence Initiative (SDI) was to reveal flaws in the economy of the Soviet Union when their competition in the arms race could not be sustained. As the Soviet Union weakened, Reagan saw that dangers existed from international terrorism and branded Iran, North Korea, Cuba, Nicaragua and Libya as terrorist regimes. He reinforced his message with a bombing raid on Libya after a 1986 bomb explosion which killed US servicemen in Berlin.

President George H. Bush was elected in 1988 apparently on the coat-tails of Reagan's popularity. As it had to ancient Rome, the Middle East again proved a trouble-spot for a super-power. The dictator of Iraq, Sadam Hussein, who fancied himself as a true successor of the ancient King Nebuchadnezzar, had been a US ally because of his enmity to Iran. CIA policy in the 1970's and 80's was often to support unsavoury leaders of grubby regimes simply because they were against Communism or simply opposed to nations out of favour with the US. The apparent failure of the CIA to forecast the danger of Iraq's invasion of neighbouring Kuwait practically ended its influence on US leaders.

Bush was quick to secure Congressional approval to act on the Carter Doctrine, and assembled allies to defend the Persian Gulf against Iraqi aggression. The allies included Arab countries such as Saudi Arabia but excluded Israel. Operation Desert Storm was successful in forcing Iraq to retreat in a very short time in January 1991, but was criticised because the allies made no attempt to capture Baghdad or Hussein. There were various reasons given for not destroying such an intransigent and belligerent regime, which, valid or not politically, simply demonstrated that the USA no longer had the will to demonstrate that it was still a super-power. The other main super-power left the scene early in 1991 when the bankrupt Soviet Union could no longer exist. China was fully occupied in integrating capitalist methods into the Communist economy to stave off bankruptcy.

The popular Clinton presidency (1993-2001) had not been able to gain increased respect for the office sufficient to weaken Congressional and bureaucratic control of the United States. The economic success of the United States in the late 1990s had been sufficient for the nation to demonstrate some world dominance of its culture.

Eight months into George W. Bush's first term as President, the September 11, 2001 Al Qaeda terrorist attacks occurred. In response, Bush announced the *War on Terror*, an international military campaign which included the war in Afghanistan launched in 2001 and the war in Iraq launched in 2003. In the latter half of 2002, CIA reports contained assertions of Saddam Hussein's intent of reconstituting nuclear weapons programs, not properly accounting for Iraqi biological and chemical weapons, and that some Iraqi missiles had a range greater than allowed by the UN sanctions. Contentions that the Bush Administration manipulated or exaggerated the threat and evidence of Iraq's weapons of mass destruction capabilities would eventually become a major point of criticism for the President. More than 20 nations (most notably the United Kingdom and faithful Australia), designated the *"coalition of the willing"*, joined the United States in invading Iraq. The initial success of US operations increased Bush's popularity, but the US and allied forces faced a growing insurgency led by sectarian groups; Bush's *"Mission Accomplished"* speech was later criticised as premature. From 2004 until 2007, the situation in Iraq deteriorated further, with some observers arguing that there was a full-scale civil war in Iraq. The Iraq war was unnecessary and so badly fought that it did nothing for the US military reputation.

The vindictive right-wing Bush was followed as president in 2008 by left-wing Barack Obama II, the first African-American to hold the office. He was awarded the 2009 Nobel Peace Prize, with the Committee citing Obama's promotion of nuclear nonproliferation and a *"new climate"* in international relations fostered by Obama, especially in reaching out to the Muslim world. Most of Obama's time was spent fighting Republican forces at home, particularly the Tea Party, and trying to financially offset the Recession (use of the word "Depression" was politically incorrect).

Only cynical observers such as myself might note that much of the US international economic expansion was based on unsound monetary practices and debt, in an age when computerised transactions can reverse huge money flows instantly. That is one risk which was apparently not being addressed. Bush and Obama followed the political policy of printing money that had proved successful in solving financial crises in the past, without apparently realising that the scale of printing money in the twenty-first century was extremely high risk. Foreign governments hold about 46 percent of all US debt held by the public, more than $4.5 trillion. At time of writing the US Federal Reserve held approx $2 trillion. The largest foreign holder of US debt is China, which owned more about $1.293 trillion in bills, notes and bonds followed by Japan $1.178 trillion. US money supply has increased by some 26% since 2008 from Quantitive Easing but the US dollar index has only devalued by 1.3%. One reason for lack of inflation and US dollar devaluation is that the velocity of money has not been affected by the increased money supply. This conundrum is apparently due to huge bank funds deposited with the Federal Reserve and thus not in the general economy. There is a risk of future inflation when such funds are used.

The other risk which I perceived was the rift in the fabric of the American Republic culture from the diminution of traditional values. The drug culture and the belief that money is the solution to all personal, corporate and government problems, has no respect for past religious, family and community values. External risk has been successfully managed in the American Republic, but has engendered a culture which, in my opinion, showed little respect for the traditions of the nation's founders.

The success of external adventures of ancient Rome was similarly the cause of the erosion of the cohesive culture of Roman honour. The risk to the Roman Republic was within, and went unrecognised until the leading generals had already commenced their civil wars. The leaders of the Roman Senate and the Assembly were too concerned with their private welfare to recognise the risk that their own lack of honour would inspire similar selfishness among the urban mob.

Erosion of leadership values in the American Republic appears to be validating decadent values in the middle and lower classes. I can perceive that same erosion of middle class values in the modern Republic, which preceded the decline of the ancient Roman Republic culture. The wealth flowing to the upper class from the debt of the middle class, and the expansion of middle class taxes required by lower class welfare, are huge risks to the USA this millennium.

The other risk which went unrecognised in Rome was the erosion of religious heritage. The religious heritage of the United States was effective in creating political unity and respect for American leaders. As America looked to have been successful in winning the Cold War, its leaders disregarded the lessons of history that a strong religion, respected by leaders and citizens alike, provides a strong cohesive element in society. There was certainly no strong religious unity in the civil protests over the Vietnam War and civil rights, despite the initiative by religious leaders. The apparent failure of political initiative by religious figures in the 1990s was to me evidence that religious respect has been lacking in the American government and the majority of the population. The *politically correct* toleration of the actions of US Muslim leaders will be seen as weakness. History suggests that, without the religious respect demonstrated to/from leadership, a culture is at risk of decline.

The Classical Greek philosopher Plato discussed a cycle of government in his writings "Republic" in which the aristocratic state degenerates into a state where only property owners may participate in government (timocracy). The next evolution is oligarchy in which money is valued over virtue, and the leaders of the state seek to alter the law to give way and accommodate to the materialistic lust of its citizens. Oligarchy then degenerates into democracy where freedom is the supreme good but freedom is also slavery. In democracy, the lower class grows bigger and bigger. The poor become the winners. Diversity is supreme. People are free to do what they want and live how they want. People can even break the law if they so chose. This appears to be very similar to anarchy.

Democracy then degenerates into tyranny where discipline has to be imposed and society exists in chaos. Democracy is taken over by the longing for actual freedom. Power must be seized to maintain order. A champion will come along and experience power, which will cause him to become a tyrant. When Plato says the tyrant is a prisoner to the lawless master, he means that if the tyrant should lose his power for any reason, his life and the life of his family would be in great danger. When the tyrant falls the cycles recommences.

I am not politically prescient but I believe that the United States Republican culture is following Plato's cycle towards tyranny. I can't see the development of the old-fashioned tyrant but I can see the evolution of a strong right-wing government in response to a financial breakdown that will bring many controls to the currently undisciplined elements of society.

The people of the United Kingdom of Great Britain did not seem to notice that their culture had lost world dominance. I suspect that the current population of the United States might prefer the entitlement culture of left-wing government to a dominant culture. The insularity of middle class America might not even notice that America is losing dominance.

> *"I have a dream - that one day on the red hills of Georgia, the sons of former slaves and the sons of former slave owners will be able to sit together at the table of brotherhood. I have a dream - that one day even the State of Mississippi, a state sweltering with the heat of injustice, sweltering with the heat of oppression, will be transformed into an oasis of freedom and justice. I have a dream - that my four little children will one day live in a nation where they will not be judged by the color of their skin but by the content of their character."*
>
> Martin Luther King, Jr. 1963

INDEX

I

K

J

L